Hanban/Confucius Institute Headquarters

Cao Xueqin

Collection of Critical Biographies of Chinese Thinkers

(Concise Edition, Chinese-English)

Editors-in-chief: Zhou Xian, Cheng Aimin

Author: Miao Huaiming
Translators: Guosheng Yang Chen
                Trevor Hay & Bo Ai
Expert: Li Ji

Nanjing University Press

《中国思想家评传》简明读本　- 中英文版 -

主 编　周 宪　程爱民

曹雪芹

著 者 / 苗怀明 Miao Huaiming
译 者 / Guosheng Yang Chen
　　　　Trevor Hay & Bo Ai
审 读 / 李 寄 Li Ji

南京大学出版社

Editor: Chen Yingjun
Cover designed by Zhao Qin

First published 2010
by Nanjing University Press
No. 22, Hankou Road, Nanjing City, 210093
www.NjupCo.com

Chinese Library Cataloguing in Publication Data
The CIP data for this title is on file with the Chinese Library.

ISBN10: 7-305-06610-8(pbk)
ISBN13: 978-7-305-06610-8(pbk)

Books available in the collection

Confucius
《孔子》
978-7-305-06611-5

Laozi
《老子》
978-7-305-06607-8

Emperor Qin Shihuang
《秦始皇》
978-7-305-06608-5

Li Bai
《李白》
978-7-305-06609-2

Cao Xueqin
《曹雪芹》
978-7-305-06610-8

Du Fu
《杜甫》
978-7-305-06826-3

Zhuangzi
《庄子》
978-7-305-07177-5

Sima Qian
《司马迁》
978-7-305-07294-9

Mencius
《孟子》
978-7-305-07583-4

Mozi
《墨子》
978-7-305-07970-2

总序

General Preface

China is one of the cradles of world civilization, enjoying over five thousand years of history. It has produced many outstanding figures in the history of ancient thought, and left a rich philosophical heritage for both the Chinese people and the entire humanity. The fruit of these thinkers was to establish unique schools that over the long course of history have been continuously interpreted and developed. Today much of these thoughts are as relevant as ever and of extreme vitality for both China and the rest of the world. For instance, the ideal of "humaneness" and the concept of "harmony" taught by Confucius, the founder of Confucianism, have been venerated without ceasing by contemporary China as well as other Asian nations.

Ancient Chinese dynasties came and went, with each new dynasty producing its own scintillating system of thought. These rare and beautiful flowers of philosophy are grounded in the hundred schools vying for attention in pre-Qin times and the broad yet deep classical scholarship of Han and Tang times and in the simple yet profound occult learning of the Wei and Jin dynasties together with the entirely rational learning of Song and Ming Neo-Confucianism. The fertile soil of religious belief was Buddhism's escape from the emptiness of the sensual world and Daoism's spiritual cultivation in the search for identification with the immortals. The founders of these systems of thought included teachers, scholars, poets, politicians, scientists and monks—they made great contributions to such disparate cultural fields in ancient China as philosophy, politics, military science, economics, law, handicrafts, science and technology, literature, art, and religion. The ancient Chinese venerated them for their wisdom and for following moral paths, and called them sages, worthies, saints, wise men, and great masters, etc. Their words and writings, and sometimes their life experiences, constitute the rich matter of ancient Chinese thought distilled by later generations. The accomplishments of Chinese thought are rich and varied, and permeate such spiritual traditions as the harmony between humans and nature, the unification of thought and action, and the need for calmness during vigorous action, synthesizing the old and innovating something new.

Nanjing University Press has persisted over the last twenty years in publishing the 200-book series, *Collection of Critical Biographies of Chinese Thinkers*, under the general editorship of Professor Kuang Yaming, late honorary president of Nanjing University. This collection is the largest-scale project of research on Chinese thinking and culture undertaken since the beginning of the twentieth century. It selected more than 270 outstanding figures from Chinese history, composed their biographies and criticized their

中国是世界文明的发源地之一，有五千多年的文明史。在中国古代思想史上，涌现出了许许多多杰出的思想家，为中华民族乃至整个人类留下了丰富的思想遗产。这些思想成果独树一帜，在漫长的历史中又不断地被阐释、被发展，很多思想对于今天的中国乃至世界而言，仍然历久弥新，极具生命力。比如，儒家学派创始人孔子"仁"的理念、"和"的思想，不仅在当代中国，在其他亚洲国家也一直备受推崇。

古代中国朝代更迭，每一个朝代都有灿烂夺目的思想文化。百家争鸣的先秦诸子、博大宏深的汉唐经学、简易幽远的魏晋玄学、尽心知性的宋明理学是思想学术的奇葩；佛教的色空禅悦、道教的神仙修养是宗教信仰的沃土；其他如经世济民的政治、经济理想，巧夺天工的科技、工艺之道，风雅传神、丹青不老的文学艺术……都蕴涵着丰富的思想。这些思想的创造者中有教师、学者、诗人、政治家、科学家、僧人……他们在中国古代的哲学、政治、军事、经济、法律、工艺、科技、文学、艺术、宗教等各个文明领域内贡献巨大。古代中国人尊敬那些充满智慧、追求道德的人，称呼他们为圣人、贤人、哲人、智者、大师等，他们的言论、著作或被后人总结出来的经验构成了中国古代思想的重要内容，在丰富多彩中贯穿着天人合一、知行合一、刚健中和等精神传统，表现出综合创新的特色。

南京大学出版社坚持20余年，出版了由南京大学已故名誉校长匡亚明教授主编的《中国思想家评传丛书》，这套丛书共200部，是中国20世纪以来最为宏大的中国传统思想文化研究工程，选出了中国历史上270余位杰出人物，为他们写传记，

intellectual accomplishments; all in all, it is a rigorous and refined academic work. On this foundation, we introduce this series of concise readers, which provides much material in a simple format. It includes the cream of the crop of great figures relatively familiar to foreign readers. We have done our best to use plain but vivid language to narrate their human stories of interest; this will convey the wisdom of their thought and display the cultural magnificence of the Chinese people. In the course of spiritually communing with these representative thinkers from ancient China, readers will certainly be able to apprehend the undying essence of thoughts of the Chinese people.

Finally, we are deeply grateful for the support from Hanban/ Confucius Institute Headquarters, and the experts from home and abroad for their joint efforts in writing and translating this series.

Editors
November, 2009

评论他们的思想成就，是严肃精深的学术著作。在此基础上推出的这套简明读本，则厚积薄发，精选出国外读者相对较为熟悉的伟大人物，力求用简洁生动的语言，通过讲述有趣的人物故事，传达他们的思想智慧，展示中华民族绚烂多姿的文化。读者在和这些中国古代有代表性的思想家的心灵对话中，一定能领略中华民族思想文化生生不息的精髓。

最后，我们衷心感谢国家汉办/孔子学院总部对本项目提供了巨大的支持，感谢所有参与此套丛书撰写和翻译工作的中外专家学者为此套丛书所做的辛勤而卓有成效的工作。

编者
2009年11月

目录
Contents

2 Contents ❨❩

引言　　遗憾的寻找

Introduction　　Regrets, Hence the Search

Life, for most people, is usually not perfect. Always, there are regrets. As the saying goes, "Of ten things in life, eight or nine are unsatisfactory." When we are admiring those in the past who have achieved so much and have had so much influence on future generations, we would often regret that we were not born at that time; otherwise we could have met them and talked with them. Although reading their written works can help, the sense of regret still lingers, particularly for those whose life stories are legendary, or even with mysterious colour. Cao Xueqin, author of *Honglou Meng* (*The Dream of Red Mansions*), is one such legendary figure to have caused later generations to have such regrets.

Today, if we were to say that Cao Xueqin is one of the world's most famous writers, not many would disagree. Some would even go further by saying that titles such as genius, great thinker, great painter, great architect and connoisseur of food, should be added to justly encompass Cao's talents. His great work has been admired by many ever since the day of its existence. That admiration has now spread beyond China's borders. The novel has received wide recognition as world-class literature. Experts and laymen alike sing its praises. The figures, stories and the poems in it are familiar to a wide readership, young and old, and have become common topics of conversation. What a pity it is then that the *Honglou Meng* we read is incomplete, with only 80 original chapters. The current compilation has 40 more chapters added to it by another writer. Did Cao complete his novel? If he did, what did he say in the chapters beyond Chapter 80? If he did, why was this part of the manuscript lost? Will it ever be found? There is no doubt that every reader asks those questions and is eager to know the answers.

Honglou Meng, to a certain degree, is like a celestial novel that contains too many puzzles and is hard to comprehend. Not much is known about its author, Cao Xueqin, an excellent writer who left behind only that great work and nothing else. Apart from a few lines of poetry written by his friends which give a description of him, there are no other direct records. The lack of reference has been a constant frustration to researchers. Ever since the

　　对大多数人来说，现实人生通常是不完满的，总是有着这样或那样的缺憾，可谓人生在世，不得意者十常八九。说起那些成就卓著、影响深远的前辈先哲，后人在景仰之余，往往也会在内心生出一种遗憾，那就是出生太晚，无法得到一睹风采、当面请教的机会。尽管可以通过阅读他们著作的方式获得一些弥补，但这种遗憾并不能完全消除，特别是对那些富有传奇甚至带有神秘色彩的前贤，更是如此。比如《红楼梦》的作者曹雪芹，就是这样一位留给后人太多遗憾的人物。

　　时至今日，说曹雪芹是一位享有世界声誉的伟大作家，恐怕已没有什么人会提出异议，有些人甚至会觉得赞美的程度不够，还要再加上一些诸如大天才、大思想家、大画家、大建筑家、大美食家之类响亮显赫的名号才觉得满意。《红楼梦》自问世之日起，就受到人们的喜爱，这种喜爱早已超越国界，这部小说也早已成为人们公认的世界文学名著，无论是专家学者还是一般读者，无不对其交口称赞，书中所写的人物、故事乃至诗词可谓妇孺皆知，深入人心，成为人们经常谈论的话题。但令人感到遗憾的是，我们现在看到的《红楼梦》是残缺的，只有前80回，后40回则是另外一位作家续写的。曹雪芹写完全书了吗？如果他写完的话，后面的部分都说了些什么？80回之后的稿子为什么会散失，将来还能找到吗？相信每一位读者都会产生这样的疑问，而且十分迫切地想知道答案。

　　从某种角度来说，《红楼梦》如同一部无法读懂的天书，里面充满了太多的谜团。对于它的作者曹雪芹，我们所知甚少。这位优秀的作家除了《红楼梦》外，再没有给后人留下什么。除了他的朋友写过几首以他为吟咏对象的诗歌外，再找不到有关他的直接记载了。资料的严重缺乏让研究者们感到头

establishment of Redology—the study of *Honglou Meng*, any tiny finding on Cao would be quite exciting and could cause a sensation in the field. Some mercenary people could not resist the temptation of wealth and fame, and went so far as to forge evidence. Sadly, that kind of forgery has ocurred several times in the 20th century. Even though many volumes of research monographs have been published on the subject of Cao, the experts actually know less about Cao than the readers might have imagined.

History is cruel. It plays hide-and-seek with human beings. While it reveals one set of facts, it hides another and hides it deep, so deep that, for the past hundred years or more, people have searched in vain for more information. The eagerness for answers and the disappointment at not being able to find them have been torturing researchers and readers for generations, and such torment will continue in the conceivable future. That is just the case with the research on Cao and his novel. It's like finding fragments of a delicate vase that was broken 200 years ago that can only give us a rough picture of what the vase looked like, but its exact image and details have been lost forever.

Nevertheless, as long as the novel exits, as long as the researchers and readers remain passionate, the quest will go on, even though everyone knows that it will be disappointing and incomplete. The quest will go on because of the irrepressible need for answers to those questions and of the respect for Cao, the great writer. As for the readers, they always want to know more, even just a little more, about the writer who has brought them such great artistic enjoyment.

痛，自《红楼梦》研究成为一门学问以来，只要是与曹雪芹有关的文献，哪怕是有一点点新的发现，都会激动人心，都会在学术界引起轰动。一些心术不正的人难以抵御名声和金钱的诱惑，则去伪造文物，这样的事情在20世纪已经发现了好几起。尽管有关曹雪芹的研究专著出版了很多，但那些专家学者们对这位伟大作家的了解并不像人们想象的多。

历史是十分残酷的，它像捉迷藏一样，让你知道一些真相的同时，往往又会对你隐瞒另外一些，而且隐瞒得很深很深，以至于人们深入挖掘了一百多年，仍所获不多，想知道答案但又无法揭开谜底的痛苦折磨着一代又一代研究者和读者，在可以想象的将来，这种痛苦还要继续下去。对曹雪芹和《红楼梦》的研究正是如此，这就像一个十分精美的花瓶，已经被打碎了二百多年，我们虽然能捡到几个碎片，看到花瓶的大致轮廓，但始终无法看到全部的细节和全貌。

不过，寻找还会继续下去。只要《红楼梦》还在，只要喜爱它、研究它的读者和研究者还在，这种寻找就会一直持续下去，尽管每个人都知道，这样的寻找注定是充满遗憾的，注定是不完满的。这种寻找既是为了满足心中难以抑制的疑问，也是为了表达对曹雪芹这位伟大作家的敬意，对这位给读者带来巨大艺术享受的作家，人们总是想对他了解得更多一些，哪怕是多知道一点点。

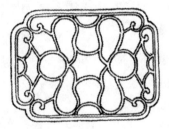

一　秦淮风月忆繁华 ——曹雪芹的家世

Chapter Ⅰ　Diminished Glories Reminisced by a Family
　　　　　　　on the Qinhuai River: Cao Xueqin's Family

In ancient China, whenever talking about someone, the family and background come first. This is not just a traditional way of thinking and faith, but a practical way of thinking of the Chinese. The ancient Chinese lived together in groups, closely bonded by clans and ties of blood. The family ties and bloodlines had an enormous impact on Chinese individual: on the environment for their growth and education, and on their future and fate in a more indirect way. Those born into noble families would have extraordinary advantages quite beyond the dreams of ordinary people.

Likewise, when discussing Cao Xueqin's life journey and literary works, we follow the same practice. Such practice is by no means routine; it is in fact of great significance. As the well-known saying goes that, "The environment changes people," the tragedy on the Cao family changed Cao's life but meanwhile made him such a great writer. It is of particular note that Cao wrote the novel with an understanding of and passion for his own family, which makes his novel autobiographical, something rarely found in previous novels and deemed a prototype of a new art form. Thus, a thorough analysis of the family composition in the novel is crucial to the decoding of its content. No matter what we discuss, either Cao or his novel, we need to start from the changes in the fate of the Cao family. This is going to be a quest that transcends life and space, and the waxing and waning of a legendary family will be laid before us.

I

Many Chinese people, for pride and honour, like to trace their family origins till they've found a famous person among their ancestors. Those researching the life and works of Cao Xueqin do likewise. Some claim that Cao is the descendant of Cao Cao, a famous politician in the Three Kingdoms Period, while others prefer him to be the offspring of Cao Bin, a famous general in the Northern Song Dynasty. Those tenuous links to the glorious families are not only hard to prove, but, even if they were real, it wouldn't have mattered to Cao Xueqin. Moreover, Cao Xueqin wouldn't have known his family history anyway, because of the long time gap in between. What could

在古代中国，谈论一个人，首先要提到的就是他的家族和出身，这不仅来自一种历史悠久的信仰和观念，而且还是一种出于现实的考虑。古代中国人通常聚族而居，生活在以宗族和血缘形成的集体中，家族和出身对个人的影响实在是太大了，既影响到一个人的成长环境和教育，往往也潜在地决定着一个人的前途和命运。出身豪门世家，对一些人意味着得天独厚的资历，对另外一些人来说，则只能是一种无法企及的人生梦想。

探讨曹雪芹的生平经历和文学创作自然也不例外，需要从他的家族和出身讲起。这并非例行公事般的俗套，而是有着特别的意义，这是因为曹氏家族命运的沧桑变化在改变了曹雪芹命运的同时，也成就了这位伟大的作家，这正如人们通常所讲的：环境改变人。尤其需要指出的是，曹雪芹还把个人对家族的认知和情感写进了他的作品中，这成为十分重要的内容，使作品带有一定的自传色彩。这在以前的通俗小说中是极为少见的，可以说是一种艺术上的创新。因此，对家族的深入剖析便成为解读这部作品的一个重要环节，或者说是一把钥匙、一个关键词。无论是探讨《红楼梦》，还是曹雪芹，都需要从曹氏家族的沧桑变迁讲起。这是一场跨越时空的追溯，它使我们看到一个具有传奇色彩的家族的荣辱兴衰……

（一）

为了家族的荣誉感，不少中国人喜欢把自己的家世往上追溯，一直追溯到一位名人作为始祖为止。对曹雪芹的家世，研究者也使用了这样的方法，有人说他是三国时期著名政治家曹操的后代，有人说他是北宋大将曹彬的子孙。这些家族荣誉且不说由于资料缺乏，无法证实，即使真的是历史事实，对曹雪芹也不会有多大影响，况且他本人都未必知道，毕竟年代太久

have really affected Cao Xueqin's life are the events in the mid-and-late Ming Dynasty. Let us use that time as a starting point and take a look at the ups and downs of the Cao family for a span of more than 100 years.

In the early years of the Ming Dynasty, a man called Cao Jun arrived in Liaoyang to take up the post of Zhihui Shi (Commander), a hereditary military position. Cao Jun settled there and his descendants carried on in that position, prospered for generations and gradually developed into a well-known family in Liaoyang. In the middle and later period of the Ming Dynasty, wars broke out between the Manchurians and the Ming, and the complacent life of the Cao family came to an end. The wars completely changed the fate of the Cao family.

In 1621, Nurhachi, the Manchurian leader, led an army and attacked Liaoyang. At that time, Cao Shixuan and his son Cao Zhenyan, Cao Xueqin's great-great-grandfather, were both the military commanders. They were defeated and captured by the Manchurian army and later became Manchurian converts. They were reduced to *nucai* (servant), or *baoyi* in the Manchurian language, in a royal family. In this way, the Cao family underwent a very important transformation, from a Han nationality to a Manchurian one, from a glorious noble family to the servants of Manchurian royal families. There were many other families that suffered the same fate. In the great turmoil of war, anything could happen.

Cao Zhenyan later followed the Manchurian army and entered inland China through the Shanhai Pass. He fought very bravely and won many military victories. He received successive promotions and was appointed to official posts in several places. He left military service and finally became a civilian. At that time, there were many other officials like Cao Zhenyan, but it was not until Cao Zhenyan's son's time that the Cao family started to prosper.

Cao Zhenyan had two sons, the elder of whom was Cao Xi, Cao Xueqin's great-grandfather. Compared to his father, Cao Xi had more of the emperor's trust and was given more important positions. The reasons are, firstly, that he was a capable man and, secondly, that he had a special relationship with the emperor. The first point is manifested in many historical records which depict his mastery of martial arts and talents in literature. Those capabilities were not the only cause of his good luck. More important was the special relationship between Cao Xi and the emperor.

Cao Xi's wife, Sun, was a nanny to Emperor Kangxi when he was very

远了。家族的变化真正能影响到曹雪芹的，则要从明代中后期说起。让我们以这个时间为起点，回顾曹氏家族一百多年间的沧桑变迁。

明初的时候，有一个叫曹俊的人到辽阳担任指挥使，这是一个武将的职位，子孙可以继承。曹俊就在此定居了下来，他的后代继承了其职位，世世代代在这里繁衍，逐渐发展为本地有名的望族。到了明代中后期，随着满族政权与明王朝之间战争的爆发，曹氏家族多年安逸富贵的生活被打乱，这场战争彻底改变了这个家族的命运。

公元1621年，努尔哈赤带兵攻打辽阳，当时在此镇守的是曹雪芹的高祖曹振彦及其父亲曹世选。他们兵败后被清军俘虏，加入满族，并成为皇家的奴才，满语称之为包衣。这样曹氏家族便发生了一个十分重要的变化，从汉族变为满族，从将门巨族变成皇家奴才。当时有着这种命运的还有很多人，在那个兵荒马乱的战争年代里，什么事情都有可能发生。

曹雪芹的高祖曹振彦后来随清兵入关，冲锋陷阵，立下许多功劳，因此他不断升迁，做了几任地方官员，其职位也从武职改为文职。在当时，像曹振彦这样的官员还有很多，曹家的真正发达是从他的儿子开始的。

曹振彦有两个儿子，其中长子叫曹玺，他是曹雪芹的曾祖父。与父亲相比，曹玺得到皇帝更多的信任和重用。之所以如此，主要有两个原因：一是他个人的才干；二是他和皇帝的特殊关系。对曹玺的才干，不少资料都有记载，说他不仅武功好，而且还有文学才能。自然，如果仅仅是因为个人的才干，曹玺可能不会有后来那么多的好运。因此，这里不能不说说他和皇帝的特殊关系。

原来曹玺的妻子孙氏在康熙皇帝小的时候曾做过其保姆。

young. In the Qing Dynasty, emperors paid close attention to their offsprings' education and up-bringing. Children of the royal family had many servants to look after their living and education. Sun was one such servant. Although she did not have a grand title, she enjoyed many benefits, which is easy to understand: A person who takes care of a prince through his childhood will certainly be rewarded later on when the prince ascends the throne.

And the rewards came rather quickly. One year after Prince Kangxi had become emperor, he granted Sun's family a good position whereby Cao Xi, Sun's husband, took up the post of Jiangning Zhizao.

Jiangning Zhizao was the post of Textile Commissioner in Jiangning County (now Nanjing city and its surrounding areas located in lower reaches of the Yangtze River). A Textile Commissioner purchased daily necessities, such as clothing, silk and satin, for the imperial court and supervised the making of silk and cloth. The position was established in the Ming dynasty and carried on in the Qing Dynasty. Ever since the Tang and Song dynasties, the southern area of the Yangtze River had escaped war damage, and its excellent natural environment was preserved. That area gradually became the national economic centre where imperial purchasing took place. There were three textile commissioners in Jiangning, Suzhou and Hangzhou respectively. Because of Cao Xueqin, we will set our focus on Jiangning Zhizao.

The position of Jiangning Zhizao was neither high in the official rankings nor high in the salary. However, many people desired the job for obvious reasons. Firstly, being a purchaser for the emperor, one could have many opportunities to make plenty of profits. Furthermore, this position was granted by the emperor himself, and the person holding that position would have direct access to the emperor and could report to the emperor in person, hence receiving the emperor's attention. In those times, such opportunities were scarce. For Cao Xi, it was therefore a great honour to be appointed to the post. The Cao family moved from Liaoyang to Beijing, and then to Nanjing. Four people in three generations of the Cao family worked as Jiangning Zhizao, and the family lived in Nanjing for over 60 years before things changed.

II

Cao Xi worked diligently at his job after arriving in Nanjing and soon had the chaotic situation of management at Jiangning Zhizao under orderly control.

在清代，皇帝很重视对后代的教育和培养，孩子生下来后，便给他们配备许多人，或照料生活，或进行启蒙教育，孙氏便是其中的一员。这个职位虽然称不上显赫，但有着许多实惠。道理很简单：整天和皇子生活在一起，接触频繁，等这位皇子长大，成为新的皇帝时，他对养育自己的人是会有所回报的。

这个回报来得很快，康熙皇帝即位第二年，就给孙氏的家人安排了一个很好的职位，那就是让其丈夫曹玺出任江宁织造。

江宁织造是个什么职位呢？说得直白一些，就是帮皇帝采买服饰、绸缎、布匹等生活用品，监督绸缎、布匹的织造。这一职位早在明代就已设置，清朝继承了这一制度。自唐宋之后，因自然环境优越、受战争破坏较少等缘故，江南地区逐渐成为全国的经济中心，皇帝的许多生活、消费用品要到这里置办。这样的职位在江南共有三个，即江宁织造、苏州织造和杭州织造。因为与曹雪芹的关系密切，这里我们只说江宁织造。

尽管江宁织造的级别并不高，俸禄也不算多，但仍有很多人喜欢这个职位。其中的原因是很明显的：给皇帝采买物品，有很大的赢利空间，可以从中得到很多好处。另外，这个职位是由皇帝亲自任命的，可以直接向皇帝上奏折，报告各种情况，因而受到皇帝的重视。在那个年代，能得到这样的机会是很不容易的。曹玺被任命为江宁织造，这是十分荣幸的事情。就这样，曹氏家族从辽阳迁到北京，又从北京迁到南京，祖孙三代四人担任江宁织造，在南京相继生活了六十多年。

（二）

曹玺到了南京之后，十分敬业，他很快控制住江宁织造署管理较为混乱的局面，使各项工作井井有条。除此之外，他还

In addition, he donated part of his salary to disaster-relieving activities, which won the appreciation of the emperor and the favour of the local people. As a result, he was granted further privileges. While the position of Zhizao was traditionally held for a period of three years, Emperor Kangxi not only let Cao Xi stay on in that position, but also made it hereditary so that Cao Xi's son could inherit the position. Such privilege accelerated the prosperity of the Cao family, which soon became prominent in the southern region of the Yangtze River. The site of the then residence of Jiangning Zhizao is not far from the present-day Daxinggong in the city of Nanjing. However, because of wars and other turbulence over the centuries, the buildings no longer exist.

The pinnacle of the Cao family's success came at the time of Cao Yin, Cao Xueqin's grandfather. Cao Yin was the elder son of Cao Xi and was very clever since childhood. It was said that when he was only four, he could already differentiate the four tones in Chinese Mandarin. When he grew up, he further demonstrated his talent in literature, especially in poetry. He befriended a lot of scholars of the time and was influential in the field of literature in the southern region of the Yangtze River. Cao Yin liked operas and composed many operatic scripts. He even owned a private opera troupe, a hobby for literati at the time, and operas were often performed in his house. Cao Yin also enjoyed reading and collecting books. Because of his affluence, he was able to amass quite a collection. According to *Lanting Shumu* (*Lanting Novel Catalogue*), the catalogue of his collections, he had over 3 200 books. Cao Yin was also appointed by Emperor Kangxi to be in charge of the preparation of the printing of *Quan Tangshi* (*A Complete Collection of Tang Poems*) and *Peiwen Yunfu* (the largest Chinese dictionary with characters listed in the order of tunes).

Under Cao Yin's management and influence for years, the Cao family became a family of scholars and a home redolent of culture. One can imagine that the atmosphere must have influenced other family members, and that Cao Xueqin's father and uncles, Cao Xueqin himself and his siblings must have all grown up in that elegant environment. While we could not find much evidence of the interaction between Cao Xueqin and his grandfather, we could conclude that a compassionate and scholarly grandfather teaching his grandson could not help but have great influence on the child. That influence became more and more obvious as Cao Xueqin grew older; we can even feel it when reading *Honglou Meng*. It is just in such a familial and scholarly environment that Cao Xueqin grew up and had his makings of a poet and qualities in literature cultivated and edified. For the Caos, the family environment closely integrated

捐赠自己的俸禄，用于救灾。这样，他不仅受到康熙皇帝的赏识，也得到当地百姓的好评。也正是为此，曹玺受到了特别的优待。本来江宁织造是三年一轮替的，但康熙皇帝不仅让曹玺长久担任这一职位，而且还将这一职位变成世袭，允许曹玺的儿子接任。这种特别的优待使曹家很快发达起来，成为江南有名的望族。江宁织造府位于今天南京的大行宫附近，原来的建筑经过数百年的战火和浩劫，早已不复存在了。

曹氏家族的鼎盛时期是在曹雪芹的祖父曹寅时。曹寅是曹玺的长子，他从小就很聪明，据说4岁时就能辨别汉字的四声。长大之后，他更是充分施展出自己的才华，善于写作诗词，与不少文人有着较多的交往，在当时的江南文坛上有着很大的影响。曹寅喜欢戏曲，曾创作了不少剧本，在家里还养着一个戏班。这也是当时文人的一种雅好，家中经常有戏曲演出。曹寅还很喜欢读书、藏书，由于家境富裕，他收藏了许多珍贵的书籍。据专门记载其藏书的《楝亭书目》记载，他的藏书多达3 200余种。曹寅受康熙皇帝的委派，还曾负责《全唐诗》、《佩文韵府》的刊刻工作。

经过曹寅多年的经营和熏陶，曹家逐渐成为一个书香门第，充满着浓厚的文化气息。可以想象，这种文化气息会感染到家族的其他成员，无论是曹雪芹的父亲、叔伯，还是曹雪芹和他的兄弟姐妹，都是在这种十分优雅的氛围中成长的。尽管由于资料的缺乏，我们还无法知道曹雪芹和其祖父交往的具体情况，但有些事实则是可以推想出来的：曹雪芹小时候应该得到过其祖父的怜爱和指教，他受祖父的影响是相当大的，特别是到后来，这种影响越来越明显，我们可以从《红楼梦》这部作品中感受到。曹雪芹的诗人气质及丰厚的学养就是在这种家庭环境中培养和熏陶出来的。家族和创作就

with literary creativity.

Cao Yin was very successful in his career. In 1684, the 23rd year of Emperor Kangxi's reign, his father Cao Xi died. A few years later, Emperor Kangxi broke with tradition and allowed Cao Yin to take over his father's position as Jiangning Zhizao. Cao Yin, in comparison with his father, was closer to the emperor, possibly because he was similar in age to the emperor and, more importantly, he had been the emperor's study companion—someone who accompanied the emperor in his childhood studies. In the Qing Dynasty, the royal court attached great importance to the education of the princes. When it was time for the princes to attend studies, some bright and clever children would be chosen from the royal and noble families to be the princes' study companions. Intimate relationships between a prince and his study companions were easily developed since they lived and studied together. When the prince became the emperor, he would naturally have trust in and bestow important positions on his study companions. Cao Yin had such a relationship with Emperor Kangxi. An indication of the closeness of their relationship was that, of the six visits he made to the southern region of the Yangtze River, Emperor Kangxi stayed four times in Cao's residence. It would not be difficult to imagine how indeed the emperor trusted and favoured the Cao family. The affluence of the Cao family was not hard to calculate either. The emperor's visits to the south are described in *Honglou Meng*, and many researchers believe that those descriptions are based on the Cao family's real experiences.

Nevertheless, being favoured by the emperor did not always turn out to be a good thing. The Cao family soon tasted the bitterness accompanying the trust and fondness: the crime of embezzlement of public funds. In those times, there were no strict financial management systems as exist today. The totalitarian ruler of the Qing Dynasty often could not differentiate his "private" assets from the "public" assets of the state. The emperor's visits to the Cao's exemplify that point. Kangxi stayed four times with the Cao family during his visits to the south. The arrival of the emperor surely was a great honour that many other ministers longed for, but one thing was clear: All expenses of the emperor and his many attendants had to be paid for by the Cao family. It would not be hard to imagine how large that expense would be, considering the luxurious lifestyle of the emperor. Additionally, the Cao family would have had to bribe the officials accompanying the emperor, be it ministers, eunuchs or princes, in order that they would not speak negatively of the Cao family in

这样十分密切地交融在一起。

　　曹寅在事业上也是十分成功的。康熙二十三年，也就是1684年，曹玺去世。过了没几年，康熙就打破惯例，让曹寅接替他的父亲，担任江宁织造。与父亲曹玺相比，曹寅与康熙皇帝的关系更为亲近，两人的年龄较为接近，而且需要指出的是，曹寅小时候曾担任过康熙皇帝的伴读。所谓伴读就是陪皇帝读书。清朝的时候，朝廷十分重视皇子的教育，到皇子们读书的时候，会从王公贵族的子弟中挑选一些聪明的孩子，陪皇子读书。这些伴读的孩子从小和皇帝在一起读书、生活，很容易形成一种十分密切的朋友关系。等到皇帝即位后，他会自然而然地信任和重用这些儿时的朋友。曹寅与康熙就是这样一种君臣加朋友的关系。两人的关系密切到什么程度，可以从一件事上看得出来：康熙曾经六次到南方巡游，其中有四次是住在曹家。由此不难想象康熙对曹家的信任和偏爱，同时也可以想象出曹家的富贵程度。《红楼梦》中也曾写到皇帝的南巡，不少研究者认为这是以曹家的经历为原型创作的。

　　不过，皇帝的信任和宠爱并不总是好事，曹家很快就尝到了信任与宠爱背后的苦涩，那就是亏空。那时候的财务管理可不像现在，一切都有严格的制度，公私分明。清朝是专制王朝，皇帝的"私"和国家的"公"经常会纠缠在一起，难以分清。比如康熙皇帝南巡，四次住在曹家，这固然是许多大臣渴望得到的恩宠，但有一点是十分明确的，那就是皇帝及其数量庞大的随从的各项开支都必须由曹家承担，以皇帝生活的豪华和奢侈我们不难想象，这该是一笔多么大的开支。除此之外，曹家还必须向皇帝随行的大臣、宦官以及皇子们行贿，以确保他们不在皇帝面前说自己的坏话。就曹家

front of the emperor. The Cao family's expenditure, with the masters and servants amounting to a few hundred, would have been huge, not to mention the assistance they often provided for some poor scholars and the valuable books they purchased, etc. As a result, all costs incurred far exceeded the family income, which gradually led to a huge debt.

For an official, the deficit of public funds was a severe crime. If the royal court were to deal with it, the official would be harshly punished. In fact, after discovering the deficit, a minister reported the Cao family to Emperor Kangxi and requested an inquiry. The emperor, trusting Cao Yin and knowing full well that the deficit had a lot to do with himself, did not want to give the Cao family a hard time. He did not approve the minister's suggestion. However, in order to placate the minister, the emperor, after some thought, set the deficit at 1.8 million taels of silver and asked Cao Yin to repay the money. Even though that figure was much less than the true amount, it still meant astronomical sums of money for the Cao family. Then Emperor Kangxi found a way to help Cao Yin by appointing him to be the Salt Administrator in Yangzhou. The position enabled Cao Yin to earn more money to pay off his debts.

In 1712, the 51st year of Emperor Kangxi's reign, Cao Yin died of malaria, leaving his son, Cao Yong, the burden of the remaining debt of 320 000 taels of silver. The death of Cao Yin was a big blow to the family, and the earlier glorious grandeur of the family he had created was impossible to restore.

After Cao Yin's death, the question arose as to whether the post of Jiangning Zhizao should be granted to another member of the Cao family. Due to his affection for Cao Yin and his regard for the Cao family, Emperor Kang-xi broke with tradition again and granted the position to Cao Yin's young son Cao Yong. Emperor Kangxi was impressed by the young successor. He considered Cao Yong intelligent and capable, and bestowed extra favours on him. Unfortunately, Cao Yong had poor health and died three years later in 1715, the 54th year of Emperor Kangxi's reign. Cao Yong had only one offspring— an unborn child, Cao Tianyou. Some people say that the child is Cao Xueqin, which is no more than a reasonable and logical speculation; some hard evidence is still needed to prove that.

The Cao family was facing a major crisis— the lack of a successor. Cao

自身的开支来说，整个家族主仆加在一起有好几百人，开销也是很大的，且不说还要资助一些贫困的文人、购买珍贵的图书，等等。这样，各项开支加在一起，已经超过家族的收入，就逐渐形成了巨大的亏空。

亏空对一个政府官员来说，是一项很严重的罪名。朝廷如果要认真追究的话，是要受到严厉惩处的。事实上，当时已经有大臣发现了曹寅的亏空，并向康熙皇帝举报，要求进行查处。康熙皇帝十分清楚曹家的亏空和自己有关，而且他又很信任曹寅，不愿因为这件事为难曹家，他并没有接受那位大臣的建议，但他又必须对其他大臣有所交代。于是他斟酌之后，确定了一个亏空的数字，即180万两白银，要求曹寅想办法填补。尽管这个数字比实际的亏空要少得多，但它仍然是一个天文数字，填补起来相当困难。于是康熙皇帝又帮曹寅想办法，派他到扬州去管理盐政，以利用这个职务获得的银两来填补亏空。

曹寅还没有来得及填补全部亏空，就在康熙五十一年即1712年因患痢疾去世了，将未填补完的32万两白银的亏空留给了他的儿子曹颙，他的去世对曹家是一个重大的打击，他所创造的家族鼎盛的神话难以再次重演。

曹寅去世后，一个新的问题被提了出来：江宁织造是不是仍由曹家人出任？出于对曹寅的怀念和对曹家的关照，康熙再次打破惯例，让曹寅年轻的儿子曹颙接任江宁织造。康熙对这位年轻继任者颇有好感，认为他聪明能干，并给予特别的关照。但遗憾的是，曹颙身体不好，只做了三年，便于康熙五十四年即1715年去世。他的后代只有一个还没有出生的儿子曹天佑，俗称遗腹子。有人说这个曹天佑就是曹雪芹，尽管很有道理，但那不过是个合乎逻辑的推想，还有待过硬、丰富的资料来证明。

现在曹寅这一支面临着缺少继承人的严重危机：曹寅只有

Yin had only one son, Cao Yong, who had already died. Cao Yin had a younger brother named Cao Xuan who had sons. With Emperor Kangxi's personal intervention, Cao Xuan's fourth son, Cao Fu, was made the successor to Cao Yin as the new Jiangning Zhizao. Under the aegis of Emperor Kangxi, Cao Fu, like his grandfather and cousins, enjoyed a comfortable life for a few years. Unfortunately, the comfort did not last long. The emperor died not long after. An old Chinese saying goes that when "the emperor goes so do his ministers." Emperor Kangxi was succeeded by his son Emperor Yongzheng, who completely differed from his father in both character and style. Now that the emperor had changed, so would all other things, including the fate of the Cao family.

III

The newly enthroned emperor had his own thoughts. Unlike his father, Yongzheng did not favour the Cao family. On the contrary, there are various indications that he even hated the Cao family. Shortly after his enthronement, Emperor Yongzheng made all sorts of excuses and picked fault with everything the family did. He accused Cao Fu of submitting reports that were not totally genuine and also criticised the quality of the brocades Cao Fu purchased. The friendliness and harmony that had existed between Emperor Kangxi and the Cao family were nowhere to be found. In only a few years' time, Cao Fu came in for increasingly severe reprimand from Emperor Yongzheng. In a totalitarian society, the fate of someone not favoured by the ultimate ruler, or the emperor, was not hard to imagine. It could be only a matter of time before a calamity befell.

In 1727, the 5th year of Emperor Yongzheng's reign, that inevitable calamity did fall upon the Cao family. In the 11th month of that year, Sai Leng' e, a chief inspector in Shandong Province, reported Cao Fu to Emperor Yongzheng for extorting money from post stations on his way back to Beijing after the procurement. Emperor Yongzheng received the report and immediately dismissed Cao Fu from his official post. Before long, he laid three new charges against Cao Fu—indecent behaviour, the embezzlement of funds as Jiangning Zhizao and the transfer of family assets. He had Cao's house raided and all assets and servants confiscated. It certainly looked more like a planned action than an improvised play by Emperor Yongzheng.

一个儿子曹颙，现在这个儿子也已去世。在康熙的亲自过问下，曹寅的弟弟曹宣的第四个儿子曹頫被过继为曹寅的继承人，并接任新的江宁织造。在康熙的庇护下，曹頫像他的父祖、兄弟一样，过了几年较为自在的生活。但这种生活是不可能长久的，因为不久康熙皇帝便去世了。中国有一句俗话：一朝天子一朝臣。康熙去世后，雍正皇帝登基。这是一个无论是性格还是作风都与其父亲迥然不同的新皇帝，皇帝换了，一切都要发生改变，其中自然也包括曹家的命运。

（三）

这位新登基的皇帝有着自己的想法，他显然不再像他的父亲康熙那样关照、偏爱曹家，从种种迹象来看，他甚至讨厌这个家族。他登基不久就开始以各种借口来找曹家的麻烦：要么批评曹頫奏折反映的情况不够真实，要么指责曹頫采买的绸缎不合格。以往康熙和曹寅之间那种君臣融洽和谐的友善气氛再也看不到了，短短几年间，曹頫不断受到雍正皇帝越来越严厉的训斥。在专制制度下，一旦最高统治者皇帝不喜欢一个人，这将意味着什么，谁都可以想象到，灾难的到来只是时间的早晚而已。

果然，到了雍正五年即1727年，这场早有预感但无法避免的灾难终于降临。这年11月，山东一个叫塞楞额的巡抚向雍正皇帝举报，说曹頫在往北京运送采买物品的途中，骚扰驿站，勒索钱财。雍正得到举报，随即免去曹頫的官职。不久，他又给曹頫罗列了三个新的罪名：行为不端、织造款项亏空和转移家庭财产，并派人抄家，没收了曹頫的全部家产及仆役。显然，这不是雍正皇帝的即兴发挥，而更像是一场有预谋的清算行动。

The result of the raid, however, surprised all. The Cao family was not as rich as everyone had imagined. Cao's family assets, compared with other rich families, looked rather shabby. Ever since the days of the great debt, Cao Yin and his two sons had worked hard to repay it but had been unable to achieve their goal. While they were able to make some money to pay off the old debts, new debts were incurred in the process of making money. In the end, that debt damaged this once glorious family. One thing worth contemplating was that, before Cao's house was raided, the family had already been on the decline. It was only trying to make ends meet and pay back its debt against enormous odds. Who would have thought that such a prosperous family could end up in such a tragic way?

Why did Emperor Yongzheng not like the Cao family? The emperor never explained the reason, so researchers can only make conclusions from and analysis of the available data. They have made several suggestions, the first of which is for political reasons. The Cao family may have been involved in the power struggle between Yongzheng and his brothers, but may not have dealt with Yongzheng properly and thus became a target of retaliation after he came to power. It may also have been for financial reasons. The Cao family did run up huge debts, which did not make Emperor Yongzheng happy. Not befriending the Caos, he simply played by ordinance and punished the Cao family severely. Due to the lack of evidence, it is now difficult to offer an explanation that would satisfy all. Nevertheless, one fact is not to be denied: Emperor Yongzheng, unlike his father, did not favour or take special care of the Cao family. After coming to power, Emperor Yongzheng took a series of actions against the Cao family, causing the hard-earned glory and prosperity of the family to vanish.

IV

A Chinese saying goes like this, "If a man achieves immortality, his dogs and chickens would also go to heaven," which means that if a man is successful, his relatives and friends would benefit along with him. On the contrary, if he experiences misfortune, his relatives and friends would suffer, too. Cao Fu's conviction was a huge blow to the whole family. After the house raid, all assets and servants of the Cao family were granted to Sui Hede, the new

不过，抄家所得的结果让所有人大吃一惊，原来曹家并不像人们想象的那么富有，其家产和当时富有者相比，甚至显得有些寒酸。自从出现亏空之后，曹寅父子三人虽然做了很多努力，但始终未能将这个无底洞补上，往往是补上了老账，又添了新账。亏空终于压垮了这个曾经十分显赫的家族。令人值得深思的是，即使没有抄家这样的厄运，曹家当时也已经相当衰落了，只是表面上勉强维持而已，内部的运转已相当困难。一个曾经十分兴旺的家族竟然以如此悲惨的方式收场，这恐怕是任何人都想象不到的。

这里有一个让人关心的问题：雍正皇帝到底是出于什么原因不喜欢曹家？由于雍正皇帝本人没有明确说过，研究者只能根据所看到的资料进行归纳和分析。他们为此提出了多种说法：一种是政治原因说，说曹家可能参与了雍正与兄弟们争夺皇位的斗争，但没有处理好和雍正的关系，结果雍正当上皇帝后，进行报复；一种是经济原因说，说曹家确实存在着很严重的亏空问题，雍正和曹家没有什么交情，按照制度来处理的话，自然会对曹家严厉惩处。限于资料的缺乏，现在还很难得出一种所有人都认可的解释。但不管怎么样，有一个事实是无法否认的：那就是雍正不再像他的父亲康熙皇帝那样关照、偏爱曹家，他登基之后一步步采取行动，打击曹家，使这个家族多年苦心经营的荣华和兴盛，瞬间化为泡影。

（四）

中国有句俗话：一人得道，鸡犬升天。意思是一个人如果发达了，他的亲友都可以从中得到好处。相反，一个人如果遇到了不测，他的亲友也都要跟着遭殃。曹𫖯的获罪使整个曹氏家族受到重大打击。抄家之后，曹家的全部家产和仆役

Jiangning Zhizao. Cao Fu and his family members, the young Cao Xueqin included for sure, were sadly dispatched from their homeland Nanjing to Beijing, and lived somewhere outside Chongwenmen in Beijing. From Beijing to Nanjing and then back to Beijing, the family seemed to have travelled in a circle. The place remained the same but people changed, so did the social and cultural environments. The comfortable and glamorous life of the past was nothing but a distant memory. Cao Fu and his family had to adjust their mindset and start a new life, a life full of hardship, a life of lower status and without dignity. This was not a temporary test for them but a permanent torture. When Cao Xi first left Beijing years before, he couldn't have imagined such tragic return for his children, to this ancient city that had given them so many dreams and expectations. Life is cruel in that it often takes away while it gives.

In ancient China all dynasties exercised totalitarian control. The fate of individuals was often held in the hands of the emperor, and there was a lot of uncertainty for each individual. Many other families suffered from fates similar to that of the Cao family. The reason we pay special attention to the Cao family is that its fate and hardship had shaped a great writer and his great literary work. When the rise and fall of a family is linked with a distinguished writer and a great novel, everything related to it gains a special meaning.

In *Honglou Meng*, Cao Xueqin weaves his personal misery into the plot. He transforms his own misfortune into the common experience of humanity. He turns his observations and personal experiences of a large family into the core contents of the novel, so that *Honglou Meng* can be also regarded as a novel about families. Some readers pay more attention to the descriptive writing of love stories than to those of the families or of politics. In fact, there are two major storylines in *Honglou Meng*. One is the love stories of young Jia Baoyu, Lin Daiyu and others. The other is the glory and decline of the families. The former is the more overt plot and the latter more of a hidden thread that often serves as background contexts. If readers do not pay attention to the descriptions of the families, they would not be able to appreciate the author's intention, nor could they fully comprehend Cao's remarkable work.

都被雍正赏赐给新的江宁织造隋赫德，曹頫及其家属，年幼的曹雪芹自然也在其中，则凄然离开故乡南京，被遣送到北京，居住在北京崇文门外的一个地方。从北京到南京，从南京再回到北京，仿佛转了一个圈，但物是人非，一切都发生了改变。安逸富贵的生活已变成不堪回首的人生记忆，现在曹頫和他的家人们必须调整心态，重新开始一种全新的生活，一种充满艰辛、没有尊严的下层人的生活。这种生活并非暂时的考验，而是永久的磨难。当初曹玺带着喜悦的心情离开北京时，他绝对想象不到，其子孙们竟然以如此悲惨的方式回到这座曾带给他们许多幻想和憧憬的古老都城。人生就是这么残酷，让你得到许多东西的同时，也剥夺了你另外一些东西。

在中国古代，由于各个朝代实行的都是专制制度，个人的命运往往掌握在皇帝手里，有很多不确定性。有着曹家同样命运的家族还有很多，我们之所以特别关注曹家，是因为这样的命运和苦难成就了一位伟大的作家，成就了一部优秀的作品。当一个家族的兴衰与一位伟大作家、一部优秀作品联系在一起时，一切都有了特别的意义。

曹雪芹在《红楼梦》中，将个人的苦难转化为创作的素材，将个人的不幸升华为人类共同的体验，他将对家族的观察和体验写进自己的小说中，使之成为作品的核心内容，所以《红楼梦》也可以称作是一部家族小说。有些读者往往只注意其中爱情的描写，对家族部分的描写则关注不够，而且还多有政治层面的解读。而实际上，《红楼梦》中有两条线索：一条是以贾宝玉、林黛玉等人为核心的青春爱情线索，另一条是以家族命运为核心的兴衰线索。前者是明线，后者是暗线，更多的时候是作为背景而存在。如果不充分注意家族的描写，就无法体会作者的苦心，无法全面、深刻地理解这部作品。

The use of personal experiences as raw material in a literary work was quite rare in ancient Chinese folk novels that were mainly based on historical stories (with relevant historical facts). There is a novel titled *Jinping Mei* (*The Golden Lotus*), which is a novel about family lives. It contains many fabricated stories and has few autobiographical features. It is very rare to find such a novel as was written by Cao Xueqin, who based the story on his own family history. Strengthened by its excellent descriptive style and vivid artistic effects, the story makes it difficult for readers to differentiate the novel from reality. They are often led to think that the figures and events in the novel could not have been fabricated but are factual.

In the novel, Cao Xueqin expresses his deep passion towards his family. Although the novel is about the Jia family, readers can apparently see the Cao family, even if to date we do not know which stories are fabricated and which tell the truth. Through figures like Jia Baoyu and others, Cao Xueqin also expresses his pride in and attachment to the family. He is not, unlike some researchers have suggested, digging the grave for his own family and giving it a last push. In fact, he wishes families like the Jia family could carry on forever and not be ruined by the few prodigals.

Naturally, Cao Xueqin's deep passion for his family was built on a critical basis of love intertwined with hatred. Cao loved his family but that did not mean he was satisfied with the situation it was caught in. He was unhappy about and even disgusted with those who refused to take responsibility and led corrupted lives. In the novel, he created figures, such as Jia Lian, Jia Zhen and Jia Rong, who benefited tremendously from the family and in the end destroyed the family. In fact, they took the major responsibility for the decline of their family. A series of incidents depicted in the novel reflect Cao Xueqin's thoughts on that. He made a grand and full display of the family's glory and decline. In the declining process, all people, from main figures in the family to the servants at the bottom, were all destroyers. The only difference was the level of the impact. A series of destructive forces gathered together and led to the ultimate calamity of the family that enjoyed glory and prosperity for many generations. Although we have not found the original ending plotted by Cao Xueqin, there is no doubt that it would be frustrating or desperate.

以个人的生活经历为素材进行文学创作，这在中国古代通俗小说中是十分少见的，因为这类小说大多取材于古代历史故事，有所依据。即使是《金瓶梅》这样以描写家庭生活为主的小说，所写也大多为虚构之事，带有纪实或自传色彩的很少。像曹雪芹这样以自己的家族生活为原型的作品是十分少见的，加上其成功精彩的写实手法，其十分逼真的艺术效果常常让读者不自觉将作品和现实混淆起来，总觉得作品中的人物和事件不可能出自个人的想象虚构，而应该是真实存在的。

在作品中，曹雪芹表达了他对家族的深厚感情，虽然作品所写的是贾家，但分明可以看到曹家的影子，尽管我们目前还难以知道，到底哪些是虚构的，哪些是真实的。曹雪芹通过贾宝玉等人物表达了他的家族荣誉感和依恋感。他并不像有些研究者所说的，渴望家族的早日灭亡，充当家族的掘墓人。事实上，他很希望像贾家这样的家族能永远延续下去，而不是被少数几个败家子毁掉。

自然，这种对家族的深厚感情是建立在批判的基础上，可谓爱恨交织。曹雪芹爱贾家这样的家族，但并不等于他对家族现状满意。他对那些拒绝承担家族责任、堕落腐败的家族成员是十分不满的，甚至带有厌恶之情。在作品中，他塑造了一批这样的人物，如贾琏、贾珍、贾蓉等。这些人从家族得到巨大好处的同时，也破坏了整个家族，他们是家族破败的主要责任者。作品通过许多事件反映了曹雪芹的这一思考。他为我们全面展示了一个家族从兴盛走向衰亡的全过程，在这个过程中，上至家族主要成员，下至底层奴仆，每个人都是破坏者，只不过程度不同而已，所有的破坏形成了一股强大的力量，彻底摧毁了一个曾经兴盛多年的家族。尽管曹雪芹有关小说结局的部分我们目前还不能看到，但它无疑是令人沮丧或绝望的。

曹雪芹画像　蒋兆和绘
Portrait of Cao Xueqin, by Jiang Zhaohe

二 步兵白眼向人斜 ——曹雪芹的生平

Chapter Ⅱ　A Scornful Look at the Reality: The Life of
Cao Xueqin

While there exists a clear picture of Cao's family history, it is much harder to put together a picture of Cao Xueqin because the facts are scarce and some of them are contradictory. Thus a huge gap forms between the desire to know more and the lack of information about him. History is mean and odd, giving us one excellent book yet hiding the secrets of it so deep, turning the pleasure of reading into a painful quest, and torturing readers generation after generation. The fact is, no matter how hard the researchers work, they could only provide a sketchy outline of Cao, with all details missing. The truth about Cao may never be told. Even though we've seen some portraits of Cao, they are the painters' told versions based on their own understanding and thus are subjective and may not be consistent with our imagination. This is a pity, yet it is not necessarily a bad thing. In a way, everyone will have a unique Cao in their mind, a Cao belonging to each reader.

I

When we talked about Cao Xueqin's family history, there was one troublesome and even embarrassing problem: We know much about Cao's great-great-grandfather, great-grandfather and grandfather, but we have not been able to identify his father. It may sound ridiculous but it is the truth. Normally, a father would have a greater and more direct influence on his child than a grandfather would do. To the father who nurtured Cao, we owe him our tribute and are obliged to know more about him. The search for more information on Cao's father would be quite meaningful rather than boring.

Why has it been unable to identify Cao's father? The reason is not difficult to understand. Cao's ancestors had been officials and had contacts with the public. Their names would certainly be found in royal records, local historical records and clan registries. However, Cao was different. He had never been an official and would certainly not appear in any official records. To the surprise

与家族历史的清晰描述相反，对曹雪芹本人的介绍将是一项十分艰难的工作，原因很简单：我们掌握的材料实在太少，就是这有限的材料有时也会相互矛盾，让人无所适从。这样，了解曹雪芹的强烈愿望便与文献资料的严重缺乏形成了十分鲜明的反差。历史就是这么吝啬和怪异，它留给了我们一部最为优秀的小说作品，但又将其中的秘密很严实地隐藏了起来，结果使本该愉快的阅读变成痛苦的追寻，折磨着一代又一代的读者。而事实上，无论研究者怎么努力，他们能提供给我们的只有曹雪芹的背影，一个轮廓还算分明但细部却相当模糊的背影，曹雪芹的真实面目我们也许永远都看不到。尽管我们可以看到不少有关的画像，但这是画家们心目中的曹雪芹，既没有什么根据，也未必符合我们的想象。这固然是个缺憾，但未必不是一件好事，这样，我们每人心目中都会有一个独特的曹雪芹，一个完全属于自己的曹雪芹。

（一）

上文在介绍曹雪芹家族历史的时候，隐藏着一个让人感到棘手和尴尬的问题，那就是我们对曹雪芹的高祖、曾祖和祖父都了解得相当清楚，但他的父亲却始终无法确定是谁。说起来这似乎有些可笑，却是一个真切的事实。按照通常的情况，父亲对孩子的影响比祖父会更直接，也更大。对这位培养曹雪芹的父亲，我们要向他献上敬意，也有理由对他了解得更多。因此对曹雪芹父亲的追寻绝不是一件无聊的事情，这是有意义的。

为什么会出现无法确认曹雪芹父亲的现象？这是因为曹雪芹的祖辈们都做过官，与外界交往较多，可以从宫廷档案、地方史志以及族谱中找到相关记载。但曹雪芹就不同了，他没有做过什么官，官方各类档案文书自然不会有他的记载。让人感

of all, Cao's information was not to be found in his clan registry, neither was his father's. Were it not for the few poems written by his friends, Cao would have vanished into thin air. How could one not shake his head in disbelief about the fact that so little information is known about such a great writer?

Since there were no records in the clan registry, how did people know Cao's grandfather was Cao Yin? That information comes from a poem written by Dun Cheng, who was a close friend of Cao and knew Cao's family very well. His description should be reliable. But the question has not been solved. Cao Yin had only one son, Cao Yong, who died at a young age with an unborn Cao Tianyou. The name Cao Tianyou was recorded in Cao's clan registry. Could Cao Tianyou and Cao Xueqin be the same person? There is no record in the clan registry or in any other literature of any connection between the two. There is insufficient evidence for a "yes" or "no" to that question.

If Cao Xueqin was not Cao Tianyou, there exists another possibility that Cao Xueqin was Cao Fu's son. It is possible but the problem is that we now know nothing about Cao Fu's children. According to the political system of the Qing dynasty, the birth of anyone important in the families of *nucai*, like the Cao family, had to be reported to the royal court. Unfortunately, we have not found any report on Cao Fu in that regard.

The problem is so tricky. If Cao Yin was Cao Xueqin's grandfather, it seems that Cao Xueqin's father could only be Cao Yong or Cao Fu. However, there is no definite answer. With so few candidates in front of us, we still cannot decide. This being the situation, there is no point in trying to solve the mystery. Let's leave the problem to future generations. Maybe they will be able to solve the mystery.

II

Even though it was hard to determine who his father was, the period in which Cao lived was identifiable. One major clue came from a piece of commentary on *Honglou Meng*, which says Cao died on New Year's Eve of the year Renwu. According to the cycle of lunar years, the year Renwu during that

到奇怪的是，就连族谱中也没有他的任何信息，更不用说他的父亲是谁了。如果不是朋友们写了几首吟咏他的诗歌的话，曹雪芹真的就像从这个世界上消失了一样。一位伟大的作家身后竟然如此凄凉，这无疑会让后人感慨不已。

既然家谱中没有记载，为什么会知道曹寅是曹雪芹的祖父呢？这是曹雪芹的好朋友敦诚在一首诗歌中介绍的。敦诚是曹雪芹交往密切的好朋友，对其身世十分了解，因此他的话应该是可信的。但问题的疑难之处在于，曹寅只有一个儿子曹颙，他很年轻的时候就去世了，只留下了一个遗腹子曹天佑。这个名字在曹氏族谱中有记载，但曹天佑是不是曹雪芹呢？族谱中没有任何交代，其他文献也同样是空白，无论说是或否，都没有足够的材料来证明。

如果曹雪芹不是曹天佑的话，就存在着另外一种可能，那就是曹雪芹可能是曹頫的儿子。这种可能性不是没有，但问题在于，目前我们对曹頫子女的情况一无所知。按照清朝的制度，像曹家这样的皇家奴才，如果有重要家族成员出生的话，都是要向朝廷报告的。但令人遗憾的是，我们没有看到曹頫有这方面的报告。

问题就是这么奇特，如果曹寅是祖父的话，曹雪芹的父亲似乎只能是曹颙或曹頫，但到底是谁，直到目前都无法确定。候选人如此集中，明明就在眼前，但就是无法确定。既然这样，我们也就不强做解人，将这个问题留给后人吧，也许他们将来能解决。

（二）

与父亲的难以确认相比，曹雪芹生活的年代则大致可以确定下来。这主要依据脂本《红楼梦》中的一条批语，上面明确交代，曹雪芹是在壬午除夕那天去世的。壬午年是乾隆二十七

time fell in the 27th year of Emperor Qianlong's reign, which was the year 1763. New Year's Eve of that year was on the 12th of the 2nd month. New Year's Eve is a very important day for the Chinese, when all family members gather together to celebrate the end of the old year and the arrival of the new. It was right on this normally joyful day of celebration that Cao Xueqin the great writer died. Celebration and death, joy and desolation mingled together on that day.

Now that we know the date of Cao's death, a clear starting point for our quest can be set. If we could further determine his age, we could then work out the year of his birth. According to the records by Dun Cheng, Dun Min and Zhang Yiquan, Cao lived for over 40 years but less than 50 years. Thus, we can work out roughly that Cao was born in the later years of Emperor Kangxi's reign although we cannot determine which year exactly. We could say that Cao lived through the reigns of three emperors: Emperors Kangxi, Yongzheng and Qianlong, a very useful piece of information for our study of the background of *Honglou Meng*.

There have been intense debates among researchers and many claims made on the year of Cao's death. Luckily, The difference betweem them is a brief period of time of one or two years. No matter who wins the debate, it will have little impact on one's understanding of *Honglou Meng*. For ordinary readers, knowing roughly each claim would be enough. There is no need to make a choice among them.

Forty-odd years as a life time is not long, actually rather short, even for the times of the Qing dynasty when science and medical facilities were not so advanced as today. Yet the value and significance of life is not measured by its length. In his 40-odd years, Cao spent at least 10 years writing *Honglou Meng*, which showed how much he treasured and loved his book and how important the book was to him.

III

According to the records concerned, Cao Xueqin's given name was Zhan,

年，也就是1763年，这一年的除夕是2月12日。除夕在中国是一个很隆重的节日，所有的家庭都要在这一天团聚在一起，庆祝旧的一年的终结和迎接新的一年的到来。这个本应充满喜庆的日子竟然成为曹雪芹这位伟大作家的忌日，欢庆与死亡，热闹与凄清，就这样奇妙地交融在一起。

确定了曹雪芹去世的具体日期，等于找到了一个清晰的时间起点。如果知道他活了多大岁数的话，就可以推知他的出生年份。根据敦诚、敦敏、张宜泉等人的记载，曹雪芹活了四十多岁，接近五十岁，但不会超过五十岁。这样一来，可以大致推断出，曹雪芹出生在康熙晚年，至于具体是哪一年，现在还难以确定。因此可以这样笼统地说，曹雪芹生活在清朝康熙、雍正、乾隆年间。确定了这一点，对了解《红楼梦》的创作背景是很有帮助的。

对曹雪芹去世的时间还有其他说法，研究者为此曾进行过很激烈的争论。好在他们提出的年份只相差一两年，无论谁对谁错，都不会影响到人们对《红楼梦》的理解。事实上，对一般读者来说，知道每种不同说法的大致内容就可以了，没必要非得在里面做出抉择。

四十多岁的人生即使是在科技不发达、医疗卫生条件不好的那个时代，也不算长，甚至可以说是相当短暂的。好在生命的价值和意义并不是以年龄的长短为标准来衡量的。在短暂的四十多年的时光中，曹雪芹至少有十年的时间用来创作《红楼梦》，由此不难看出他对该书的重视和珍爱程度，由此也不难想见这部小说对曹雪芹该有多么重要。

（三）

根据相关记载可以知道，曹雪芹名霑，字梦阮，雪芹是他

his courtesy name was Mengruan, and Xueqin was his *hao*, an alternative name or title. In addition, he also had Qinpu and Qinxi Jushi (the dweller of Qin Creek) as his *hao*. In ancient China, names were given by parents who invested their wishes and expectations in the children. The *hao*, or title, was what a person wanted himself called, and normally illustrated his life goal or pursuit.

Cao was born in Nanjing. Although at the time of his birth his family was declining, it was a few years before the family was raided in the 5th year of Emperor Yongzheng's reign. The extravagant lifestyle of song and dance, wine and red lanterns, and the coming and going of guests was very familiar to Cao. He lived in a luxurious and peaceful family environment for some time and met various kinds of people and attended different events. More importantly, the affluence of the family enabled him to receive good education and be culturally enriched. They were very significant to his writing later on. Those happy days cast a very deep impression on Cao and became an unforgettable memory for him, especially during the hard times later on.

There must have been reasons for the decline of the Cao family, but it was too hard on a child. He had not yet fully benefited from the glory of the family and yet he would have to suffer all the bitterness due to the decline. The dramatic changes in life would inevitably affect the development of his character and his future. Fate was surely unfair to Cao, exposing the darkest side of life to him at too early an age.

When his family was raided, Cao was only a child of about 10 years old. It was a time when a boy starts to observe the world with curiosity, and to analyse and try to comprehend things happening around him, using the unique logic of children. The sudden changes in the family may not have been fully comprehensible to him but he would have understood to some degree, when watching the misery and sadness on the faces of his relatives. It was only after moving to Beijing that he finally understood what changes had really happened in his life. If Cao were born in a poor family, just like Ban'er in *Honglou Meng* who learned to support his family at a young age out of necessity, the experience of all sorts of sufferings would not have meant as much. However, Cao was born into the family of Jiangning Zhizao. He fell from wealth into

的号，此外还有芹圃、芹溪居士等名号。在古代中国，名字是由父母所起的，包含着长辈对孩子的期待和祝愿。号则通常是个人所起，反映了不同的人生理想和追求。

曹雪芹出生在南京，虽然他出生时曹家已走过了最为辉煌的时期，但离雍正五年的抄家尚有一段时间，家族内部依然歌舞升平，灯红酒绿，迎来送往，热闹非凡。曹雪芹就是在这样的环境中度过了一段富贵繁华、快乐安逸的贵族生活，见识了家族的各类人物、诸种排场，更为重要的是，富裕的家庭条件也使他受到良好的教育和文化熏陶，这对他日后的小说创作有着十分重要的影响。这段幸福快乐的生活给曹雪芹留下了十分深刻的印象，成为他终生难以割舍的一个情结，特别是当他陷入困顿时。

曹家的衰落固然有其必然的原因，但对一个孩子来说，则是过于残酷了。他还没有充分享受家族兴旺带来的好处，就要承受家族破败带来的种种苦难，戏剧性的人生变化将不可避免地影响到其性格的形成与日后的命运。对曹雪芹来说，命运注定是不公平的，它过早地向这个孩子展示了人生中最不美好的东西。

曹家被抄家那一年，曹雪芹不过是个十来岁的孩子，这个年龄的孩子正用充满好奇的眼光打量着眼前的世界，似懂非懂地以孩子的独特逻辑来观察和理解着身边发生的一切。对于家族突然发生的变故，他未必知道究竟是怎么回事，不过从家人苦痛、伤心的表情中，他也许可以明白一些。只有迁居到北京后，他才能真正明白自己的生活到底发生了哪些改变。如果曹雪芹出生在一个贫民之家，就像《红楼梦》里所写的板儿那样，穷人的孩子早当家，这一切不幸和苦难也许都算不了什么。可他偏偏出生在江宁织造府里，转眼间，从富贵跌入贫困，从贵

poverty, from the life of a nobleman to that of a pauper. The change of environment was so sudden and the contrast so huge that it would be too complicated for a child to comprehend, yet he had to adjust to it.

A grand family in the southen area of the Yangtse River, famous and respected, was suddenly reduced to the status of prisoners and slaves in the blink of an eye. Cao was there to experience such dramatic change. That change altered his life path completely. The days of luxury with no worries were gone with the wind of yesterday, and could only be a sweet memory buried deep in his heart. The struggle on the poverty line, so sharp a contrast to his life before, made him feel the hardships of life, and gave him a deeper and more profound understanding of the harshness of reality. It wouldn't be hard to imagine how he had been influenced and devastated by all that experience. The glories of the Cao family on the Qinhuai River could only be a bitter memory to linger in Cao's mind forever.

The decline of a family was a disaster that no one would willingly accept. Yet, viewed from the perspective of literary creation, the disaster and misfortune were rare experiences in life as well as a source for creative inspiration. Without such experiences in life, Cao would not have had such a thorough understanding of the intricacies of family life and reflected so thoroughly and comprehensively on the subject, nor would he have had the strong impulse to begin his writings. A great work like *Honglou Meng* may have never existed. A well-to-do young man who lived in a comfortable environment would never have the passion for literary creation, let alone the persistence required to embark on such an arduous work. The sufferings destroyed a family yet developed a great writer. Was that a misfortune or a fortune? It would be hard to agree on either answer, which shall be the true logic of history.

Obviously, the Cao family would need to adjust all aspects of lifestyle and, more importantly, their own status and their mindset after arriving in Beijing. One could imagine how difficult it would be for the senior members of the Cao family. Cao would have seen a lot of tears and heard a lot of sighs. One thing would be certain that the whole family could not avoid doing the

族沦为贫民，生活环境改变之快，前后相比反差之大，对一个还不怎么懂事的孩子来说，这一切都太复杂了，但他必须去适应。

一个显赫百年、无比尊崇的江南望族，转眼间沦落为潦倒失意、低人一等的阶下囚，身为家族成员的曹雪芹亲身经历了这一极富戏剧性的巨大变迁。这一变迁彻底改变了他的人生道路，安享富贵、快乐无忧的日子如风而逝，只能成为深埋心底的一份温馨记忆，低层生活线上的挣扎使他倍感人生的艰辛，人生前后色彩极为鲜明的反差使他对人间冷暖、世态炎凉有着更为丰富、深刻的体验和理解，其心理由此所受到的冲击和影响是可以想见的。"秦淮风月忆繁华"，这是终生萦绕在其心头的一种挥之不去的情结。

家族的破败固然是一场灾难，没有人会心甘情愿地接受它，但从文学创作的角度来看，苦难与不幸又何尝不是一笔难得的人生财富和创作资源。没有这一阅历，曹雪芹就不会对家族内部的诸种内幕了解得如此透彻，其反思就不会如此全面、深刻，因而也就不会有如此强烈的创作冲动。否则，很难想象会有《红楼梦》这部小说的产生。一个整天泡在温柔乡里的纨绔子弟既不会有这种创作激情，也不会有揽下这份苦差事的毅力。苦难摧垮了一个兴旺的百年望族，却成就了一位伟大的作家。这到底是不幸，还是该感到庆幸？也许很难给出一个统一的答案，这就是历史的真实逻辑。

曹家到了北京之后的生活是可以想见的，大家不仅要在生活上适应这一意外变故，更要从身份、心理上去适应。可以想象，这对曹雪芹的长辈们来说，该有多么艰难。同时也不难想象，曹雪芹所看到、听到的，肯定是大人们的泪水和叹息。不管怎样，有一件事情是无法回避的，那就是曹家的上上下下、

hard work themselves of providing for their own daily needs.

According to records, Cao had worked in Zong Xue, a school for the royal and noble families, where he met two brothers Dun Cheng and Dun Min who became his good friends. The three were of a similar age and had similar family tragedies. The Dun family was related to the royal court and had declined when it came to their generation. The previous family glory and fortune could not solve their real life problems. Having similar family histories, the three had a lot in common. They encouraged each other to face the hardships in life.

Unfortunately, there is so little information about Cao's life in Beijing that we don't have enough to paint even a sketchy outline of him. We can imagine that Cao's life in Beijing, where he came to meet people of various identities, status and natures and witness the decline of many prosperous families, must have had a great influence on Cao. All those experiences enriched him and later became major resources for his writings.

In the last 10 years of his life, perhaps out of poverty or the need for a quieter place for writing, Cao moved from inner Beijing to a small village in the city's western suburbs where many a few people lived. He led an even poorer life. The whole family lived on gruel, and for Cao Xueqin a glass of wine became a luxury that he had to ask for on credit. It was in such a difficult situation that Cao continued to write and revise his work.

In such hardship, one's family was the last support and hope for anyone. But fate was so cruel that it ripped away Cao's last comfort by taking his youngest son's life. This was no doubt a big blow to Cao. He fell ill but had no money to see a doctor. His health deteriorated and he died on the New Year's eve in 1763, the 27th year of the reign of Emperor Qianlong, leaving behind all his hatred, disappointment, and his unfinished work, away from the world not worth remembering.

大大小小必须为生计而奔波。

据记载，曹雪芹曾在当时的宗学中任过职。在那里，他认识了两位好朋友，即敦诚、敦敏兄弟。兄弟俩和曹雪芹年龄相仿，个人的境况也有相似之处。他们虽然出身皇族，但到他们这一代时，已经走向破败，祖辈的荣耀和富贵并不能解决现实中的困境。相似的境遇使他们有着许多共同语言，大家相互安慰，共同面对艰难的人生。

遗憾的是，有关曹雪芹在北京活动的资料实在太少了，我们甚至连他的背影都无法勾勒出来。可以想见，在北京的生活经历对曹雪芹的文学创作当有着十分深远的影响，在这里，他可以看到各种身份、地位及面目的人，也可以看到那些从兴旺走向衰败的家族，从这些世情百态中，他获得了独特的人生经验，这些后来都成为他作品中的重要素材。

在曹雪芹人生最后的十数年间，可能是由于生活困顿的原因，也可能是出于安心创作的需要，他从北京城内迁居到西郊一个人烟稀少的小山村里。在这里，他过着更加贫困的生活，全家人靠喝粥来维持生活，连喝酒都成为十分奢侈的事情，需要赊账。就是在这样艰难的环境中，曹雪芹仍坚持创作，不断修改自己的作品。

在如此困顿失意的生活中，家庭将是最后的归宿和安慰。可是上天实在太残酷了，连这一点起码的安慰都不愿意给曹雪芹。不久，小儿子不幸夭折，这对曹雪芹无疑是一个重大打击。他因此感伤成疾，由于无钱请医，病情恶化，大约在乾隆二十七年即1763年的除夕，带着满腔的怨恨和遗憾，留下了这部未完成的小说，离开了这个并不值得他留恋的世界。

IV

According to the descriptions in *Zaochuang Xianbi* (*Essays from the Date Tree Lodge*) by Yu Rui, Cao is "fat with wide forehead and dark complexion, eloquent with elegant taste, sentimental at nature." Yu Rui put these words down according to what he had heard from his older relatives who befriended Cao. His words were trustworthy to some extent. This was the only available description of Cao's appearances. Cao, according to Yu Rui, had a voluptuous figure with a big forehead and dark complexion. Such ordinary appearance may have disappointed some readers as Chinese scholars normally are thought to be quite slim in figure with a white complexion—the standard portrait of an educated scholar. Different from romance novels depicting scholars and beauties, however, in reality one's appearance would unnecessarily have any connection with his talent.

Luckily, we are able to gain a vague picture of him from the descriptions of Cao's friends in their poems. Even though not many poems have been written by Dun Cheng, Dun Min and Zhang Yiquan about Cao, rough sketches of him can still be drawn. Portraits of later times were all made based on those poems. We learn from the poems that Cao was open-minded, bold, and unconstrained. He was conceited and would not easily compromise. Towards the people and things that he did not approve of, he would not hesitate to show his contempt, just as the famous literati Ruan Ji and Ji Kang had done in the past. Such behaviour reflected the nature of Cao Xueqin as well as the direct effect of his living environment.

However, he was quite happy when with his friends. He was humorous and eloquent. He liked drinking, to the extent of being an alcoholic, which was common among many scholars; there had been many legendary writings on literati and wine. People with such distinct and unique characters as Cao's may be impossible for normal people to endure, but luckily he had good friends like Dun Cheng and Dun Min. The small number of good friends did not bother him, as the most important thing was to have someone to confide in and be happy with.

Cao was multi-talented. He wrote good poems, as was manifest in

（四）

据裕瑞在《枣窗闲笔》一书中记载，曹雪芹"其人身胖头广而色黑，善谈吐，风雅游戏，触境生春"。裕瑞是听前辈亲友中与曹雪芹有过交往的人说的，有一定的可信度。这也是目前见到的有关曹雪芹相貌的唯一一则材料。按照裕瑞的描述，曹雪芹身材富态，头大，皮肤较黑。如此普通的相貌显然会让一些读者失望，因为按照中国人对才子的想象，他应该身材瘦削，皮肤白皙，一副文质彬彬的样子。但这仅仅是想象，毕竟人不是生活在才子佳人小说中，相貌和才气没有必然的联系。

好在曹雪芹的好友们都见过曹雪芹，通过他们的诗歌，可以依稀想象曹雪芹的音容笑貌。敦诚、敦敏、张宜泉等好友吟咏曹雪芹的诗歌虽然数量不多，但却十分形象地为我们勾勒出曹雪芹的神采和风貌。后人心目中的曹雪芹形象，主要是通过阅读这些诗歌作品得来的。通过这些诗歌作品我们知道，曹雪芹生性豁达豪放，恃才傲物，他不是那种随便妥协的人，对自己看不惯、看不起的人和事，会像著名的文人阮籍、嵇康那样，用眼神来表达自己的蔑视之情。这既是曹雪芹个性的表现，也是生活环境影响的结果。

不过当和好朋友在一起时，他还是表现得挺开心的，诙谐、健谈。他喜欢饮酒，并达到迷狂的程度，这也是许多才子们共同的爱好，在历史上曾流传着许多文人和美酒的佳话。如此鲜明、独特的性格在一般人是难以接受的，好在他还有敦诚、敦敏等好友。朋友不在乎多少，只要能真正谈得来，大家在一起开心就好。

曹雪芹具有多方面的才华。他的诗歌写得也很好，这可以

Honglou Meng. He created many characters in his book and many of them were able to compose poems that matched their roles. Those poems he composed for Lin Daiyu, in particular, were a good demonstration of his extraordinary talents. Cao's poems were similar in style to that of Li He, the famous poet in the Tang Dynasty; they both were brilliant and novel. Friends sang highly of his poems and some even compared him to Cao Zhi, a famous poet in the Three Kingdoms Period.

Apart from composing good poems, Cao was good at painting. He painted rockeries, mountains and rivers, and he painted to express his feelings. Unfortunately, none of his poems and paintings can be found. We could only find two lines of his poems, apart from those in *Honglou Meng*.

A short and hard life may be commonplace and normal. However, when such a life is linked with *Honglou Meng*, the most excellent ancient novel in Chinese history, everything is different, and all becomes meaningful. It certainly is regrettable that there is little information about him, but Cao's success showed us the highlights, or the most colourful pages, of his life. Who would have thought the down-and-out literati would become a famous writer admired by the world, and that the quest to know more about him and his work would become Redology, a discipline attracting thousands of researchers worldwide? Now, years after many emperors and royal families were buried in history, what normal people cannot forget are those folk heroes who do not appear in historical records. It is just like a verse in the first chapter of *Honglou Meng*, which says, "Where have they gone, emperors, ministers, and generals in history? In graves under the wild grasses."

Hence, gains and losses, glory and shame, being in power or just being a normal citizen, can no longer be judged against the same standard. It is wise to look to the future rather than have too many complaints about one's current situation. Fate is fair. If it is to impose hard labour on one's back and to frustrate one's mind, it would certainly make that person good enough for something great, for example, carrying on the heritage of Chinese culture.

从《红楼梦》中看得出来。在作品中，他为不少人物拟写了符合他们身份、性格的诗歌，特别是为林黛玉所写的那些，显示出其过人的才华。曹雪芹诗歌的风格和唐代著名诗人李贺较为相似，才华横溢，以奇取胜。朋友们对他的诗歌评价很高，把他和历史上著名的诗人曹植相比。

此外，曹雪芹还擅长丹青，喜欢画奇石、山水，通过绘画来表达个人的感情。遗憾的是，无论是诗歌还是绘画，现在都已经失传了。如今除了《红楼梦》外，我们能看到的只有他的两句残诗了。

坎坷多艰的短暂人生看似平淡无奇，但当它和中国古代最优秀的小说《红楼梦》发生联系后，一切都改变了，一切都变得有意义。资料缺乏带来的诸多人生空白固然意味着遗憾，但曹雪芹成功地让我们看到了其生命中最为精彩、亮丽的一页。谁能想到这位失意落魄的文人日后会成为人人景仰的世界级作家，围绕其个人与作品的研究竟然成为一门学问，吸引了全世界成千上万名专业研究人员和业余爱好者。几百年后，显赫一时、养尊处优的帝王将相早已湮没于历史的陈迹中，人们念念不忘的偏偏是那些史籍无载的民间文化英雄，这正如《红楼梦》第一回中所说的：古今将相在何方？荒冢一堆草没了。意思是说：古往今来的帝王将相都在哪里呢？不过湮没在荒草坟墓中而已。

可见，人世间的得与失，荣与辱，显与隐，都是不能一概而论的，正所谓牢骚太甚防肠断，风物长宜放眼量。造化是公平的，它既然要劳其筋骨，苦其心智，必然会降下承传民族文化薪火的大任。

題芹溪居士 姓曹名霑字夢阮號芹溪居士其人工詩善畫

愛將筆墨逞風流。廬結西郊別樣幽門外山川供
繪畫堂前花鳥入吟謳。羹調未羨青蓮寵苑召難
忘本立羞借問占來誰得似野心應被白雲留。清
新典雅自在流行

傷芹溪居士 其人素性放達好飲又善詩畫年未五旬而卒

謝卓池邊曉露香。懷人不見淚成行。北風圖冷魂
難返。白雪歌殘夢正長琴裏壞囊聲漠漠。劍橫破
匣影鋨鋨。多情再問藏修地翠登空山晚照涼。

张宜泉《春柳堂诗稿》中关于曹雪芹的诗作
Poem about Cao Xueqin by Zhang Yiquan

三 不如著书黄叶村 ——曹雪芹的创作

Chapter Ⅲ　Writing in the Village: Cao Xueqin's Work

People face many choices in life. Whether one choice is right or not depends on a number of considerations. Would the choice give one a sense of achievement and meaningfulness? Would the public regard it as a contribution to society and humanity? Cao, in his short life, made the greatest choice to write *Honglou Meng*. There was a great risk associated with his choice. At that time, novels were looked down upon by the public, who used them for relaxation after tea as they could not bring any actual benefit. Furthermore, they could bring unexpected troubles. Cao started his writing in such a disadvantageous environment, and he was sure to have encountered many obstacles but he persisted. A writer who succumbed to others' expectations would never be successful. A true writer should go far beyond the times he lived in, and because of this the writer would feel lonely and bitter. However, history will always be fair. It has compensated the writer who contributed so much to the times and society in which he lived, even though the compensation came late.

I

Before discussing the circumstances of the writing of *Honglou Meng*, we must answer the fundamental question, a simple and even ridiculous question: Is Cao the writer of *Honglou Meng*?

The very reason we must begin with this question is that two hundred years have gone by since the first appearance of *Honglou Meng*. Many people think Cao is the writer while many others think otherwise. The latter group of people even suggested some other candidates. Even though in current times Cao is commonly accepted as the writer of *Honglou Meng*, some people still have doubts. Readers believe they have the right to know who the writer really is. As for the researcher, it is their obligation to find a proper answer to that question. Based on the two reasons above, I'd like to start discussing the question that who wrote *Honglou Meng*.

According to *Honglou Meng* itself, Cao seems to be only an adaptor, as it is made clear in the book that the story is copied from a magical stone. The

人在一生中会面临很多选择，选择得正确与否，一要看个人的感受，自己是否有成就感，觉得有意义；二要看他人的评价，在别人看来，是否对社会有贡献，是否有益于人类。曹雪芹在其短暂的一生中做了一个最大的选择，那就是创作《红楼梦》。这个选择是带有很大风险的，因为在当时人们看不起小说，认为它不过是茶余饭后消遣的玩意儿，并不能为个人带来实在的好处，相反还可能会遇到意想不到的麻烦。在这样不利的环境中，可以想象曹雪芹在创作《红楼梦》时，一定会遇到不少阻力，但他坚持了下来。完全顺从他人意志的作家注定是没有出息的，一位真正优秀的作家往往会走在时代的前面，因为超前，所以会感到孤独和痛苦。但历史最终是公平的，那些为时代和社会做出贡献的人会得到补偿的，尽管这种补偿来得稍迟了些。

（一）

在探讨曹雪芹创作《红楼梦》的诸种情况之前，我们必须回答一个基本的，但看起来有些幼稚甚至可笑的问题：曹雪芹究竟是不是《红楼梦》的作者？

之所以要从这个最基本的问题开始，是因为从《红楼梦》面世到现在，二百多年过去了，既有很多人认为曹雪芹是《红楼梦》的作者，也有不少人反对这一看法，他们为此还提出了其他一些候选人，即使是在曹雪芹为《红楼梦》作者成为常识的今天，仍是如此。对读者来说，知道作品的作者到底是谁，这也是他们的权利，研究者有责任弄清这一问题。基于这两个原因，笔者愿意从原点开始，探讨《红楼梦》的作者问题。

从《红楼梦》自身的记载来看，曹雪芹似乎只是一个改编者，因为书中交代得很明确：这部书原先刻在一块神奇的石头

stone was intelligent and could talk like a human being. With the help of a Buddhist monk and a Taoist priest, the stone came down to the worldly human society. After experiencing the ups and downs of human society, it recorded all it had experienced. Later, a Taoist priest with the title of Kongkong Daoren (Void Reverend) copied the story from the stone. Based on the words on the stone, Cao, in his study called Daohong Xuan, "spent ten years reading and editing, and revised the manuscript five times, putting the text under different chapters and giving each one a title." He named the book *Jinling Shi'er Chai* (*Twelve Beauties in Jinling City*). It is a folk novel with chapters and titles.

Some researchers claim that Cao is only an adaptor and the real writer is actually the magic stone. It sounds reasonable but does not stand up under closer scrutiny. The prerequisite of this theory is that the story of *Goddess Nu Wa Repairing the Sky* must be genuine. What must also be genuine is the story in it that only one stone left behind from the repairing job went down into human society. And it is necessary that the stone should have the ability to talk and write. Obviously, there is no way these can be proved. The use of legendary stories can only be regarded as the writer's story-telling techniqne and not the evidence that a stone wrote the book.

Cao creates a wonderful and surreal world, using the mystical writings of Goddess Nu Wa repairing the sky and the stone going down to the worldly human society. These stories become the major thread of the whole book, along with the descriptions of the crimson pearl flower fairy and her tears, and the illusory land of great void. Such is the writer's unique design and it is very important in revealing the spiritual contents of the book. It also creates a wonderful artistic effect that is both mystical and pseudo-genuine. We need to understand those descriptions from an artistic perspective and not treat them as reality.

However, from the contents we can tell that the writer was not trying to hide his identity. On the contrary, all information is telling the readers that Cao Xueqin is the writer.

At the beginning of the book, a poem has indicated Cao's authorship. It reads, "This book seems to contain ridiculous words, yet it is full of the tears

上。这块石头具有灵性，能像人一样说话，他曾在一个僧人和一位道士的帮助下，到世间去，经历了一番人情寒暖，回来后把自己看到的一切记录下来。后来有个叫空空道人的人把石头上的故事抄录下来，曹雪芹在此基础上，于悼红轩中"批阅十载，增删五次，纂成目录，分出章回"，则题曰《金陵十二钗》。意思是，曹雪芹曾经用十年的时间来批阅这部书，先后增删了五次，并且将这部书分成章回，撰写目录，使它成为一部章回小说。

有的研究者据此认为曹雪芹不过是个改编者，真正的作者是那块神奇的石头。这一看法似乎很有道理，但细细推敲，它是不能成立的。因为这个观点有一个基本前提，那就是《红楼梦》开头所讲的女娲补天、石头下凡的神话故事是真实的，都是现实生活中发生的真事，那块神奇的石头确实能像人一样说话，会写字，能写书。很显然，这一点是没有办法证明的。这一段神话故事只能作为作者的艺术手法来看，而不能当成判断《红楼梦》作者的依据。

《红楼梦》开头有一段女娲补天、石头下凡的神话描写，这一神话贯穿作品的始终，和绛珠还泪、虚幻仙境等故事一起，构成了一个超越现实人间的奇妙艺术世界，在作品中占有重要地位。这些描写是作者独具匠心的艺术构思，对揭示作品的思想内涵具有重要意义，同时也具有一种神秘莫测、虚实相生的奇妙艺术效果。对这些描写，只能从艺术的角度去理解，而不能落到实处，视作现实生活的真实写照。

不过，从《红楼梦》一书的相关内容来看，它并不想隐瞒作者的姓名，而且明确地告诉读者：本书的作者就是曹雪芹。

在作品开头，有一首标明曹雪芹所写的诗歌："满纸荒唐言，一把辛酸泪，都云作者痴，谁解其中味。"全诗的大意是：

of sorrow. Everyone says the author is insane, yet who really understands the message in the book?" There is not much argument about the authorship of this poem— Cao Xueqin. Let's chew on it a little bit more. Doesn't it sound like the author's monlogue? He is talking to his readers and wishes they could really understand him. If Cao were only an adaptor who compiled the story, he would have had no need and no authority to write in such a manner. Cao also uses the term "author" in that poem.

Obviously, Cao wants his readers to know his true identity as the author. Even though he does say that the stone has written the book, and that Kongkong Daoren has copied the words from the stone, he does not intend to make the author's identity a puzzle for the readers. After all, this is a book on which he has spent more than ten years. How many ten years does one have in a lifetime? The reason for him to put his name in his book is that he has confidence in the book and is sure that the contents are not ridiculous and they would be passed on. He also wishes that the readers would really understand his message about the "tears of sorrow." If he had decided not to reveal his name, he could have easily omitted it rather than give a detailed account of his work. He could have followed the example of the author of *Jinping Mei* by using a pen name such as Lanling Xiaoxiao Sheng (Laughing Man from Lanling), thus leaving an everlasting puzzle for the readers. It would be wrong for anyone to ignore the author's own indication in the book and to deny Cao's authorship. That would be disrespectful to the author. The concern that Cao expressed a couple of hundred years ago, "yet who really understands the message in the book," is not without justification. People who live after him have had so many different interpretations of his work, and even his authorship is challenged.

Let's take one step back and presume that there were a stone that had written the book, and that Kongkong Daoren had copied the words from the stone. It was Cao who had "spent ten years reading and editing, and revised the manuscript five times, putting the text under different chapters and giving each chapter a title." Cao's version of *Honglou Meng*, with fundmental changes made, would have been greatly different from the original manuscript, perhaps totally different. Such kind of work should not be simply described as

字里行间所写的都是荒唐的文字，但它的背后却隐藏着辛酸的泪水。人们都说作者有些痴迷，谁能理解其中的真正蕴涵呢？这首诗是曹雪芹写的，读者和研究者基本上没有什么异议。细细体会，这分明是作者的个人独白，以作者的口吻和读者进行对话，希望他们能真正理解自己的一番苦心。如果曹雪芹仅仅是个改编者，他没有必要、也没有资格这样写，何况其中还直接用到了"作者"一词。

显然，曹雪芹是希望读者知道他的作者身份的。他虽然使用了石头作书、空空道人传书这种艺术手法，但他并不想含糊作者问题。毕竟这部小说凝结着他十多年的心血，在短暂的人生中，能有几个十年？他之所以特意署上自己的名字，说明他对自己的作品很有信心，相信它并非"荒唐言"，而是能够永久流传的，他渴望后人能真正解味，读懂隐藏在作品中的"辛酸泪"。否则，如果真的不想让别人知道自己姓名的话，他可以很容易地做到，完全没有必要点出"曹雪芹"这个名字，把自己所做的工作交代得那么清楚。他可以像此前的小说《金瓶梅》的作者那样，署上一个"兰陵笑笑生"之类的名字，给后人留下一个永久的谜团。偏离作品自身明确的交代，武断地否定曹雪芹的著作权，这种做法正是作者本人所担心的，也是对作者的不尊重。可见，曹雪芹几百年前"谁解其中味"的担心并非多余，因为后人不仅对这部书的理解千差万别、千奇百怪，有些人甚至连他的著作权都生硬地剥夺了。

退一步来讲，即使真有那么一部石头所创、空空道人传抄的书稿，在经过曹雪芹十年修改、五次增删、纂成目录、分出章回这一番脱胎换骨的工作之后，不难想象它与今天所看到的《红楼梦》的差别该有多大，完全可以用面目全非一词来形容。这样的工作是改编一词所不能涵盖的，而是一种具有原创性的

adaptation. It was an artistic recreation from an original piece of work. Hence, if a manuscript had existed before, it could have only served as source material for Cao's revision, editing and compilation. Cao's authorship is not to be denied.

In the history of Chinese literature, it had been a common phenomenon for authors to use some other works as source materials to create their own work. Those kinds of work are considered recreations or readaptations, not just adaptations. *Romance of the Three Kingdoms*, *Water Margin* and *Pilgrimage to the West* had all been written as new books. The original forms of the three books are *Historical Records of the Three Kingdoms in Plain Languages*, *Collections of Forgotten Tales of the Xuanhe Period of the Great Song Dynasty*, and *Pilgrimage to the West in Plain Languages* respectively. There arc also many operas based on the three novel. However, the current versions of the novels absorbed many materials from the previous works, and Luo Guanzhong, Shi Nai' an and Wu Cheng' en are recognised as the authors, not adaptors. The case with *Honglou Meng* should be no exception.

Besides, Cao himself has indicated that he is the author, though expressing it in an artistic way. Anyone who does not have a biased view would be able to figure out Cao's identify.

Apart from Cao's own indications, there is other strong evidence that could prove his authorship. The evidence falls into three categories. The first category is the commentaries written by Zhiyanzhai (Rouge Inkstone) and others. While writing *Honglou Meng*, Cao's good friends including Zhiyanzhai read and commented his work. Many commentaries confirmed that Cao is the writer. The second category is the affirmation by people who lived in the same times as Cao. Not long after the appearance of *Honglou Meng*, there were records about its creation and circulation. Those records can be proof that Cao is the writer. The last category is the various records made after the printing of the book. There were a number of records but they were made a long time after Cao's time. Even though those records were not convincing, they represented the views of a number of people. Cao's authorship was not acknowledged academically until 1921 when Hu Shi issued his "Textual Researches on *Honglou Meng*." Prior to that, the most popular and prevailing view had been that Cao was the writer.

Based on the theories mentioned above, we could confidently say that Cao

文学创作。因此，在曹雪芹进行修改、增删、篡成、分出等工作之前，所谓的书稿即使存在，充其量也只能称作创作素材，而不是小说作品。因此，曹雪芹的著作权是动摇不了的。

在中国古代小说史上，以其他作品为素材，在此基础上进行新的创作，这是一种很常见的文学现象，人们通常将这种工作称作创作，而不是改编。在《三国演义》、《水浒传》、《西游记》成书之前，分别已有《三国志平话》、《大宋宣和遗事》、《西游记平话》小说和大量的三国戏、水浒戏、西游戏。《三国演义》、《水浒传》、《西游记》显然从前代文学作品中汲取了不少营养，但人们仍然称罗贯中、施耐庵、吴承恩为作者，而不是改编者，《红楼梦》自然也不能例外。

恰恰是曹雪芹本人说出了自己的作者身份，他只不过用艺术的手法表达而已，如果不是抱有成见，做过多发挥的话，由此推断出曹雪芹的作者身份是不成问题的。

再者，除了曹雪芹本人的亲自交代外，还有不少其他过硬的材料可以支持他的著作权。这些材料有三类：一是脂砚斋等人的批语。曹雪芹在创作《红楼梦》时，他的好友脂砚斋等人就开始进行评论，这些评论有不少明确说明曹雪芹是《红楼梦》的作者；二是曹雪芹同时代人的证言。在《红楼梦》流传初期，就已有关于该书创作、流传情况的记载，这些记载都明确点出曹雪芹的作者身份；三是《红楼梦》刊刻之后的各类记载。这些记载数量较大，虽然距曹雪芹生活的时间稍远，不够权威，但它代表了当时不少人的看法。尽管在1921年胡适发表《红楼梦考证》一文之前，曹雪芹的作者身份还没有得到学术层面正式的确认，但在有关《红楼梦》作者的诸多说法中，曹雪芹为《红楼梦》作者的说法是最为流行、影响最大的。

基于上面的理由，我们可以有把握地说，曹雪芹就是

is the writer, not an adaptor, of *Honglou Meng*. Various other claims of authorship are not as convincing. They either lack strong evidence or are based on imagination or on the misinterpretation of historical evidence. Thus, the presumption that Cao is the writer is tenable and it is worthwhile writing a biography of Cao.

II

The next question we must answer is why Cao wrote *Honglou Meng*. What were his motives and goals?

Since Cao clearly had spent a lot of effort and time in writing this book, he must have had a goal in his mind. Apparently it was not fame, money or other material things, even though he lived in poverty and must have had the need for them. Compared with other rather commercial novelists prior to his time, Cao did not write the book in a quest for commercial benefits or fame, nor for his self-entertainment. To him, writing the book was a serious career, just as was for Pu Songling, who lived before Cao's time and devoted himself to the writing of *Liaozhai Zhiyi* (*Strange Tales from a Chinese Studio*). Pu regarded his work as an achievement of value in life. Cao, wanting to confide and to express something, wanted his readers to remember and treasure those important things. He also wanted to share his unique views on society and life. Otherwise, had he not been so eager to express and so disappointed at the world, Cao could have kept silent and would have taken the story along to his grave. After all, writing *Honglou Meng* was not something imposed on him. It was totally his own choice to write.

By reading Chapter 1 of *Honglou Meng*, we understand that Cao wanted to express, through his book, two kinds of feelings. One is repentance, and the other is commemoration. He wanted to repent to himself, as well as to his family. He said, "I have let down my father and brothers who had educated me, and have ignored my teachers and friends who had persuaded me to follow a

《红楼梦》一书的作者，而不是改编者。其他关于《红楼梦》作者的诸多说法要么证据不足、不够过硬，要么建立在对资料曲解、臆测的基础上，远不如曹雪芹作者说可信。因此，以曹雪芹为《红楼梦》作者的前提是可以成立的，为曹雪芹写传记也是值得去做的。

（二）

接下来我们必须面对另外一个问题：曹雪芹为何要写《红楼梦》？他写作的动机和目的究竟是什么？

曹雪芹既然在《红楼梦》这部书上花费了如此多的心血和精力，显然是为了达到某种目的，但这种目的显然不是金钱、名声、娱乐等现实的东西，尽管生活在贫困中的他也很需要这些。与此前商业意味十分浓厚的通俗小说相比，曹雪芹的创作没有商业、名利等功利色彩，也不是为了消遣和娱乐。对他来说，这是一项很严肃的事业，就像他之前的小说家蒲松龄那样，把《聊斋志异》当作体现自己人生价值的重要标志。他想倾诉、想表达，想让读者记住那些他认为需要珍惜、不该被遗忘的东西，想表达他对社会和人生的一些独到思考和想法。否则，如果没有表达的欲望、对这个世界彻底绝望的话，曹雪芹完全可以保持沉默，把一段历史和故事永远带进坟墓，毕竟撰写《红楼梦》不是一项别人强加的任务，写和不写，主动权完全在他本人。

从《红楼梦》第一回的交代来看，曹雪芹想借助这部小说传达两种感情：一种是忏悔，另一种是纪念。忏悔是指向个人和家族的，内容包括"背父兄教育之恩，负师友规劝之德，以至今日一技无成、半生潦倒之罪"，意思是说：违背了父辈兄长们对自己的教诲，辜负了老师朋友们对自己的规劝，以至于

virtuous path. Hence, I have acquired few skills, and have been poor and frustrated half of my life." His commemorations were for women. "There have been some females of strong and good personalities. I can't, for the protection of my own shortcomings, let them perish without a trace." These two kinds of feelings have been fully expressed in the book. The former one was woven into the story of the family while the latter became the elegies for the youths. The latter is the core subject of the book, as is said in the book "mainly about romance."

The above-mentioned two kinds of feelings are the highlights of Cao's life experiences and contain his unique understanding of life and the world. He has done away with his personal hatred and hardship, and has brought them to a higher level of the sacredness of humanity. His work is enlightening even for us today. We can thus see that a real piece of art endures the test of time. Readers used to pay too much attention to the descriptions of the females in the book instead of Cao's repentance, which is just the key to understanding the book.

Another question rises from here. Now that we know the author wanted to express such solemn and sacred feelings, why did he choose the novel over other literary forms to convey his message? We all know that in ancient China, only poetry and essays were highly recognised. Novels, especially folk novels, were looked down upon, with their values not acknowledged by the then society.

Cao did not give an answer to that question. By analysing the book, however, we can try to find the answer via the study of the development of folk novels at the time.

Cao might have chosen the art form of folk novel for three reasons.

Firstly, folk novels would have a large readership and therefore an extensive and long-lasting influence. The popular folk novels could be easily passed down from generation to generation. The long-time circulation and great influence of *Romance of the Three Kingdoms*, *Water Margin* and *Pilgrimage to the West* are strong proof of that. Cao would have known it well and adopted the art form of folk novel, in the hope that his work could be passed down and his experiences and enlightenment be drawn upon by future generations.

现在连一技之长都没有，半辈子穷困潦倒；纪念则是指向女性的，"闺阁中本自历历有人，万不可因我之不肖，自护己短，一并使其泯灭也"，意思是说：女性中还是有不少十分优秀、出色的，不能因为我的不争气，自我掩饰，使这些女孩子湮没无传。这两种感情在作品中都得到了较为充分的表达。前者为家族叙事，后者为青春挽歌，而且以后者为核心，正如作品所说的"大旨谈情"。

这两种感情可以看作是曹雪芹人生体验的浓缩，其中包含着他对世界、对生命的独特理解，他摆脱了个人的恩怨和苦难，并将其升华为一种人类共同的神圣情感。即使是在今天，这些见解也很有启发意义。由此我们也可以体会到，真正的名著是永远都不会过时的。这也是理解这部小说的关键所在，以前人们通常关注作者对女性的描写，对他所表达的忏悔之情则注意不够。

由此又引出另外一个问题：既然要表达如此珍重、神圣的感情，为何选用通俗小说而不用诗文等其他艺术形式呢？要知道，在中国古代，只有诗歌和散文才被人们承认，小说特别是通俗小说则受到歧视，它的价值是得不到社会认可的。

对于这个问题，曹雪芹并没有做出明确的回答。不过我们可以通过对《红楼梦》的分析，并结合中国古代通俗小说在当时的发展状况来揭开其中的谜底。

曹雪芹之所以采用通俗小说文体，大概有如下三个考虑：

一是通俗小说这种艺术样式读者面广，影响大，作品可以广泛、永久地流传下去。此前《三国演义》、《水浒传》、《西游记》等小说的广泛流传和巨大影响证明了这一点。曹雪芹对此十分清楚，他想借助这种文体，让自己的作品永远流传下去，为后人提供人生经验和启迪。

Secondly, folk novels have large volumes that could include many characters and events; all other literary forms could be used in them as well. Through a folk novel, the author could express his meaning easily and display his talents fully, which could not be achieved through a single art forms of poetry or essay.

Thirdly, a novel could hide personal factors. In a novel the author could use imagination and fabrication to make things up so that his personal feelings and experiences could be transformed to the more universal experience of humanity.

Apparently Cao could also use this literary form so as to avoid the danger of persecutions on literature as a result of the stories he told. He did it for the purpose of self-protection. Cao was writing on noble families and experiences using his own experiences and family history, which could easily attract the attention of the officials at the time. To be a dissident and to express different, especially dissatisfactory, views could incur severe punishments. The use of folk novel, for example, the use of imaginations and fabrications, could serve as a disguise to avoid unwanted trouble.

Overall, the literary form of folk novel satisfied all of Cao's needs for his literary creation. As for folk novels, it was an honour that Cao used the form for his work. Through the intricate design of Cao, the great architect, the literary form of the folk novels reached a higher level and a new stage of development.

When talking about Cao's motive for writing *Honglou Meng*, there is one more thing worth mentioning. That is, whether Cao has woven an important message of historical mystery that was not supposed to be told, be it an important hidden message that manifested a change of regime, or a major crime in the royal courts, as has been suggested by some researchers. According to them, the main purpose of *Honglou Meng* is to highlight the struggle among ethnic groups and to make an accusation of the corruption of the royal court. When researchers read *Honglou Meng* as an historical work and try to find the sublime hidden codes with deeper meanings, it is figurative methods that they have adopted.

From the contents of the book, and all other related materials, we can see that Cao had only wanted to write a novel, not an historical record or an autobiography. There is no special hidden message in it, and we shall focus our attention more on the literary side.

二是通俗小说容量大，再多的人物、事件都可以容纳；文备众体，各种文体都可以穿插进来。通俗小说这种文体可以充分表达个人的感情，充分发挥个人的才华，其他文体如诗歌、散文则无法做到这一点。

三是淡化个人因素。利用通俗小说特有的想象、虚构特征，将个人的生活体验转化为人类普遍的感情，写出人性中的共性来。

当然，其中也可能会有避免文字狱、个人自我保护的考虑。因为曹雪芹在作品中使用个人的家世和经历作为素材，容易引起官方的注意。当时官方对持不同政见、表达不满情绪者的处罚是十分严厉的。使用通俗小说这种以想象、虚构为基本特征的文体可以有所掩饰，避免意外的麻烦。

总的来看，是通俗小说这种艺术样式满足了曹雪芹的艺术表达需要。对通俗小说来说，这种选择则意味着一种荣幸，因为经过曹雪芹的苦心经营，通俗小说的艺术品格得到提升，达到一个新的艺术高度。

说到《红楼梦》的创作动机，这里还有一个值得深思的问题，那就是曹雪芹是不是通过这部小说作品隐藏了一段不可告人的历史秘闻，或许是隐含着某些改朝换代的重要信息，或许是隐藏着宫廷大案，就像一些人所研究的那样。按照这种研究，《红楼梦》的主旨是斗争和控诉，反映了民族斗争，控诉了朝廷黑暗。这种将《红楼梦》当历史著作来阅读，通过各种语言密码来寻找微言大义的研究方法，人们通常称作索隐式研究法。

结合作品及相关资料来看，曹雪芹确实是要写一部小说，而不是史书或个人自传，里面并没有隐藏什么特别的信息，我们应该更多地从文学角度来解读。

III

Among so many versions of *Honglou Meng* available today, there is one known as the Jiaxu Version. It was produced in the year of Jiaxu, which is one of the names of the Chinese lunar calendar years. Researchers commonly regard it as the earliest handwritten copy of the original manuscript because of one sentence in it that says, "When Zhiyanzhai copied the book and commented on it again in the year of Jiaxu, the title *Shitou Ji* (*The Story of the Stone*) is kept."

The year of Jiaxu fell on the 19th year of Emperor Qianlong's reign, which was the year 1754. It means that as late as 1754, Cao had already completed writing the book; otherwise, he would not have said he had "spent ten years reading and editing, and revised the manuscript five times, putting the text under different chapters and giving each chapter a title." Besides, it is the year when Zhiyanzhai commented for the second time on the book. We also know that the book seemed to have more than one title, *Shitou Ji*, as the word "kept" indicates. From all the above, we can estimate that Cao began his writing of *Honglou Meng*, at the latest, in the 10th year of Emperor Qianlong's reign, which was the year 1745, when he was around thirty years old. We can also work out the approximate time which Cao spent writing the book. For a writer, the age of thirty is a golden age to have abundant life and social experiences as well as energy and literary talents.

Some other questions still exist:

Firstly, is it an exact or rough number when it says "spent ten years reading and editing, and revised the manuscript five times"? If the numbers are true, as many researchers agree, then why have these numbers been the same in other handwritten copies even though they have been copied at different times? Why didn't other copies record that the manuscript had been read and commented within eleven or twelve years and revised six or seven times? Why were all the numbers the same? Are the numbers just rough ones? If they are, then during which period was *Honglou Meng* written? That is truly a question worth contemplating.

Secondly, if Cao had completed the writing of *Honglou Meng* by the year of Jiaxu, then why are other later handwritten copies, such as the Jimao and Gengchen versions (both Jimao and Gengchen are the names of the Chinese

（三）

在现在所能看到的《红楼梦》的众多版本中，有一个版本叫甲戌本，研究者通常认为它所依据的底本抄录时间是最早的。因为该书中有这么一句话："至脂砚斋甲戌抄阅再评，仍用《石头记》。"意思是说，脂砚斋在甲戌年这一年抄录阅读，并再次进行评论，仍然沿用《石头记》这个书名。

甲戌年是乾隆十九年，也就是1754年。这表明至少在1754年，曹雪芹已大体上完成了全书的创作，否则他不会在作品开头说"批阅十载，增删五次，纂成目录，分出章回"这句话了，何况这一年脂砚斋已经对该书做了第二次评点。而且当时的书名似乎也不只是《石头记》一个，"仍"字表明了还有其他书名。由此可以推断，曹雪芹开始创作《红楼梦》，最迟当在乾隆十年，即1745。这一年曹雪芹三十岁左右。由此我们可以知道《红楼梦》创作的大致时间。对文学创作者来说，这是一个黄金年龄，既有丰富的社会阅历和人生体验，又有旺盛的精力和才情。

不过这里还存在着一些疑问：

第一，作品中所说的"批阅十载，增删五次"到底是实写还是虚写？如果是像许多研究者所认可的、是实写的话，后来的其他抄本抄录的时间并不一样，为什么它们也都是这样交代，而不是说批阅十一载、十二载，增删六次、七次呢？为什么不同时间、不同次数的修改都使用同样的数字，莫非它们是虚指？如果是虚指的话，《红楼梦》的创作到底是在什么时候？这确实是个值得深思的问题。

第二，如果到甲戌这一年，曹雪芹已大体写完了《红楼梦》的话，为什么后来抄录的其他版本如己卯本和庚辰本还那样残

lunar calendar years) incomplete? For example, both the Jimao and Gengchen versions lack Chapters 64 and 67; in the Gengchen version, Chapters 17 and 18 are not separated as in other versions. Also, in the Gengchen version, Chapter 19 does not have a sequential number nor a title; Chapter 22 is incomplete, and the famous Mid-autumn poems by Jia Baoyu and others are missing from Chapter 75, and so on. These signs indicate that the copies were not made from a complete book but rather a half finished work. The years of Jimao and Gengchen fell on the 24th and 25th years of Emperor Qianlong's reign respectively (1759 and 1760), three or four years before Cao's death. Does this mean that Cao had not completed the book when he died? If it were the case, why did he claim that he had completed the book a few years earlier, i.e., in the 19th year of Emperor Qianlong's reign? How did he write and revise his work? Without much information, this again is a very difficult question.

While some details could never be known, there is one thing we can be sure of, which is that Cao had spent tremendous time and effort on his book. He revised it over and over, making minor changes or huge alterations, as described in the introduction in the Jiaxu version, "Each and every character seems to have been written with blood. The works in the ten years are extraordinary." With this in mind, we would easily forgive some minor discrepancies in the book, for example, Jia Baoyu's age, the issue of Qiao Jie (Sister Qiao) and the inconsistency of locations in the book. Suh problems could have happened due to the many times that Cao had revised the contents. Cao would have completed the early drafts of the book and kept revising it and did not finalise the details before he died. Hence, some discrepancies were not picked up and corrected.

The name of the book was also puzzling. *Honglou Meng* seemed to be the first name used, as Yong Zhong, Fucha Mingyi and those who saw the book all used this name in their descriptions. Zhiyanzhai, the commentator, seemed to prefer *Shitou Ji* and used it in his commentaries. After Cheng Weiyuan and Gao E published their version, *Honglou Meng* became the most popular name and has remained the most popular name ever since. Other names, such as *Qingseng Lu* (*Records of a Monk's Feelings*), *Fengyue Baojian* (*Holy Mirror of Love Affairs*) and *Jinling Shi'er Chai* are mentioned in the book, but we do not

缺不全呢？比如己卯本和庚辰本都缺第六十四、六十七回，庚辰本第十七、十八回没有分开，第十九回缺少回次和回目，第二十二回未写完，第七十五回少贾宝玉等人的中秋诗，等等。这显然不像全书已写完的样子，倒更像一个创作中的半成品。己卯、庚辰年分别是乾隆二十四年（1759）和乾隆二十五年（1760）。这个时间在离曹雪芹去世前三、四年，莫非曹雪芹直到去世时都没有完成全书？如果真是这样的话，那他为什么早在乾隆十九年就告知全书已完成的信息呢？他的写作及修改方式又是怎样的呢？由于资料缺乏，这确实是一个很难回答的问题。

有些细节可能永远都无法还原了。不过有一个事实则是可以基本确定的，那就是曹雪芹为了创作《红楼梦》这部小说，曾投入大量的时间、精力，经过多年不断的修改，其中有大改，也有小改，正如甲戌本的凡例中所说的"字字看来皆是血，十年功夫不寻常"，意思是说：每个字读来都是用鲜血写成的，十年所下的功夫确实不同寻常。明白了这一点，对小说中出现的一些疏漏，比如大小宝玉的问题、巧姐的问题、故事地点变移不定的问题等，也就比较容易理解了，这应该是修改过程中出现的问题。曹雪芹也许很早就完成了这部小说的初稿，但后来一直不断修改，大概到去世的时候都未能完成，于是，书中存在的一些疏漏没有来得及弥合而保留下来。

书名问题也让人感到困惑。作品最早似乎叫《红楼梦》，因为当时看到这部小说的永忠、富察明义等人用的都是这个书名。那位评论者脂砚斋则更喜欢《石头记》这个名字，并用在其批点本中。程伟元、高鹗的刊本出版之后，《红楼梦》成为最为流行的书名，一直到今天，这仍然是该书流传最广、影响最大的名字。至于《情僧录》、《风月宝鉴》、《金陵十二钗》等

know whether they have been used. More importantly, we need to respect Cao's say in the name of the book. However, due to the lack of information, it seems impossible to find out now.

According to relevant records, apart from *Honglou Meng*, Cao also wrote a book called *Fengyue Baojian*. What kind of book is it? What is it about? Unfortunately it can no longer be found. We can but make presumptions and speculations.

Knowing that Cao had written *Fengyue Baojian*, people would naturally wonder whether it has any relation to *Honglou Meng*. In Chapter 12 of *Honglou Meng*, there is a magical mirror by the name of "Fengyue Baojian." This could not have been a pure coincidence. Cao must have included it in *Honglou Meng* for good reasons. Some researchers even claim that *Fengyue Baojian* is the original draft of *Honglou Meng* and it contained descriptions of love affairs between men and women and the law of cause and effect. Perhaps because of the sexual descriptions in the book, Cao revised it into *Honglou Meng*, a book that has greater educational significance and is at a higher literary level. It has been passed on for generations. The evolution from *Fengyue Baojian* to *Honglou Meng* indicates the transformation of Cao's thought as well as the development of his literary talent. This theory, again, is reasonable but still needs further evidence to back it up.

IV

The current version of *Honglou Meng* is incomplete with 80 original chapters written by Cao. The remaining 40 chapters that go along with it, whether by Gao E or by someone else, were not written by Cao. On this point there is almost a consensus in the academic world. A series of questions remain unsolved: Did Cao complete his final version? If yes, why is the whole

书名，作品中虽然也曾提及，但不知道是否真正使用过。更为重要的是，曹雪芹本人对书名究竟有何想法，毕竟他是作者，我们要尊重他的意见，但限于资料，今天已无法知晓了。

根据相关记载可以知道，曹雪芹在《红楼梦》之外，还曾写过一部名为《风月宝鉴》的书。《风月宝鉴》到底是一部什么样的书，是讲什么的？遗憾的是，现在我们已无法看到，同样没有答案，只有种种假设和推测。

知道曹雪芹写过《风月宝鉴》一书，人们很自然地会产生联想，这部书和《红楼梦》之间是不是存在着某种关系？从《红楼梦》的相关描写来看，两书似乎存在着一定的关联，因为作品第十二回中提到并描写了一面神奇的镜子，它的名字恰好就叫风月宝鉴，这显然不是偶然的巧合，它既然在《红楼梦》中出现，自有作者的深意在。一些研究者甚至提出，《风月宝鉴》就是《红楼梦》的原稿，它是一部讲男女风月、谈因果报应的小说，可能里面有不少男女欢爱、床第之事的描写，曹雪芹在此基础上，脱胎换骨，将其改造成一部寓意更为深刻、艺术水准更高的传世名著，即《红楼梦》。从《风月宝鉴》到《红楼梦》，既反映了曹雪芹思想的变化，也体现了创作水平的提高。这个看法有一定的道理，但同样需要更多的材料和更为充分的理由来证明。

（四）

我们现在看到的《红楼梦》是不完整的，只有前80回，与它一起流传的后40回不管到底是不是出自高鹗之手，但它确为后人所续，并非曹雪芹所作。关于这一点，学界的看法还是基本一致的。这里就有一系列的问题需要解决：曹雪芹是否写完了全书？如果已经写完的话，为什么现在无法看到？如果没有

book not available? If he did not complete it, then why?

These questions could be answered in two ways.

Firstly, Cao's artistic conception has shown us that he had the overall design of the ending of the book as well as the fate of the main figures. This can be proved in the first few chapters in the book, especially in Chapter 5. In the fifth chapter, the discriptions of the "Illustrations of the First Rank of Jinling City's Twelve Beauties" and the "Second Rank of Jinling's Twelve Beauties" as well as the overtures of *Honglou Meng* have provided clear and detailed ending of the main characters in the novel. Obviously this could only be possible after the author's careful consideration and planning of the overall plot. Furthermore, different skills, such as foreshadowing, hinting, symbolism and telling in advance, are used to foretell the fate of the figures and the ending of the book, responding to the arrangements in the first few chapters in the book. This was also a common practice in literary creations where authors would have a comprehensive design and well-developed plan before writing. It would not be possible for a great writer to think as he writes. For such a literary work that has taken him so many years' hard work, Cao wouldn't have written it randomly and casually.

Secondly, according to the facts available, Cao had written the latter part of his book or at least he completed part of the latter part. Commentaries by Zhiyanzhai revealed some of the details that can be found, for example, in Chapter 22 of the Gengchen version. Comments on a kite riddle by Tanchun read, "This is a prediction of Tanchun's marrying afar. If this person did not go far away when the family calamity comes, the children of the family wouldn't be scattered around." The "marrying afar," "family calamity," and "scattered around" are not mentioned elsewhere in the original 80 chapters. Obviously Zhiyanzhai had read the contents beyond Chapter 80. Otherwise how could he know such details?

Now that we know Cao had an overall planning of the fate of the figures and the ending of the book, also that he had completed at least part of the chapters beyond Chapter 80, how did those manuscripts go missing? Maybe another piece of commentary from Zhiyanzhai could disclose the tip of the iceberg of the puzzle. In Chapter 20 of the Gengchen version, a comment reads, "Once when I was copying the manuscript, five or six sections, 'Baoyu

写完，又是出于什么原因呢？

对这些问题可以分两个方面来回答：

首先，从曹雪芹的艺术构思来看，他对全书的结局以及主要人物命运的安排是有比较成熟的想法和具体的考虑的。这可以从《红楼梦》前几回，特别是第五回中看出来。这一回所描写的金陵十二钗正钗和副钗图册、红楼梦套曲等，对小说主要人物的结局有着较为明确、详细的交代。显然，作者必须对全书的结构布局进行通盘的考虑后，才会这样写。此外，作者在作品中还不断使用伏笔、暗示、象征、预叙等手法预示全书的结局及人物的命运，与前面的描写形成呼应。这也符合文学创作的一般规律，作者只有在进行较为成熟的构思后，才能动笔写作，而不大可能是边写边想，写到哪儿算哪儿。对这样一部花费了许多心血的精心营构之作，曹雪芹是不会这样随便草率的。

其次，从实际创作情况来看，曹雪芹已经写到了后半部，最起码是写了其中的一部分。脂砚斋所写的批语透露了一部分后面的情节。比如庚辰本第二十二回探春的风筝谜下有一条这样的批语："此探春远适之谶也。使此人不远去，将来事败，诸子孙不至流散也。"意思是说：风筝谜是探春将来要远嫁的预言。如果探春不远去的话，将来贾府出现变故，其子孙们也不至于流散。这里面所透露的"远适"、"事败"、"流散"等情节，在前80回中都没有写到，显然，脂砚斋看到了80回后的内容，否则他怎么能知道这些情节呢？

既然曹雪芹对全书的结局及人物的命运有着完整、统一的考虑，80回之后又写了至少一部分，那么这些稿子是如何遗失的呢？脂砚斋的一条批语也许能揭开冰山一角。在庚辰本第二十回有一条批语："余只见有一次誊清时，与'狱神庙慰宝玉'

Being Consoled in the Detention Centre' and others, were missing because of the borrowers. Pity. Pity." From these comments we know that some manuscripts are lost after some people had borrowed them. However, there is one question on the "five or six sections." We are not sure of its exact meaning. Were there five or six chapters lost or were they five or six copies of the manuscripts? Seeing that there were many handwritten copies of manuscripts available now, we can assume that there were many versions of handwritten copies of manuscripts in circulation when the book was first drafted. Another problem arose. The loss of part of a handwritten copy should not have affected other versions copied. Why are the latter parts of the book missing from all handwritten copies? Why? Did the loss happen while Cao was still alive or after his death? If it happened before his death, why didn't he rewrite them? Didn't he have enough time? There have been no convincing answers to these questions.

There is a story about the loss of the manuscripts. After Cao's death, his wife did not have money to buy incense paper money to burn in his commemoration. She found a pile of paper in the house and used them as paper money. That pile of paper turned out to be the manuscript of the chapters beyond Chapter 80. But this is only a story that could not be proved.

On another account, Cheng Weiyuan, in the forewords of *Honglou Meng*, said, "The Table of Content of the original has 120 chapters. However the current versions are not completed, all having 80 chapters. ...The book has a Table of Contents indicating 120 chapters, and how could it be possible that there isn't a complete book?" Another piece of writing provides a support to this view. Cheng's analysis is similar to the account in Yu Rui's *Zaochuang Xianbi*. Perhaps Cao had already planned the structure of the book. But he did not have enough time to complete it before his death.

等五六稿被借阅者迷失，叹叹。"意思是说：我看到有一次稿子誊写清楚时，带有"狱神庙慰宝玉"情节的稿子被借去阅读的人弄丢了，真是可叹啊。可见其中有些稿子是被人借走后迷失的。什么是"五六稿"，"五六稿"到底有多少，是五、六回还是五、六册？这也是一个难以弄清的问题。同样令人疑惑不解的是，从《红楼梦》现存诸多抄本的情况来看，该书在早期流传时，有多种抄本存在，其中某一个抄本的部分迷失应该不会影响其他抄本的流传，何至于多个抄本的后半部全都迷失了呢？原因到底何在？迷失是在曹雪芹生前还是死后？如果在曹雪芹生前的话，他为什么不再补写呢？是时间来不及吗？这些问题现在都没有令人信服的答案。

有这么一个民间传说：曹雪芹去世之后，他的妻子没钱去买纸来祭奠他，看到家里有一叠厚厚的纸，就把它拿来烧了。而这一叠纸正是曹雪芹的手稿，上面写的是80回后的内容。但这仅仅是一个民间传说，无法证实。

另外，程伟元在《红楼梦》序中曾有这样的交代："原目一百廿卷，今所传只八十卷，殊非全本。……是书既有百廿卷之目，岂无全璧？"意思是说：原书的目录有120卷，现在流传的都只有80卷，不是全书。……这部书既然有120回的目录，哪能没有全书呢？这一点在裕瑞的《枣窗闲笔》一书中得到印证："八十回书后惟有目录，未有书文，目录有'大观园抄家'诸条，与刻本后四十回'四美钓鱼'等目录迥然不同。盖雪芹于后四十回虽久蓄志全成，甫立纲领，尚未行文，时不待人矣。"意思是说：80回之后只有目录，没有正文，这个目录中有"大观园抄家"等记载，和刻本后40回"四美钓鱼"等迥然不同。大概曹雪芹虽然准备写成全书，但只写好了大纲，还没有来得及动笔，就去世了。

The Table of Contents which contained 120 chapters and had been sighted by Cheng Weiyuan and Yu Rui, must have existed. But it's a pity that it can't be found now.

Cao did write the latter part of his book. However we do not know how much he had written. One thing is certain. He must have had a very thorough plan. We can't rule out the possibility that he had completed the whole book, but the latter part was lost, hence leaving the full Table of Contents of the book. Even if he had only completed a section of the latter part of the book, he could have written the full Table of Contents because of his thorough plan for it. History is so mean that it would not allow us to view the contents beyond Chapter 80; it would not show us even the Table of Contents of the latter part.

V

When talking about Cao's *Honglou Meng*, we must mention one person, or a few persons. However, we know little about them, and there have been different opinions on this. Let us choose one called Zhiyanzhai, obviously a pen name rather than his real name.

The reason for us to mention his name is that he enjoyed very close relationship with Cao in two ways.

Firstly, his identity is special. The mysterious Zhiyanzhai, who had a very close relationship with Cao, knew many things about Cao's writing of *Honglou Meng*. He knew many secrets that no one else was able to know, for example, Cao's life, motives of writing, the writing process, the meanings behind the words and the plot arrangements. He demonstrated his knowledge in his commentaries. In the past, there had been other commentators for other novels, such as Mao Zonggang's commentaries on Luo Guanzhong's book, Li Zhi and Jin Shengtan on Shi Nai' an's, also Zhang Zhupo on Lanling Xiaoxiao Sheng's. There had been a time gap between the authors and the commentators of at least 100 years. It would not be possible at all for those commentators to have contacts with the authors of the book they commented on. The intimate relationship between Zhiyanzhai and Cao is very rarely seen, almost unique, in Chinese history of novels.

Secondly, the time is special. Usually, commentators of novels lived long

这个120回的目录程伟元、裕瑞都看到过，应该是真实存在过的，但遗憾的是，现在已无法看到了。

曹雪芹确实进行了后半部的创作，虽然写到什么程度我们不知道。但他已有通盘的考虑则是确定无疑的。如果他已写完全书，自然会有后半部的目录，丢失了后半部，但前面的目录仍在，这种可能性并不是没有。即使他只写了其中一部分，在有通盘考虑的情况下，列出全书的回目也未尝不可。历史真是太吝啬了，不让我们看到80回的正文不说，就连目录都不肯让我们看一眼。

（五）

说到曹雪芹创作《红楼梦》，还必须提到一个人，也许是几个人，由于我们对其了解实在太少，而且意见不一，姑且就以一个人为代表吧。此人叫脂砚斋，显然这是一个别号，不是他的真实名字。

之所以提起这个名字，因为他和曹雪芹的关系十分特殊，这种特殊主要表现在如下两个方面：

一是身份特殊。这位神秘的脂砚斋和曹雪芹过从甚密，对曹雪芹创作《红楼梦》的各种情况十分了解，知道许多他人无法知晓的秘密，比如作者的生平情况，创作的动机、过程，作品的寓意、结局的安排等等，并通过批语的形式透露出来。此前的小说评点家与作者，如毛宗岗与罗贯中，李贽、金圣叹与施耐庵，张竹坡与兰陵笑笑生，等等，中间都隔着至少上百年的时间距离，相互之间根本没有认识、往来的可能性。像脂砚斋与曹雪芹这种十分密切的亲友关系在中国古代小说史上是十分少见的，甚至可以说是绝无仅有的。

二是时间特殊。通常情况下，小说评点者与作者所生活的

after the authors' time and the commentaries appeared many years after the circulation of the books. The case of Zhiyanzhai is different. He started his commentaries while Cao was writing the book, parallel to Cao's writing time, what we call "Zero Time Difference Commentary." What became more special is that Zhiyanzhai was not satisfied with purely commentating and that he actually participated in the writing and revising of the book. Some of his suggestions could have been taken by Cao.

Zhiyanzhai had commented many times, with thousands of entries of comments registered. The commentaries, by a commentator and an insider, are of extremely high value in both literary and historical senses. Zhiyanzhai commented on different aspects of literary ideology. The commentaries also provided very important information on the author's life and the situations under which he wrote the book.

Now, who on earth is Zhiyanzhai? What is his relationship with Cao? This is an unsolved puzzle, and many suggestions are put forth. Some say Zhiyanzhai is Cao's brother while other argue that they are the same person; some say Zhiyanzhai is Cao's uncle and some even suggest it is Shi Xiangyun, one of the core female figures in *Honglou Meng*. There are others who believe Zhiyanzhai is a liar who did not know Cao at all, and the commentaries are pure fabrications.

Some of these suggestions are not tenable and can be eliminated straightaway, for example, the claim that Zhiyanzhai is Cao. It is because in his commentaries, Zhiyanzhai had clearly stated that he and Cao are not the same person. Some other claims could not be proved by any information available, for example, the Shi Xiangyun version. Whether Shi Xiangyun is a real person or only a figure in the book is a question of its own right, let alone determining she is Zhiyanzhai. Actually, the two suggestions make sense to a certain degree, but they need to be carefully considered and backed up by solid evidence. Nevertheless, we have not been able to identify Cao Xueqin's father; it would be even more difficult to know who his uncles and cousins were, and to determine whether Zhiyanzhai was a cheat or not.

No matter what, there is no question about the fact that Zhiyanzhai is very close to Cao. He may be a family member, a relative or a friend. He knew a lot about the writing of *Honglou Meng* and he participated in the writing in a very

年代往往隔着较长的时间，评论一般是在作品流传多年之后进行的。但脂砚斋则不然，他在曹雪芹创作《红楼梦》的同时就已着手进行评论，可以说是与创作同步，堪称零距离批评。而且更为特殊的是，脂砚斋并不满足于单纯的评论，他实际上还参与了小说的创作和修改，其意见有时也会被曹雪芹采纳。

这位脂砚斋前后批点多次，写了上千条批语。评点家兼知情者的特殊身份使脂砚斋的评论具有文学与史料的双重价值：它一方面对作品思想艺术的各个方面进行点评，另一方面又透露不少有关作者生平及创作情况的珍贵信息。

那么，这位脂砚斋到底是什么人？他与曹雪芹究竟是什么关系？这也是研究者十分关心但一直悬而未决的一个难题，为此研究者提出了多种说法：有人说脂砚斋是曹雪芹的兄弟，有人说脂砚斋就是曹雪芹本人，有人说脂砚斋是曹雪芹的叔父，还有人说脂砚斋就是作品中的主要人物史湘云。当然，也有人说脂砚斋是个骗子，他根本就不认识曹雪芹，他的批语是编造出来的。

这些说法有些不能成立，是可以直接排除的，如脂砚斋是曹雪芹本人的说法就是如此，因为脂砚斋在评论中明确交代他和曹雪芹并非一人，这一点还是比较可信的；有些则是根据现有的资料无法论证出来的，比如史湘云说，史湘云是否真有其人还很难说，更不用说把她和脂砚斋划等号了。其实两种说法都有一定的道理，但同样需要仔细斟酌，需要过硬的证据来证明。不过，在连曹雪芹的父亲是谁都没有办法弄清楚的情况下，再来谈论他的兄弟、叔父是谁，更是困难重重，无法解决。至于脂砚斋是不是骗子，要证明这一点同样十分困难。

不管怎样，脂砚斋与曹雪芹关系密切，可能是家人，可能是亲戚，也可能是朋友，这一点是没有什么问题的。他熟悉和了解《红楼梦》的创作情况，以特殊的形式参与了创作，他的批语对

special way. There is consensus that his commentaries provided great assistance to the further understanding of all aspects of *Honglou Meng*. We need to thank him because we would have known much less about Cao without him. As to the question of who this mysterious person really is, it would be a puzzle that may never be solved. Indeed, we know too little about *Honglou Meng* and the people related to it. It seems to be a little pessimistic yet it is the right beauty of *Honglou Meng*. The less we know, the more we want to find out. If we had known everything, the *Honglou Meng* boom would not be as fervant as it is now.

我们深入理解《红楼梦》的各个方面有着较大的帮助，这一点读者和研究者还是存在共识的。我们感谢脂砚斋，如果没有他，我们对曹雪芹的了解将更加贫乏。至于这位神秘的人物究竟是谁，恐怕只能是个永远无解的谜了。围绕《红楼梦》与它有关的人和事，我们知道的确实太少了，这似乎有些悲观，不过《红楼梦》的魅力也正在于此，越是不知道的，人们越想知道，如果什么都了解得一清二楚的话，也许《红楼梦》的研究就不会像现在这么热了。

大观园
Grand View Garden

四　不是情人不泪流 ——曹雪芹的思想

Chapter Ⅳ　Sentimental Tears: Cao's Thoughts

The simplest laws of nature always seem to be the most easily ignored. The research on the profound and complex themes in the epic novel *Honglou Meng*, seemingly provides proof of this. Over the last century, a great number of Hong experts have been searching other classics for traces of records about the author, his family, and various versions of the novel. These experts, looking for "needles in a haystack," managed to find records that revealed several different possibilities of Cao's ancestries, tracing all the way back to the Three Kingdoms Period. We can't say that their arduous work has been in vain, yet all the complexity seems to have overshadowed a simple truth that, no matter how grand or how excellent *Honglou Meng* is, it is only a popular novel, a sad story that reveals the tragedies of life. It is not an encyclopedia, nor a medicine that can heal the world, and it certainly does not reveal any historical secrets. Yet it is for this reason that *Honglou Meng* has remained popular since its creation, and also the reason why so many readers have come to love the novel.

Different people of different experiences, views, interests, and education would naturally view *Honglou Meng* differently. The famous writer Lu Xun had an interesting and vivid take on such phenomenon. He said, "The Orthodox see *Change* in it; moralists see pornography; scholars see romance; revolutionaries see anti-Manchurian actions; gossips see royal court secrets and scandals..." Everyone sees different things in *Honglou Meng*. Nevertheless, it does not mean the novel can't be fully comprehended, nor does it mean one can easily understand all. Behind the chaotic and glorious scenes, we have some consensus about what lies between the lines.

Honglou Meng, despite its rich contents and the fact that it could be viewed and understood from different angles and at various levels, is after all, as readers would agree, a work of tragic novel. Even though, seen from the surface, the book is all about stories of family to-dos and romance, we can still feel the tragic atmosphere and sadness between the lines, and hear a sad song for life being chanted.

最浅显的道理往往最容易被人忽略，看似高深莫测、博大精深的《红楼梦》研究似乎也在验证和重复着这个道理。近百年来，数量庞大的红学家们在浩若烟海的各类典籍中苦苦寻觅，对《红楼梦》的作者、家世、版本等问题极尽大海捞针之能事，将曹雪芹的远祖一直追溯到三国时，为曹雪芹找了好几个祖籍。不能说这些辛劳没有价值，但在繁琐复杂的红学研究背后，恰恰掩盖了这样一个再简单不过的事实，那就是《红楼梦》无论如何优秀，如何伟大，它也只是一部小说，一部抒写社会人生悲剧的通俗小说，它不是百科全书，不是救世良药，更不是什么历史密码。而这正是《红楼梦》面世以来流行不衰的根本所在，也正是广大读者喜爱这部小说的奥秘所在。

因读者经历、观念、趣味及学养的不同，在阅读《红楼梦》时，自然会产生各种不同的看法和见解，著名作家鲁迅对这种现象曾有十分生动、精彩的描述："经学家看见《易》，道学家看见淫，才子看见缠绵，革命家看见排满，流言家看见宫闱秘事……"意思是说：经学家从书中看见易经的道理，道学家从书中看见淫乱，才子从书中看见缠绵的爱情，革命家从书中看见对满族的排斥，流言家从书中看到宫廷秘闻，每个人都可以从《红楼梦》中读出不同的东西来。但这并不是说，《红楼梦》是不可理解的，或是说是可以随便理解的，因为在纷繁芜杂的喧闹表象背后，人们还是有着一些基本的共识。

《红楼梦》的思想内容虽然十分丰富，可供多角度、多层次地解读，不过总的来说，它是一部悲剧小说，相信读过这部小说的读者会有同感。尽管全书从表面上看，不过是一些家庭琐事、闺阁闲情的描写，但字里行间无不弥漫着一层浓重的悲剧氛围和感伤色彩，它所吟唱的是一首凄婉哀伤的人生挽歌。

I

Before the philosophical thoughts of *Honglou Meng* is talked about, it is necessary to give a brief introduction of the story outline.

The stories happen mainly in the family of Jia. The ancestors of the Jia family are two brothers, Duke Ning and Duke Rong. They fight for the country and have been significantly successful. They are rewarded by the emperor and become a well-known noble family. The descendants of the two brothers enjoy royal benevolence, power, and wealth. However, these descendants, being complacent and without any ambition, indulge themselves in pleasures and fail to carry on the family glory, and the family inevitably goes downhill. The author depicts the whole process of the Jia family's decline from glory.

In the Jia clan, Duke Ning's position is inherited by his eldest son, Jia Daihua, whose title passes on to his second son Jia Jing after his death. However, Jia Jing is more interested in finding a Taoist's way to immortality and cares little about other things. The house affairs of Duke Ning then falls on Jia Jing's son, Jia Zhen, who is not an ambitious man and likes luxury and women, as well as gambling. His wife is from a You family. Like father like son. Jia Rong, Jia Jing's son, is also a playboy. He marries Qin Keqing who dies young. Jia Jing also has a daughter, Jia Xichun.

Duke Rong's position is inherited by his eldest son, Jia Daishan. Daishan's wife, known as Grandma Jia in the book, comes from a famous Shi family, another grand family at that time. After the death of Jia Daihua and Jia Daishan, Grandma Jia, being the most senior member in the Jia clan, becomes the most powerful person. Her granddaughter, Shi Xiangyun, is a very straightforward girl and pays frequent visits to the Jia family. After Jia Daishan's death his eldest son Jia She inherits his title. However, Jia She indulges himself in women and wine, and has little time for family affairs. Jia She and his wife, who comes from a Xing family, have two children: a son, Jia Lian, and a daughter, Jia Yingchun. Jia Lian's wife is Wang Xifeng, Madame Wang's niece. Jia Lian has a daughter by the name of Qiao Jie. Wang Xifeng is very capable and takes charge of many affairs in the House of Duke Rong. Jia Lian has a concubine called Ping'er, who is an assistant to Wang Xifeng.

Jia She has a younger brother, Jia Zheng, and a younger sister, Jia Min. Jia

（一）

在谈及《红楼梦》的思想之前，有必要先对这部小说的主要故事内容进行一番简要的介绍。

故事主要发生在一个姓贾的家族内。这个家族的祖先为宁国公、荣国公兄弟俩，他们历经沙场征战，立下赫赫功勋，受到皇帝的封赏，缔造了一个地位显赫的望族。其后代们享受着前辈传下的恩宠、权势和财富，但他们大多贪图享乐，好逸恶劳，不求上进，无法将家族的辉煌延续下去，整个家族在走下坡路。作品描写了贾氏家族从繁盛走向衰落的全过程。

在贾氏家族中，承袭宁国公职位的为其长子贾代化。贾代化死后，其第二个儿子贾敬承袭父职，但这位贾敬的兴趣却在修仙成道上，对家族事务在内的其他事情漠不关心。宁府主要由贾敬的儿子贾珍来管理。贾珍不求上进，生活奢侈，贪色好赌。他的妻子姓尤。贾珍的儿子贾蓉也是这样一个人，年纪轻轻就开始堕落，成为一个游手好闲的不良青年。其妻子叫秦可卿，去世较早。此外，贾敬还有一个女儿叫贾惜春。

承袭荣国公职位的为其长子贾代善，他的妻子来自一个姓史的显赫家族，小说中称其为贾母。贾代化、贾代善死后，贾母便成为贾氏家族中年龄最长者，有着很高的威望和地位。她有个外孙女叫史湘云，性格豪爽，经常往来贾府。贾代善死后，承袭其职位的是长子贾赦，但他整日沉湎于酒色之中，很少关心家族的事务。贾赦的妻子姓邢。他有两个孩子：儿子贾琏，女儿贾迎春。贾琏的妻子王熙凤是王夫人的侄女，两人生有一个女儿叫巧姐。王熙凤很有才干，管理着荣府内部的诸多事务。贾琏有一个妾叫平儿，是王熙凤的助手。

贾赦的弟弟叫贾政，妹妹叫贾敏，其中贾政受到皇帝的恩

Zheng is granted a position in the royal court while Jia Min marries an official called Lin Ruhai and gives birth to a daughter, Lin Daiyu. Jia Min dies when Lin Daiyu is very young.

Jia Zheng's wife is from a known family. In the book she is named Madame Wang. She has three children. Their eldest child, a son, is Jia Zhu who dies very young, leaving behind his wife Li Wan and a son Jia Lan. Jia Zheng's second child is Jia Yuanchun, who becomes the emperor's consort and brings honour to the Jia family. The youngest is Jia Baoyu, the hero of this novel. Jia Baoyu is born with a piece of jade in his mouth, and because of this, he is treasured by his grandmother, Grandma Jia, and receives lots of privileges in the house. Jia Zheng also has two children with his concubine Auntie Zhao. The two children are Jia Tanchun, the elder sister, and Jia Huan, the son.

Madame Wang's younger sister is known as Auntie Xue because she marries a merchant from a Xue family. Xue dies young and leaves behind two children. The elder is a son called Xue Pan, a troublemaker, and his younger sister is Xue Baochai.

Those are the main figures in the Jia family and its relatives. There are also many servants and maids. Even though they are of lower social status, all of them have their own characteristics and aspirations. Examples include Xiren, Qingwen, Sheyue and Qiuwen, maids for Jia Baoyu; Zijuan and Xueyan, maids for Lin Daiyu; Yuanyang, a maid for Grandma Jia; Jinchai and Yuchai for Madame Wang, etc. A fair amount of descriptions are devoted to those people.

The stories of *Honglou Meng* develop among those people. There are a great number of them, and their relationships are complicated. Their stories cover various aspects of the ancient Chinese society.

The stories begin with Lin Daiyu's moving into the Jia Mansion. Lin, whose mother dies when young, is sent to live with her grandmother, Grandma Jia. Grandma Jia takes Daiyu under her full protection and cherishes her dearly. Jia Baoyu and Lin Daiyu live together from a young age and become close to each other. The natural feelings between them are pure and romantic love as they grow up together. Xue Baochai follows her mother and brother to the capital city to live in the Jia Mansion for a long time. Xue is adored by all because of her generosity and easygoing disposition. Xue is also close to Jia

赐，在朝中做官；贾敏嫁给一个叫林如海的朝廷官员，生了一个女儿林黛玉。贾敏在林黛玉很小的时候就去世了。

贾政的妻子来自一个姓王的显赫家族，小说中称其为王夫人，他们生有三个孩子：其中长子为贾珠，他在很年轻的时候就去世了，留下妻子李纨和儿子贾兰。其女儿为贾元春，她嫁给了皇帝，成为地位尊崇的贵妃，为贾氏家族带来了荣耀。第三个儿子叫贾宝玉，是小说的主人公。当他出生的时候，嘴里竟然衔了一块美玉，这一奇迹使他受到祖母贾母的特别宠爱，在家族中享有很高的地位。此外，贾政和他的妾赵姨娘还生了两个孩子：长女叫贾探春，次子叫贾环。

王夫人的妹妹嫁给一个姓薛的商人，小说中称其为薛姨妈，她的丈夫很早就去世，留下两个孩子，长子叫薛蟠，是个无事生非的莽撞公子哥，次女名叫薛宝钗。

上面介绍的是贾府的主要家族成员和他们的亲戚，围绕着这些家族成员，还有许多仆从和丫环们，他们虽然地位低下，但都有着自己的个性和追求，比如贾宝玉身边的袭人、晴雯、麝月、秋纹，林黛玉身边的紫鹃、雪雁，贾母身边的鸳鸯，王夫人身边的金钏、玉钏，等等。作品用了不少篇幅来描写这些人的生活。

《红楼梦》的故事主要在上述这些人中间展开，全书人物众多，关系复杂，写到了中国古代社会的各个层面。

作品以林黛玉进贾府为正式开场。林黛玉因早年丧母，贾母将她接到自己家中抚养，对其十分疼爱。贾宝玉、林黛玉从小生活在一起，青梅竹马，两人来往密切，建立了十分深厚的感情。等他们逐渐长大时，这种感情就变成了纯洁、浪漫的爱情。后来，薛宝钗也随着母亲、哥哥到京城投奔亲戚，长年住在贾家。薛宝钗为人大方、随和，受到周围人们的喜爱。她与

Baoyu, a situation not happily received by Lin who has always been sensitive and suspicious. Jia and Lin often argue because of Xue and minor things around their lives. However, it is through those arguments that Jia and Lin get to know more about each other and win trust from each other. They would often have tacit agreement. The love affair between them is morally unacceptable and it is not approved by elders in the family. They have to hide their feelings and go on in secret and subtle ways. In the old times in China, parents and grandparents decided who their children would marry. The young normally had no choice of their own.

Jia Baoyu loves being with the girls and is friendly to his servants and treats them equally. He does not like studying books and does not want to become a government official. He often befriends actors, who at those times are looked down upon in society. Because of his rebellious characteristics, Jia Baoyu is not understood and accepted by people around him. He is regarded as a lunatic and is once punished very harshly by his father Jia Zheng. However, nothing could change Jia Baoyu and he goes on living like always. The Jia family, in order to welcome the visiting imperial consort, Jia Yuanchun, builds an enormous garden, the Grand View Garden. Jia Baoyu, Lin Daiyu, Xue Baochai, Jia Yingchun, Jia Tanchun, Jia Xichun and others move into the garden and have enjoyed a pleasant period of time.

Jia Baoyu's life is closely connected with the fate of the Jia family. Due to the fact that most members of the Jia family are complacent and have indulged themselves in pleasures, they become corrupt and do whatever they want. They ruin their family's wealth and cause their family to decline. The signs of decline have become very obvious by Chapter 80 of the book.

To our disappointment, we can only read the first 80 chapters written by Cao Xueqin, and the rest are lost. According to the hints in the first 80 chapters, we could work out that there would be great changes befalling the Jia family beyond Chapter 80. The Jia family would be raided because some members broke the law. The life of Jia Baoyu, as well as that of many others, would change dramatically. They would fall into poverty and the whole family would receive a heavy blow.

The later 40 chapters in the current popular 120-chapter version were not considered by many to be written by Cao but by someone else, and was called

贾宝玉也有比较密切的交往，这引起了敏感、多疑的林黛玉的不满。贾宝玉、林黛玉因薛宝钗及身边一些生活琐事多次发生争吵，并在这种争吵中相互试探，取得对方信任，达到了心灵上的默契。但这种爱情在当时是不符合道德规范的，也没有得到家族长辈的认可，因而只能以较为隐秘、含蓄的方式进行。在中国古代，青年男女的伴侣通常由他们的父母、祖父母等长辈决定，本人通常是没有选择权的。

贾宝玉喜欢和女孩子们在一起，对待仆人、丫环们也很友善，能够较为平等地对待他们。他不愿意读书，也不愿意走做官的道路，还经常和当时受到社会歧视的伶人交往。他的这些思想具有叛逆性，不能为周围的人理解和接受，被视为疯癫，为此父亲贾政曾将其毒打一顿。但这些都未能改变贾宝玉的性格和思想，他仍然按照自己的意愿生活。贾府为了迎接贵妃贾元春的探亲，修建了一座很大的庭院，叫大观园。后来，贾宝玉和林黛玉、薛宝钗、贾迎春、贾探春、贾惜春等人搬到这里生活，度过了一段十分美好的时光。

贾宝玉的生活和贾家的命运密切地联系在一起。由于贾府的主要家庭成员贪图享受，荒淫堕落，胡作非为，坐吃山空，导致了整个家族的衰落。到小说第八十回的时候，这种衰落的趋势已十分明显。

令人遗憾的是，我们目前只能看到曹雪芹所写的前80回，后面的部分已找不到了。不过根据作品前面的提示，我们可以知道，80回之后，贾府将出现重大变故，因家族成员们违法乱纪等原因，贾府被朝廷抄家，贾宝玉等人的生活由此发生戏剧性改变，陷入贫困的状态。整个家族受到打击，走向破败。

现在流行的120回《红楼梦》中的后40回，通常认为并非出自曹雪芹之手，而是另外一个人续写的，属于《红楼梦》的

a continuation of the original book. The continuation was often published with the previous 80 chapters and was also quite popular. Here is a brief introduction.

In the later 40 chapters, Grandma Jia disapproves of Jia Baoyu and Lin Daiyu's love affair. Unbeknowing to him, Jia Baoyu is deceived by Madame Wang, Wang Xifeng and others, and marries Xue Baochai instead. Lin Daiyu dies because of her illness and anger. All those events make Jia feel extremely hurt and guilty about Lin. Later, Jia Yuanchun dies of illness and the Jia family loses its biggest supporter. The Jia family is stricken when it is raided due to some criminal acts. After this, the family is no longer a prestigious and wealthy family. Wang Xifeng, Grandma Jia, Jia Yingchun and Auntie Zhao die one after the other. Jia Tanchun gets married and moves to a faraway place; Jia Xichun leaves home and becomes a Buddhist nun while Jia She and Jia Zhen are dismissed and sent to remote place to work as labourers. Jia Baoyu, suffering from the marriage trauma, the death of relatives, and the family decline, experiences great mental torture and becomes disillusioned with the world. Eventually, after taking part in the official-selection exam, he retreats from the world and becomes a Buddhist monk. Even though the Jia family has a chance to revive, as hinted by the author of the later 40 chapters, the past glories of the Duke Ning and Duke Rong, after Jia Baoyu becomes a monk, could not be restored. The sufferings of losing family members could not be forgotten easily. Thus, the later 40 chapters carry on with the stories in the previous 80 chapters and focus on a family tragedy.

II

Honglou Meng mainly demonstrates to us a family tragedy and a complete story of a family's decline from glory. This is the main plot of the book, travelling many decades, depicting hundreds of people. The decline of the family was like the toppling of a gigantic mansion, or the burst of a river, with far-reaching repercussions. In this main story, the misfortunes and sufferings of individuals in the family flowed together and formed a great river of sadness. The misfortunes no longer belonged to any individual, yet it became a collective expression of sadness, a sadness of the whole society and even of the whole humanity.

Many people commented that Cao, like Jia Baoyu, hated his own family

续书。这个续书经常和前80回一起刊行，影响很大。这里对其内容稍作介绍：

在后40回中，由于贾母等人的反对，贾宝玉被王夫人、王熙凤等人蒙蔽，在不知情的状态下娶薛宝钗为妻，而林黛玉则在疾病和悲愤中死去，这让贾宝玉感到极为痛苦和愧疚。其后贾元春病逝，贾氏家族失去后台，由于违法乱纪，被朝廷抄家，受到严重打击。家族的声望和财富不再，一些人如王熙凤、贾母、贾迎春、赵姨娘等相继去世，贾探春嫁到很远的地方，贾惜春出家为尼，贾赦、贾珍也被发配到外地服役。婚姻的不如意、亲人的死去、家族的破败，等等，这一切都使贾宝玉陷入巨大的痛苦之中，也使他对这个世界产生厌倦之感。他终于在参加科举考试之后，出家为僧。尽管后40回的作者预示，贾宝玉出家之后，贾氏家族还有复兴的可能，但这更多的是一种心理安慰，因为宁国公、荣国公当年所创造的家族辉煌是不可能再出现了，家族成员去世离散所带来的痛苦也不是马上就能遗忘的。因此，后40回延续了前80回的故事，写的仍然是一个家族悲剧。

（二）

《红楼梦》首先展现的是一出家族悲剧，它较为完整地展现了一个家族从兴旺发达到破败衰落的全过程。这是全书的一个主线，它延续数年，涉及数百人，仿佛大厦崩塌、洪水决堤，具有十分强烈的震撼效果。在这一大背景下，个人的不幸和苦难如涓涓细流，逐渐汇成家族的悲伤长河。这种不幸不仅仅是属于个人，它更是一种集体感伤情绪的传达，传达的是整个社会乃至人类的哀伤。

从作品的具体描写来看，曹雪芹并不像有的研究者所说

and wanted to have nothing to do with them and wanted be their grave-digger. However, from the detailed descriptions in the book, Cao was not like that. On the contrary, via Jia Baoyu, Cao expressed his strong passion towards his family, his pride in it and his sense of pity when the family fell. For example, in Chapter 5, Duke Rong and Duke Ning, the ancestors of Jia Baoyu, had told the Fairy in Illusory Land to "assist him to jump out of the circle of illusion and walk on the correct path." The two brothers hoped that Jia Baoyu could take up some responsibility in the family and take the righteous path. In Chapter 13, before her death, Qin Keqing appeared in Wang Xifeng's dream and left a message "to save up in times of glory in readiness for times of calamity. In this way, the family could be protected for generations." In other words, she was asking Wang Xifeng to be prepared in advance so as to find a path for retreat when the time came for the family to collapse. Also, the descriptions of the ancestor ceremony on New Year's Eve, in the House of Duke Ning in Chapter 53, was so solemn and sincere, and the author's feeling was obvious. The above-mentioned scenarios, be it conversations between people or descriptions of the events, were written with earnestness. There was not a hint of sarcasm or irony and Cao was grateful and paid tribute to the founders of the family. Obviously he wanted someone to carry on the glory of their family and develop it further.

Seen from a different angle, Cao was like the Goddess Nu Wa, repairing the hole in the sky. He wished his offspring could carry on and develop the family glory, instead of destroying it. Even though he had expressed criticisms and condemnations towards the dark sides of the family, his deep passion for his family should not be disregarded just because of his sharp criticism. To sing highly of something is a way to express one's feelings. To criticise something is another way. There is a saying that "the harsher the criticism, the deeper the love." Who would not wish his family to prosper and develop? Who would want his family shattered and with no descendents? Cao was someone who lived in the time of the Qing Dynasty, over 200 years ago and he would not have modern ideas like those of our times. People nowadays would not hope for bad luck to their family. In the last 40 chapters the descriptions of achieving high in government and family prosperity were heavily criticised and even abused by some researchers. When we look at the full picture, taking

的，让笔下的主人公贾宝玉厌恶自己的家族，要与家族决裂，成为家族的掘墓人。而事实上，他通过贾宝玉流露出对家族十分深厚的感情，有着强烈的家族自豪感，对家族的破败怀有深深的惋惜之情，这可以从作品的相关描写中看得出来。比如在第五回，荣国公、宁国公这两位贾宝玉的祖辈对幻警仙姑曾有过这样的嘱咐："使彼跳出迷人圈子，入于正路。"他们希望幻警仙姑规劝贾宝玉，让他负起家族的责任，走上正路。比如第十三回，秦可卿临死前，给王熙凤托梦，说了这样的话："于荣时筹画下将来衰时的世业，亦可谓常保永全了。"希望王熙凤提前做些准备，避免家族的衰亡，或面临衰败时，留条后路。再比如第五十三回"宁国府除夕祭宗祠"对祭祖场面的描写，十分庄重、虔诚，由此不难看出作者的感情取向。以上无论是人物的对话，还是场面的描写，作者都是郑重其事的，丝毫看不出有任何反讽、嘲弄的色彩。对家族基业的那些开创者们，曹雪芹是充满敬意和景仰之情的。显然，他希望能有人将家族的基业传下去，并发扬光大。

因此，从这个角度来看，曹雪芹是个补天者，他希望子孙们能延续、光大祖先传下来的家族事业，而不是去破坏它。他虽然对家族内部的种种弊端颇多批评和指责，但不能因为这些尖锐、辛辣的批评就否定其对家族的深厚感情。歌颂是一种表达感情的方式，批评同样也能传达这种感情，只不过表达的方式不同而已，正所谓爱之愈深，恨之愈切。作为一个正常人，有谁不希望自己的家族兴旺发达、常保永全，而整天盼着它分崩离析、断子绝孙？要知道曹雪芹生活在二百多年前的清朝，他不可能有现代人的想法。即使是在今天，人们也未必会这样做。在后40回中，兰桂齐芳、家道中兴的描写曾受到不少研究者的严厉批评、指责甚至漫骂，但是，如果对前80回有着全面、

the first 80 chapters into consideration, we can tell that the story was not at all a matter of low tastes. It reflected Cao's own sentiments perfectly.

Deep passion and pride need not be expressed in terms of high praise. Cao chose another pattern. His description of family is very reflective. He did not blindly uphold and praise everything about the family. On the contrary, using his discerning eye, he scrutinised various defects of the family, pondering over the root causes of the decline. In his book, the relationships and conflicts between father and son, mother and son, husband and wife, wife and concubine, among brothers and cousins are all vividly described. All conflicts mingle together and form a very strong force which eventually destroys the hundred-year family and led to its inevitable tragedy and downfall.

As to the reason for the family tragedy, Cao had his own clear understanding. He demonstrated his detestation for the corrupt family members, their incompetence, and conspiracies against others, as shown in Chapter 74 via the words of Jia Tanchun. However, his comments are constrained. He did not simply vent his feelings. He used understated descriptions and left his readers to explore the meanings between the lines.

The complete darkness of the Jia family is vividly and comprehensively exposed. Descriptions are extensive: from core family members who hold extreme power to young female servants of inferior social status; from external dealings with officials to the internal conspiracies against others; from excessive indulgence and lewdness of men and their wanton tastes to rivals of jealous and trouble-making women; from extravagant funerals to greedy anticipation of monthly profits and usurious loans. All these are the reasons for a family decline. In sum, they form a very strong force that destroys a family.

Such panoramic exposure of the family has its significance. Using vivid characters and events, Cao shows us a once grand family of over one century

深切了解的话就会发现，这样的情节安排一点都不庸俗，它和曹雪芹的思想恰恰是一脉相承的。

深厚的感情和自豪感并不一定非得用赞美的口吻来表达，曹雪芹就选择了另一种方式，他对家族的描写是带有反思色彩的。他不是毫无原则地维护和赞美家族的一切，而是用挑剔的眼光审视着家族内部存在的种种弊端，思考着家族从盛到衰的深层根源所在。在作品中，家族成员父子、母子之间，夫妻、妻妾之间，兄弟、嫡庶之间，主仆之间等等，几乎家族内外的所有关系及矛盾都得到了十分充分的描写和展现，各种矛盾交织在一起，形成一股巨大的破坏力量，最终摧毁了这个百年旧族，造成了整个家族不可避免的悲剧。

对造成家族悲剧的根源，曹雪芹有着很清醒的认识，对家族主要成员的堕落、无能与勾心斗角，他表现出一种特别的愤恨，在作品的第七十四回借助探春之口表达了这种情绪。不过，他在作品中的感情流露还是很有节制的，他没有不加控制地宣泄自己的情绪，而是通过冷静、从容的叙述，让读者从字里行间看出其感情取向，明白其用意所在。

作品对贾府家族内部存在的诸多弊端给予全方位的揭露，无论是高高在上的家族骨干，还是身份低微的丫环仆从；无论是对外的交通外官，还是内部的勾心斗角；无论是男人们的荒淫无耻，坐吃山空，还是女人们的争风吃醋，惹是生非；无论是丧礼上的大肆挥霍，风光无限，还是月例的借贷生利，延期发放等等，都得到了较为充分的描写。而这些都是导致家族破败的根由，它们逐渐汇集起来，成为一支强大的破坏力量，摧毁了整个家族。

这种家族全貌式的展示自然是有其深意的，曹雪芹以具体可感、生动形象的人物、事件描写让读者看到一个显赫一时的

of history in decline, from its full-blossomed glory to its bleak emptiness in the end, and also reveals the root causes of the decline. The description is not an outburst of feelings but an in-depth contemplation of the past. To Cao, the fall of the family is not caused by one single person overnight. It is an explosion of long accumulated and inevitable conflicts. In this process, all family members, low or high in their status, male or female, are all sufferers of the tragedy and at the same time the creators of their own tragedy. In other words, they bury themselves. The corrupt Jia She, Jia Lian, Jia Zhen, Jia Rong and others are certainly to blame; Jia Baoyu's rebellious behaviour also has shocked the foundation of the house; Wang Xifeng, being the housekeeper, has caused chaos in the house because of her abuse of power in deciding family affairs and in pocketing public benefits. The turbulence in the kitchen caused by Wang also has a destructive impact upon the house. Cao's revelations surpass those of other literature in terms of comprehensiveness and profoundity.

The overall picture is that the author did not hide anything when he disclosed the internal defects of the family, his criticism is so clear and so sharp. He spared no effort, especially in disclosing those male members of the family who are the real culprits. Perhaps because the author had experienced such things before, his sadness and anger are palpable.

The fall of a family is not an isolated social phenomenon. Even though each family has its own uniqueness and sustainability, the family glory and decline are closely related to the outside world by various cultural factors. Those factors could be good and they could also be fatal. In the book, Cao's main focus is on the Jia family and he peppered it with some descriptions of other families. Those families include Xue, which is described in a bit more detail, and the Shi, Wang and Zhen families which are mentioned when they interact with the Jia family. They could be regarded as a huge social contextual background for the stories in the book. Cao uses one family as an example to reflect on the whole society. The descriptions of one family have revealed a lot

百年望族从鲜花着锦、烈火烹油的盛况沦落到一片白茫茫大地真干净的沧桑巨变，并点明其根源所在。这并非情绪的宣泄，而是冷静的思考，达到了一定的深度。在曹雪芹看来，贾府走向破败、衰落，并非一人一时之力可成，它是各种矛盾冲突经过长时期积累之后的总爆发，有其历史必然性。在这一过程中，家族的每位成员，无论身份高低，无论性别如何，他们既是悲剧的承担者，同时也都是悲剧的制造者，也就是说，是他们自己动手埋葬了自己。贾赦、贾琏、贾珍、贾蓉等人的荒淫堕落、胡作非为固然是导致家族悲剧的直接因素，但贾宝玉的叛逆和反抗同样从根本上动摇了支撑家族的基石；身为管家的凤姐以权谋私、中饱私囊，将整个家族一步步带向万劫不复的深渊，厨房内部的种种风波不断扩大，同样也可以形成推翻大厦的致命力量。这种揭示全面而有深度，是先前的同类小说作品所无法企及的。

　　总的来看，作者在揭示家族内部的种种弊端时，笔无藏锋，批判色彩是很鲜明的，也是很尖锐的。特别是对那些家族的男性成员们，他们对家族的衰败负有主要责任。作者对其毫不隐恶，予以无情揭露。这也许与作者特殊的生活经历有关，从作品的字里行间，我们可以分明感受到其带有忧伤、悲愤色调的沉痛心情。

　　家族的衰落、破败并不是一个孤立的社会文化现象，尽管每个家族都有其独立性、自足性，但它们都不是完全封闭的，它的盛衰兴亡与外界诸多社会文化因素的影响息息相关，这些因素可能是有利的，也可能是致命的。作品实写贾府，虚写他家。除对薛家着墨较多之外，史、王、甄等家基本上是虚写，只是在与贾府发生关系时才会被写到，它们可以说是作为社会背景而存在的。写一个家族实际上是写了其他各个家族，贾府

of common elements. Problems that exist in the Jia family exist more or less in other families.

The revelation of the problems inside a house is linked to the outside world, which is the social and cultural background of the stories. The author gives detailed descriptions of society. In Chapter 4, we see Jia Yucun abuses his legal power and does his old friend a favour; in Chapter 13, we see Dai Quan, a eunuch, uses his power and gains some benefits. Other examples include the conversation of Qin Zhong with the judge from the Nether World and the small ghosts before his death; and in Chapter 72 we see Eunuch Xia and Eunuch Zhou's unreasonable demand for money. Those incidents are all related to families and also fall in the category of social issues. Generally speaking, the author criticises the society from his point of view and reveals different sorts of defects and vice practices of the society.

Tragedies of different individuals and families become social tragedies. The extensive descriptions of lives in the society make the book a song of mourning. Using his unique senses and intuitions as a writer, Cao is able to touch on the deeper level of the society and is able to expose darkness and misfortunes, expressing his sense of crisis and anxiety. He does this through his highly descriptive language, creating thrills in the readers' heart.

III

Honglou Meng is a symphony of sadness. Tragedies of different people in the book are the different musical notes that extended to various levels of social lives, filling the whole book with sadness. The tragedies of love and marriage are the ones remembered most by the readers.

The book depicted different love stories and marriages—love stories of masters and of servants, from the imperial courts to all walks of life, from the grown-up to the young—most of which ended in tragedy. During one's lifetime, one has to make different choices. The choices may include life goals in different periods of time. The choice of love and marriage would be of utmost significance, being one of the most sacred in one's life. When the right of this kind of goal is ripped away, when one's individual happiness and fate

不过是其中的代表。作品对家族生活的描写具有一定的普遍性，贾府存在的问题在其他家族也不同程度地存在着。

揭露家族的弊端必然会涉及到围墙之外的大千世界，这是家族故事展开的社会文化背景。作品对此有较为充分的展示，比如第四回贾雨村的徇私枉法，第十三回太监戴权的以权谋私，第十六回秦钟临死前判官与众鬼的对话，第七十二回夏太监、周太监的索要钱财，等等。这些事件都与家族有关，也都是属于社会的。总的来看，作者是以批评的眼光来审视这个社会的，对其中存在的种种弊端和恶俗给予了揭露。

各种人生、家族的悲剧归结在一起，形成了整个社会的悲剧。小说以宽广的生活面描写强化了这种意识，使整部作品如同一首哀伤的挽歌。曹雪芹以作家特有的敏感和直觉触及到社会的深层，更多地写出了其阴暗、不幸的一面，表达了一种深沉的危机感和忧虑感，并以生动可感的语言展现出来，造成一种扣人心弦的艺术效果。

（三）

《红楼梦》如同一支深沉哀婉的悲剧交响曲，全书大大小小的人生悲剧组成各种不同音色的声符，这些悲剧触及到社会人生的各个层面，使整部小说弥漫着一种凄清幽怨的感伤情调，其中受到最多关注的自然是那些刻骨铭心的爱情婚姻悲剧。

《红楼梦》一书描写了形形色色的爱情和婚姻，从主子到奴仆，从宫廷到民间，从成人到少年，不过大多是以悲剧而收场的。人在一生中会面临各种选择，而这些选择实际上包含了一个个具体的人生目标，爱情婚姻无疑是其中最为核心的一个。这种选择是人类最为神圣的权利之一，当这种权利被粗暴地剥夺，个人的幸福和命运掌握在他人

lie in others' hands, tragedy is inevitable. The ailing situation of the society is reflected in the misfortunes of the individuals. When the love and marriage of a couple are not in their own hands, when they have no say in their own life, when love and marriage become a tool that a family uses to gain benefits, human beings are merely a pawn on the chess board, a sacrifice at the mercy of others. Even though some did eventually unite in marriage, they would only experience a change of social titles and lifeless family life. When these kinds of benefit-oriented marriages become a norm in the society, true love would look too different and too sharp a contrast against the pragmatic arrangements of the rest of the world. Love becomes very fragile and could only result in a tragedy—a life tragedy disguised as a love story. Examples are to be found everywhere in *Honglou Meng*.

In the book, the main movements of symphony are a tragedy of love and a tragedy of marriage, i.e., the love between Jia Baoyu and Lin Daiyu, and the marriage between Jia Baoyu and Xue Baochai. From the moment of their acquaintance to the beginning of their love, and to their eternal parting, Jia and Lin's love is like a clear spring running down the mountains. They love each other from the bottom of their hearts. Not only do they appreciate each other's appearance, they understand each other perfectly. They used to have doubts, one about the other, and have misunderstandings and arguments. They have had conflicting views and had clashes in personalities, sometimes very strong clashes. But they are able to have in-depth communication and harmony in their souls, which is the most beatutiful and moving thing about love. Different from common love stories where scholars and beauties fall in love at first sight, where they make pacts through poems, the love stories in *Honglou Meng* are more authentic and the description is unprecedented. The love stories are like those of modern days. But those who are ahead of their times always suffer. Jia Baoyu's unique thoughts and behaviour make him stand out from the normal people in society. On the other hand, Lin Daiyu is a self-respecting girl and she despises society. She understands Jia and supports him. The love between them is unconventional and rebellious, and is out of tune with orthodox views. Under extreme pressure, their love is fragile and could only flourish for a moment, never coming to fruition. Their tragedy is inevitable.

Jia Baoyu, with a predestination of Wood and Stone confronting him and Lin, has another choice, a Gold-and-Jade combination between him and Xue Baochai.

手中的时候，悲剧也就不可避免。从个人的不幸往往可以看出社会的病态，当爱情婚姻脱离美好的人性和意愿，与当事双方无关，成为家族用以谋取利益的工具和手段时，个人不过是家族大棋盘上一颗随意移动的棋子，从婚姻中得到的也不过是社会角色的改变与毫无生气的所谓家庭。当这种以利益为筹码的婚姻成为社会常态的时候，真正符合人性的爱情就显得颇为另类，与这个世界格格不入，变得十分脆弱，其最后的结果只能是悲剧，以爱情悲剧为表象的人生悲剧。这一点在《红楼梦》中得到了充分的描写和体现。

在小说中，贾宝玉和林黛玉的爱情悲剧以及他与薛宝钗的婚姻悲剧构成整个悲剧的主声部。从相知相爱到生死两别，贾宝玉和林黛玉的爱情始终如清澈的山泉，纯洁无瑕，发自真心。两人不仅在形貌上相互吸引，更多的则是彼此理解基础上的情投意合。他们也曾经猜忌过、误会过、争吵过，其中既有观念的矛盾，又有性格的冲突，有时候甚至相当激烈，但最终达到了灵魂深处的沟通和默契，这正是爱情的奇妙动人之处。与以往才子佳人小说中一见钟情、诗书订盟的戏剧化爱情故事相比，《红楼梦》对爱情的描写更为真实，达到了一种前所未有的深度，同现代社会的爱情理念有颇多相合之处。走在时代前面的人并不都是幸运儿。由于贾宝玉思想观念与行为方式上的特立独行、卓然不群，林黛玉性格的孤芳自赏、不同俗流以及她对贾宝玉的理解和支持，他们的爱情本身就具有一种异端性和叛逆性，与当时正统的思想观念格格不入。在强大的社会重压之下，这种爱情显得格外脆弱，注定是只能开花而不能结果，以悲剧而告终也就在所难免。

对贾宝玉来说，在他与林黛玉的木石前盟之外，还有与薛宝钗的金玉良缘乃至更多的姻缘可以选择。

Xue Baochai, a beauty with scholarly talent, is considered by men to be a good wife and loving mother. In contrast to Lin's seclusion from society and indulgence in her artistic world, Xue is more amenable to worldly happiness. She is able to control her feelings and behaves according to the norms. Her thoughts are more acceptable to all and she also maintains good relationship with others. She, despite what many Hong experts have claimed, does not whole-heartedly want to marry Jia Baoyu; she hasn't tried all she can to please everyone, as a sinister and ruthless secret agent would do. In fact, she is a nice lady with her own principles. Otherwise, it would be hard to understand why she would try to convince Jia Baoyu to pursue further studies and prepare for the national official-selection examinations. Even though Xue knows Jia wouldn't be happy if she did this, and that doing so would push her away from Jia and make Jia lean toward Lin Daiyu, it is out of her firm belief and strong sense of responsibility that she behaves in such a manner. She does it out of care for Jia, not purely for her own selfish purpose of becoming the wife of Jia. Whether Jia would accept her advice is not her concern. In the past, a lot of people had a stong prejudice against Xue that she does not deserve.

The choice between the Wood-Stone Predestination and the Gold-Jade Combination might be regarded as a conflict between love and social conventions. But for Jia, it is more a choice of survival—to live for himself or to live for other people. He chooses the former without hesitation. His choice of Lin does not mean that there is anything wrong with Xue. Love should be a perfect match for two and should not be considered right or wrong. The contradiction caused by a third party should not be overemphasised.

In the later 40 chapters of the book, all stories come to an end dramatically. The change of brides, not clever but effective, makes everything very easy. Lin dies in the happy music of Jia and Xue's wedding, leaving the Wood-Stone Predestination an eternal sadness of tears. However, the Gold-Jade Combination eventually makes Xue a victim, too. The departure of Jia makes Xue's expectation for a good life a distant dream. In the love triangle, no one is a winner. Jia, Lin and Xue are all victims. The tragedy is not their fault. It results from the social environment and etiquette system, mainly the system of marriage, which suppressed individuality and freedom. It is quite

薛宝钗也是才貌兼具的绝世佳人，是许多男人心目中的贤妻良母。但与近乎不食人间烟火、生活在艺术中的林黛玉截然相反，她更向往滚滚红尘间的各种快乐，善于控制自己的感情，言行举止无不合乎礼节，思想合乎社会道德规范，有着良好的人际关系。她并不像有些红学家说的，一心想嫁给贾宝玉，为此没有原则地讨好别人，像个特务一样阴险狠毒。事实上，她是一个善良的女性，有着自己做人的原则和立场，否则就很难理解，她为什么多次规劝贾宝玉读书仕进，尽管她明明知道这会激起贾宝玉的反感，将自己推到贾宝玉的对立面，使其感情天平更偏向林黛玉，是坚定的信仰和强烈的责任感促使她这么做，而且她这样也确实是为贾宝玉着想，并不见得是出于想做宝二奶奶的私心。至于贾宝玉能否接受，那是另外一件事。过去人们对薛宝钗有着太深的偏见，这是不公平的。

这种木石前盟与金玉良缘的选择，固然可以看作情与礼的冲突，但对贾宝玉而言，更多的则意味着生存方式的选择，是诗意地栖居还是现实地生存，他毫不犹豫地选择了前者。选择林黛玉并不等于薛宝钗的人格有问题，爱情需要的是情投意合，不存在是非正误，不应该过于强调三人之间的矛盾。

在后40回中，所有的恩怨都被戏剧性地完成了，一个并不高明但很有效的调包计使一切变得十分简单。在宝玉、宝钗成亲的鼓乐声中，林黛玉泪尽而逝，木石前盟伴着如雨的泪水化作永久的遗憾。但金玉良缘最终使薛宝钗成为无辜的受害者，贾宝玉的撒手而去使其对生活的美好愿望变成遥遥无期的等待。在这场爱情、婚姻的角逐中，没有最后的胜利者，宝、黛、钗三人都是失败者和悲剧人物。悲剧并非源自三人的性格缺陷，而是来自那个压抑个性和自由的社会氛围

meaningful when the author says, in Chapter 5, that this book contains "sadness for Gold and condolences for Jade."

The love tragedy of Jia, Lin and Xue is not a competition and rivalry among the three young people, as no one is a winner in the end. This heart-struck love story ended in tragedy, leaving Lin dead and the other two desperate. No doubt, the fates of Jia and Lin are both tragic. But Xue, criticised by readers for the last 200 years, has not gained any happiness in the love affair and in the eventual marriage. Not to mention being a sufferer of all sorts of family worries, Xue is also a sacrifice for her own marriage. Xue does like Jia a lot, and it would not be her fault even if she wanted to marry him, because she has the right to love. It is not wrong to love someone, nor it is wrong to love one that he or she should't have loved, yet it is real fault to push two people with no mutual affection into marriage. The Jia family and the marriage system that has been supporting the family, rather than Jia or Xue, are to take the blame. The Gold-Jade Combination is an ideal match and an irresistible life attraction for Xue and her family, After all, Xue is a per-mature girl raised traditionally; she has to think for herself and more for the family. With her identity and status, and under the then social conditions, her marriage with Baoyu wouldn't have been more suitable.

If love were not a factor, the story of the three would be a struggle for marriage. Jia and Xue have good reasons to get married, and their marriage would benefit the family, a view shared by many, including readers. However, because of Lin, everything is different. It is her love that has changed everything and is the origin of tragedy. True love, with its basis and essence in true feelings, is totally against external obstacles, such as family origin, clans and wealth. Even though Xue impresses the family by what she does and says,

和礼法制度，特别是与之有关的婚姻制度。小说作者在第五
回中称该书"悲金悼玉"，还是大有深意的。

对贾宝玉、林黛玉、薛宝钗之间这场有些三角恋爱色彩的
爱情婚姻来说，它并不是一场三个青年男女之间的竞争和较量，
因为谁都不是最后的胜利者。这场刻骨铭心的爱情以凄惨的夭
折而告终，它葬送了所有的主角，有人失去了性命，有人因此
而绝望。贾宝玉、林黛玉无疑是一对悲剧人物，对二百多年来
一直饱受读者指责的薛宝钗来讲，她又何尝从这段感情纠葛和
其后的婚姻中得到过快乐。且不说其家庭内部纠纷带来的种种
烦恼，即使是这场小范围的爱情婚姻，她又何尝不是殉葬品。
确实，她对贾宝玉有着相当的好感，但即使是有想嫁之意，也
并不是什么不可原谅的过错，因为她有爱别人的权利，爱一个
人不是过错，爱一个不该爱的人也不是过错，而两个不相爱的
人因外力因素被生硬地推向婚姻，这才是真正的过错，但过错
的责任不在贾宝玉，也不在薛宝钗，而在这个家族和维系这个
家族的婚姻制度。金玉良缘对于她以及她的家庭来说，是十分
理想的婚姻，是一种难以抵御的人生诱惑，毕竟她是一个早熟
的女孩，身上有着更多传统的因素，她要为自己考虑，更需要
为家族着想。以她的身份和地位，在当时的社会条件下，缔结
这门婚姻是再合适不过的事情。

如果不考虑爱情的因素，这确实会成为一场婚姻较量，双
方都有着结亲的充分理由，这场婚姻为家族带来的好处是谁都
可以想见的，事实上他们周围的很多人包括旁观的读者们也多
是这样来看的。但是，因为有了林黛玉，一切都发生了改变。
是爱情使一切都发生了改变，这才是导致悲剧的根源。对以感
情为纽带、为核心、为基础的爱情来说，门第、家族、富贵等
所有一切统统成为了外在因素，成为了爱情的阻碍物。薛宝钗

she could not win Jia's heart. Not that there is anything wrong with her as a person. After all, friend and lover are two completely different concepts, and love needs no reasons. Xue could be a good friend to Jia but by no means a lover because there is a sharp contrast between her and Jia in terms of interests and character. In our current society, things might be much easier. People of different interests may not so easily be forced together by marriage. However, the interests of the two families have tied two unwilling people together in a knot of marriage.

A girl as clever as Xue, however conservative and smooth she may be, wouldn't fail to understand what the arranged marriage would mean to her. For a girl who has studied all sorts of books, it wouldn't be hard to understand that "the saddest thing in love is to face a cold heart." In fact, after figuring out the unbreakable bond of love between Jia and Lin, Xue has decided to nip her dream of love for Jia in the bud. She voluntarily withdraws from the game of pain. However, the situation is beyond her control. What she has thought of is also thought of by others. What she does not want is now imposed upon her. Xue is innocent of Lin's death and of the dramatic bride-swap. She does not have to be morally responsible for any of the accusations. Xue seems to be free and unrestrained, but she has no choice on critical matters and has to obey her parents' manipulations. Compared with Jia and Lin, Xue is even more miserable: Jia and Lin have truly fallen in love and they do not care whether they would face death or escape. Xue has not truly been loved by anyone and she has not loved anyone. She ends up a pawn in a chess game, ultimately ruining the game. Xue's tragedy may be different from that of Jia and Lin, but the tragic ending is the same. After Jia's escape from his loveless and lifeless family, where could Xue go? Is there anything more heartbreaking?

Love brings happiness, even though that love comes to nothing. Apart from Jia, Lin and Xue, the book depicts love tragedies of Si Qi, a female

固然可以靠她得体大方的言行得到全府上下的一片喝彩，但得不到贾宝玉内心深处的爱情，这并不是说她的品格有什么问题，毕竟朋友和情人是两种性质完全不同的关系，爱情不需要更多的理由。她可以成为贾宝玉很好的朋友，但注定不能成为他的情人，因为两人在志趣、性格方面有着太大的反差。如果是在现代社会，这是再正常不过的事情，道不同者不相为谋，缺少爱情的婚姻可以最低限度地发生，但是，双方家族的利益还是将两个并不情愿的人紧紧地拴在了婚姻这条绳子上。

以薛宝钗之聪明睿智，她再保守、再世故，也不会不明白没有爱情的婚姻对自己意味着什么，"哀莫大于心死"的古训对饱读诗书的她并不是什么难以理解的人生大道理。事实上，在她弄清宝玉、黛玉之间牢不可破的爱情之后，她已经将刚刚萌生的爱情种芽扼杀在心底，自觉地退出了这场痛苦的爱情游戏。但是，她已经无法置身事外，自己想得到的早已被别人得到，自己想逃避的偏偏找上门来。不管是黛玉的泪尽而逝，还是戏剧般的调包计，她都是无辜的，不必为之承担道义上的责任。虽然平日里看似自由自在，但到了关键时刻，她并没有多少选择权，只能听从长辈们的摆布。与宝玉、黛玉相比，她应该更为痛苦，因为别人毕竟还曾真诚地相爱过，不管是死亡还是逃避，都还有一个充分的理由，而她却从来没有被人真正爱过，也没有用心地爱过别人，最后被用作打扫残局的棋子。与宝、黛二人的悲剧相比，也许薛宝钗悲剧的意义性质不同，但最后的悲惨结局则是相同的。当贾宝玉脱离这个没有爱情、缺少活力的家庭时，她又能逃到哪里呢？还有比绝望更痛苦的事情吗？

拥有爱情，是一种幸福，哪怕这样的爱情没有结果。在贾宝玉、林黛玉、薛宝钗之外，作品也写到了其他一些人的爱情

servant. For most of the servants in the Jia family, the fact that they do not have freedom means that they would never have love. They have been deprived of the right to love. All they can expect is a marriage arranged by their masters. They live in a world of pot luck and their fates totally depend on their masters. They live in a gamble and are the stakes waiting to be placed anywhere on the gaming table. Their tragedies have begun the moment they went into the Jia family. Marriage initiated under their masters' whips only accelerates the onset of tragedies and makes the tragedies more miserable.

The servants' situation is as such yet the lives of their masters are no better. They may have had more freedom but they also long for love, which is a luxury item. They have the opportunity to enjoy the abundance of their family, and they should take up more responsibilities, especially in times of hardship. Now that their lives are closely connected with the fate of their family, their marriage could not be regarded as personal affairs. Their marriages are treated as public affairs in which every member of the family has a say. If their personal choice is in conflict with the interests of their family, it is the individual that is to be sacrificed. This is the internal mechanism of society. When faced with the power of society, the struggle of an individual would only be in vain and could only result in tragedy.

IV

No one can deny that, among all figures depicted in the book, most pages of *Honglou Meng* are dedicated to those young, innocent, and lively girls. At the beginning of the book, when talking about his intention in writing, the author said he wanted to "write the stories of the girls into history" so that they wouldn't be forgotten. The author seemed to have a special respect towards girls. He, via Jia Baoyu, said, "Girls are made of water and men of mud. When I see girls I feel light, yet when I see men, I feel disgusted by their odour." The

悲剧，其中也包括像司棋这样的奴仆的爱情悲剧。对贾府里众多的奴仆们来说，没有人身自由的人生注定与爱情无缘，他们已完全失去恋爱的权利，唯一能做的就是等待，等待主子分配给他们的婚姻。他们生活在一个充满偶然性的世界里，前途命运完全取决于主子的秉性和好恶。生活就像一场赌局，就看主子将他们这些赌注押在哪个地方。悲剧在他们进入贾府的时候就已经开始，皮鞭之下萌生的爱情不过使悲剧来得更快，更为惨烈而已。

奴才们如此，生活优越高雅的主子们又何尝快乐，他们也许生活得更为自由些，但爱情对于他们来说，又何尝不是奢侈品。他们既然充分享受了家族优越的人生资源，也就必须为这个家族承担更多的责任，特别是当苦难到来时。既然他们的人生与家族的兴衰荣辱紧密地联系在一起，其爱情婚姻就不能仅仅看作是个人的私事，它必须成为家族成员们皆有发言权的公共事业。一旦个人的选择与家族的整体利益发生矛盾时，被牺牲的只能是个人，这就是那个时代社会运作的内在逻辑。在强大的社会面前，个人的反抗不过是徒劳，只能是一场惨烈的悲剧。

（四）

没有人否认，在《红楼梦》所描写的众多人物形象中，着墨最多、最显灵性的是女性，尤其是那群天真烂漫、洋溢着青春活力的妙龄少女。作品开头在谈及创作意图时，说要"使闺阁昭传"，意思是说：要为平生见过的一些女性立传，以免湮没无传。作者对女性有一种近乎崇拜的态度，他借贾宝玉之口提出了一个很别致的观点："女儿是水作的骨肉，男人是泥作的骨肉。我见了女儿，我便清爽；见了男子，便觉浊臭逼人。"

author, when praising the girls, had a strong sense of self-pity. The self-pity did not mean the author had a mental problem. He was only disappointed that he was a male. He wanted to keep some beautiful things in humanity, for example, purity and innocence. In ancient China where the male was dominant and the female of little importance, the author's ideas were too original to win any agreement.

Even though he liked the girls so much, Cao did not follow the trend of conventional novel of the past in designing a good ending for the girls. Normally, in that kind of novel, heroines would marry a handsome, talented husband who had achieved the highest scholarship, or Zhuang Yuan, and would live a wealthy and respected life with many children. Cao, however, composed a song of sadness for those kind and beautiful girls. In Chapter 5 of *Honglou Meng*, when Jia Baoyu is dream-visiting the Grand Illusion Land, the tea and the wine being served are named "Qianhong Yiku" (one thousand girls in one cave) and "Wanyan Tongbei" (ten thousand beauties in the same cup). The implied meaning, through two pairs of homophones, is "a thousand girls crying" and "ten thousand beauties in sadness." The author tried his best to show us the best and brightest side of the girls as well as the whole process of them being engulfed and defiled by ugliness and savageries. What Cao intended and what he actually did are a sharp contrast and have left behind something the readers keep recalling.

From the book, we see most girls could not escape tragedy, either Tanchun who had been struggling agaist her destiny, or Yingchun who had been accepting reality as it came upon her, or Yuanchun who is an imperial consort. Nor could Miaoyu, who had devoted herself to the religious world, let alone those humble maids who enjoyed no freedom. They were people of the lowest status in society and could have no control over their fate. They were born to face hardship and misfortune. Be it the ladies in the noble families or the humble maids who are busy waiting on masters all day, they are all lambs to the slaughter for the dominant male and are the victims of the family. It is through these descriptions that the tragedy becomes most poignant.

The author meticulously designed the Grand View Garden, a world for females and a paradise for the girls. He also gave them Jia Baoyu, a passionate and sentimental protector. In the garden, they form a poets'

在崇拜女性的同时，他也流露出一种深深的男性自卑感。这种自卑并非心理有问题，而是对作为社会主要角色的男性的失望，希望能留住人性中一些最美好的东西，比如青春少女的那种纯洁和天真。这在男尊女卑的中国古代社会，可谓石破天惊的怪论，难以得到一般人的认同。

崇拜归崇拜，赞美归赞美，曹雪芹没有像以前的才子佳人小说那样为女主人公设计一个美好的结局：嫁给才貌双全的状元丈夫，过着富裕、尊贵的生活，生一群孩子。他为自己笔下这些美丽、善良的女性唱的是一首凄清的挽歌。在小说的第五回，贾宝玉梦中游览太虚幻境时，所饮的茶、酒名为"千红一窟"、"万艳同杯"，实则是暗喻"千红一哭"、"万艳同悲"之意，要为这些千红万艳来唱哀歌。作者极力写出了这些青春少女最美好、最亮丽的一面，同时又展现了她们被丑恶野蛮吞噬、玷污的全过程，两者构成极为鲜明的对比，让人读后久久难以释怀。

在作品中我们可以看到：无论是与命运顽强抗争的探春，还是逆来顺受的迎春，无论是人在宫廷的元春，还是身在方外的妙玉，她们都逃脱不了悲惨的结局，这就更不用说那些没有人身自由、身份卑微的众多丫环仆女了，她们生活在社会的最底层，无法掌握自己的命运，从出生那天起，便无可避免地要面对种种苦难和不幸。无论是家族里尊贵的小姐还是终日忙碌的仆女，皆是如此，在主宰整个社会的男人面前，她们只能任人宰割，成为家族的牺牲品。唯其如此，这种悲剧性也就显得特别突出。

作品精心描绘了一个女性的世界，为她们设计了一个人生的乐园——大观园，并为她们安排了一个惜香怜玉、颇有儿女情肠的看护人——贾宝玉。在大观园中，她们结社赋诗、宴饮

society, write poems and play without any worry. They enjoy their youth and freedom and demonstrate the best and most beautiful qualities of young girls. It is the descriptions of those happy and romantic moments that become the vivid contrast to the sad scenes of the deaths or separations of the girls. The Garden is not an isolated place; it is encircled and contaminated by the dirty world outside. All pleasures are temporary. The happy scenes are soon destroyed and become nice memories only for the girls. The girls, leaving the Grand View Garden one by one, disappear into the darkness outside. They either get married, they age, they die young or they are destroyed. What awaits them is degradation or death. The contrast between the destructive corruption and the innocence of young girls, happiness and bleakness, beauty and ugliness, engrosses the readers even more.

Young girls symbolise the most beautiful things in life. Their life tragedy is the tragedy of the entire society. If a society did not allow the most beautiful things, youth, romance and true feelings, to exist, and would even destroy them, it is abnormal and its sustainability is to be questioned. When young girls were dying, the end of the world would not be too far away.

V

Life is full of choices. But for many people in *Honglou Meng*, Jia Baoyu for example, choice is a luxury. His life is at the mercy of the society and his family, and his growth is a story of giving in. Naturally, no one would willingly accept others' manipulation, even that of his own parents. Hence choosing and giving in, responsibility and cowardice, become the major contradictions between Jia and his seniors and other family members. Faced with a strong family power and social pressure, personal choice could only become a struggle in vain; Jia's tragedy could be envisaged. Whoever rejects society would in turn be rejected by society, becoming a redundant person and then a tragedy. The tragic effect is the most overwhelming in the case of Jia Baoyu.

嬉戏，无拘无束，尽情享受生命所赋予的青春活力和个性自由，展示了青春少女最为美好的品质。也正是这种充满欢快、浪漫气息的详尽描绘，后来少女们的死亡离散才显得格外凄清悲凉。但是，大观园不是孤立存在的，它被污浊的世界包围着、侵蚀着。一切都是暂时的，欢快热闹的场面很快被破坏，成为少女们埋在心底的美好回忆。其后，这些少女们便一个个从大观园中走出，消失于茫茫的黑暗世界，或婚嫁、或衰老、或夭折，被无情吞噬、毁灭，等待她们的是沉沦或死亡。小说描写了腐朽、没落对少女、青春的毁灭，欢乐与凄凉、美好与卑俗，就这样形成了十分鲜明的对比，增强了全书的感染力。

青春少女象征着人间最美好的事物，她们的人生悲剧也是整个社会的悲剧。一个社会如果连世间最美好的东西如青春、浪漫、真情等都不允许存在，都要无情摧毁的话，那它显然是不正常的，其存在的合理性应该受到质疑。当红消香断、群芳凋零的时候，末世的降临真的是不远了。

（五）

人生是一个不断选择的过程，但对《红楼梦》里的不少人物比如贾宝玉来说，选择是一个颇为奢侈的字眼。因为按照社会和家族对其人生的设计，他的成长只能是一个不断服从的过程。自然，没有人会甘心接受他人的摆布，即使是自己的父母。于是，选择与服从、责任与逃避，就构成了他与长辈及其他家族成员的矛盾，在强大的家族势力和社会压力面前，个人的选择只能变成一种徒劳的挣扎，其不幸的结局也是可以想见的。谁拒绝了这个社会，这个社会就要抛弃谁，他注定要成为一个多余的人，悲剧由此而生。这一悲剧在作品主人公贾宝玉身上体现得最为突出。

People who have strong personal characteristics and do not want to drift along with society, suffer all the time the loss of choice and the helplessness of yielding to social conventions. In the end, life is nothing but emptiness and tragedy. This is not a Buddhist's passive thinking; it is real life. In a normal society everyone would have their own rights to choices of their future and their belongings, even though they'd have a choice that may lead them to a winding path. In *Honglou Meng*, Jia does not have such rights. He wants to live the way he likes. He hates the set writing style of Bagu (eight-part essay); he has no intention of becoming an official. He only wants to study anywhere and everywhere; he wants to be with the girls. All these are against the expectations of the society and the family, so it is natural that people think him strange. After Lin's death, Jia decides to "let go of the cliff" and devotes himself to the hermit's life. He makes his most resolute struggle against the time through self-imposed exile.

The destruction of different behaviours, be it Jia Baoyu's rebellion or the corruption of Jia Lian, Jia Rong, Jia Huan and Xue Pan, is the same when family is concerned. These people's choices in life are reflected in the book through the detailed descriptions of the society at that time. The corrupted ones, like Jia Lian, Jia Rong, Jia Huan and Xue Pan, carry on the luxurious lifestyle of their elders, take advantage of their family's abundant resources and indulge and overspend themselves in life. They have abandoned their responsibilities and moral obligations. Such are their choices, a kind of choice mostly taken up by people from rich families. By doing so, they become one link in the family's process of decline and can never break away from their family. Furthermore, they accelerated the decline of their family. In front of them lies an inevitable trap set by themselves. When the family crashes, they would be left with nothing but bitter wine brewed by themselves.

The corrupted would go down the abyss while the rebellious end up in tragedy. The former is a commonplace tragedy seen in feudal families while the latter would have a totally different implication. For Jia Baoyu, who is rich and adored, and who does not need to worry about his livelihood, his major pursuit is spiritual. His thoughts and pursuits are at a higher level beyond others' understandings. He wants to gain control of his own life, not simply

对《红楼梦》中那些个性鲜明、不同俗流者来讲，他们时时刻刻感受到丧失选择的痛苦和屈从世俗的无奈。结果，人生到头来不过是一场无常和虚无的悲剧，这并非佛教的刻意宣传，而是活生生的现实。在一个良性发展的社会里，每个人都应有选择自己前途和归宿的权利，哪怕这种选择有问题，会走弯路。但贾宝玉就失去了这些，他想按照自己喜欢的方式来生活，厌恶八股，无意仕进，喜欢"杂学旁收"，与姐妹们厮守，这与社会对他的定位、家族的期待是相悖的，因此被世人视为叛逆异端也很自然。黛玉死后，他最终弃绝俗世，"撒手悬崖"，以自我放逐的方式与那个时代进行了最为决然的抗争。

不管是贾宝玉这样的叛逆者，还是贾琏、贾蓉、贾环、薛蟠这样的堕落者，尽管他们言行各异，但对家族的破坏作用则是一致的。全书通过日常琐事的描写展示了这批年轻贵族面对社会人生的不同选择。对贾琏、贾蓉、贾环、薛蟠这样的堕落者来说，他们只继承了长辈们安逸享乐的传统，充分利用家族的丰厚资源来享受人生、透支人生，完全放弃了对家族的责任和道义，这就是他们的人生选择，也是富贵家族子弟最容易走的一条人生之路。这样，他们不过是家族盛极而衰过程中的一环，他们不能使家族走出这一怪圈，反而加速了家族的破败，在他们的前面是早已铺设的人生陷阱。家族破败了，他们就什么都没有，只能喝下自己酿制的苦酒。

堕落者走向的是深渊，叛逆者所走的又何尝不是悲剧之路。前者不过是封建家族经常上演的悲剧，后者的悲剧则有着全然不同的意义。对贾宝玉来说，物质生活的富足、个人所受的恩宠使他不必为衣食住行之类生活琐事担忧，因而他更注重精神层面的追求。这样，他的思考和追求也达到了一个新的高度，一个常人难以理解的高度。他想得到对人生之路的自主选择权，

live his life in the family arrangements. He does not want to sit for the scholar tests, nor does he want to take up the responsibility of carrying on his family glory. What he wants is to choose his life companion, to live according to his will. He has his unique view on his dreams and the society. However, his thoughts are so ahead of the times that society is not ready for him. His rebellion against and reliance on his family often put him in a dilemma. Sometimes all he can do is vent his emotion. He could not have comprehended the situation that clearly, so his rebellion would be aimless and in vain. When the family is on the decline, people around him start to disappear and he suffers more and is more desperate than anyone else. Eventually he chooses one of the common ways that ancient Chinese escape from the the real world: He renounces it and becomes a Buddhist monk. This is his only ultimate struggle. In fact, no matter how Jia chooses to live his life, either by obeying his family's arrangements or insisting on his own way, he would inevitably end up in tragedy. When the whole family crumbles, personal choices and decisions have no impact at all.

Tanchun, as a chamber maid, is a contrast to the men described in the book. She has a strong sense of family responsibility. She is "clever and ambitious." She wanted to "repair the sky" like Goddess Nu Wa. She demonstrates her abilities that are not inferior to those of men in a short period when she deals with daily affairs. Born in the male-dominant society, however, she would never be able to realise her ambitions. No matter how capable she is, the family corruption reduces everything to an illusion. She has to leave home and marry afar. The poem which hints at her fate reads, "luck diminishes as birth is delayed," reflecting the harsh and cruel reality.

Unfortunate marriages, declining glories and bitterness of life are fully demonstrated in the crash and tumble of the whole family. The Jia family, once a clan with scholarly demeanour and etiquette, had extremely luxurious times when food was cooked in huge bronze vessels and where grand bells were rung to make announcements. The detailed description of Qin Keqing's funeral is an example. Because some family members, especially the men in charge, are incompetent and destructive, the grand family of over a century's glorious

而不是在家族规定好的场地里活动。他不想走科举之路，他不想承担振兴家族的责任，他想自己选择人生伴侣，他想按照个人的意愿生活，他有自己的个人理想和对社会人生的独特认识。但是，这一切实在是太超前了，当时的社会还没有为此做好准备。一方面是对家族的叛逆，另一方面则是对家族的依赖，这就是贾宝玉面对的尴尬人生困境。于是，他的个人意愿和人生选择只能以一种情绪宣泄的方式表达出来，他不可能想得这样清楚，其反抗也只能是徒劳的和没有目标的。当自己身边的情人知己烟消云散，当家族走向破落，他比别人更痛苦，也比别人更绝望，最后他选择了古代中国人常用的逃避方式——出家。这是他唯一的一次决然的反抗。其实，对贾宝玉来说，无论是顺从家族的意愿还是坚持个人的选择，都不可避免地要走向悲剧，当整个家族走向没落之际，个人的选择无论方向如何，都只能是一种徒劳。

　　与这些男性形成鲜明对比的是探春，她虽然身为闺阁秀女，但"才自精明志自高"，志在"补天"，对家族有着强烈的使命感。她曾在短暂管理家务的过程中显示出不让须眉的见识和才干，但在男权社会中，她的女性身份就注定了其最终的抱负难展，不管如何有才干，家族的腐朽没落使这一切成为泡影。弃亲别家、离乡远适的结局使"生于末世运偏消"这句话显得分外沉重和枯涩。

　　婚恋的不幸、韶华的远逝、人生的悲苦，所有这些最终以整个家族的没落和衰败表现出来。诗礼簪缨之族、钟鸣鼎食之家的贾府，曾经有过"烈火烹油，鲜花着锦"的极盛时光，这可以从小说中对秦可卿葬礼的精细描绘中略见一斑。由于家族成员特别是那些身负家族重任的男人们的无能和破坏，整个家族辉煌百年、盛极一时之后，终于无可奈何地走上日暮途穷的

history finally goes down. Throughout the pages of *Honglou Meng*, we see extravagant indulgence, conspiracies, grandstanding and flattery. We also see that senior men in the family are either greedy, like Jia She, or complacent and doing nothing, like Jia Zheng. The younger men in the family are a gang of gamblers, brothel-goers, like Jia Zhen, Jia Lian, Jia Huan and Jia Rong. They, as well as Jia Baoyu, lead to the family's crisis of not having an ambitious person to carry on the family glory. Jia's advanced thinking and the disgraceful corruption of others form a strong force that tolls the death knell of the family. Finally in the end of the book, the Jia family is raided and ruined and "all the monkeys scattered when the big tree fell." In a poem, the author's description is, "just like the scene when the food is gone and the birds are back in the trees, leaving a piece of empty bleak land."

Living in the halcyon days of Emperors Kangxi and Qianlong, Cao cast his eyes on the scenes behind the glory, which made him the best novelist in ancient China. When reading the book, we have an intertwining feeling of loss and sadness, not simply because of the deaths of characters and the family's decline. The colourful, story-telling words of the author has depicted for us the most magnificent scenery of life and society.

末路。翻开作品，家族成员的奢侈浮华、靡费铺张，相互间的勾心斗角、欺骗献媚，种种丑行，随处可见。老一代的男人，要么如贾赦贪婪荒淫，要么如贾政庸碌无为；年轻的一代，如贾珍、贾琏、贾环、贾蓉等更是一群聚赌嫖娼、淫纵放荡之徒。家族后继无人的危机并不仅仅体现在贾宝玉一个人身上，超前的异端和无耻的堕落形成一股强大的破坏力，共同敲响家族的丧钟。终于，在小说的结尾，贾府被抄，彻底走向破败，"树倒猢狲散"，正像作者所形容的："好一似食尽鸟投林，落了片白茫茫大地真干净。"

作者身处康乾盛世，目光却投向了种种奢华表象背后的没落，也正是这份敏锐和危机感使曹雪芹成为中国古代最优秀的小说家。阅读小说时那种交织着失落和惆怅的复杂感觉并非简单的人物死亡、家族破败所能概括，随着作者如泣如诉、充满诗情的笔墨，我们领略了人生、社会之间最为奇丽的风景。

林黛玉画像

Portrait of Lin Daiyu

五　三寸柔毫能写尽 ——曹雪芹的才华

Chapter V　The Three-inch Brush Writes It All: Cao's Talent

For every novelist, it would be a great challenge to be able to clearly sort out all clues, among so many characters and so many scenes. It would require even more talent for a writer to relate the stories to big and small events at correct times. We don't see many such books among a great number of ancient novels in China. *Honglou Meng* is an exception with superb achievements and has become a pre-eminent classic among China's narrative works. Readers and scholars alike have all been amazed by the literary skills demonstrated in the book.

I

When reading *Honglou Meng*, the readers are most impressed by the characters in the book. The beautiful, elegant, yet sad Lin Daiyu, the kind, diligent and easy-going Xue Baochai, the spicy-tempered and capable Wang Xifeng, and, the kind and smiling-faced Grandma Jia are full of character and they all seem so vivid as if they lived around us. It is hard to imagine that they are characters made up in a book. They seem more realistic than those in historical biographies. Besides the major characters in the book, trivial people who only appear a few times, such as Xiaohong, the Stupid Sister, Jiao Da and Mingyan, seem so full of life in between the lines and are unforgettable.

Because of the successful depictions, and the liveliness of the characters, readers think these people could not have been fabricated, and that the prototypes must have existed. Some went on a quest for the prototypes, only to be disappointed. We know so little about Cao and his writing process. It is almost impossible to find the prototypes.

If we are to think from an artistic perspective, we would have to ask another question. Why are the characters in *Honglou Meng* so vivid and alive? Or what kind of writing method did Cao use?

纷繁的头绪，众多的人物，琐细的事件，多变的场景，这对每一位小说家来说，都是一场并不轻松的考验和挑战，而要将其安排得条理分明，疏密得当，张弛相宜，各得其所，恰如其分，这确实是需要大手笔的。在众多的中国古代小说作品中，能达到这种水准的并不多见，《红楼梦》一书就做到了这些，而且做得非常优秀，成为中国古代叙事文学的经典之作、巅峰之作。从古至今，无论是一般的读者还是专门的研究者，无不惊叹于《红楼梦》高超的艺术手法。

（一）

阅读《红楼梦》，印象最深的要数那些鲜活、真实的人物了。无论是美丽高雅、多愁善感的林黛玉，还是温柔贤惠、精通人情世故的薛宝钗；无论是性格泼辣、干练精明的王熙凤，还是慈眉善目、笑态可掬的贾母，无不刻画得十分逼真，性格独具，仿佛就在眼前，仿佛就在身边。很难想象他们是想象虚构中的文学形象，甚至觉得他们比历史传记中的人物还要真实。且不说那些浓笔重墨描绘的主要人物，就连出场不多的小人物如小红、傻大姐、焦大、茗烟等，都一个个跃然纸上，让人难以忘怀。

也正是因为《红楼梦》写实手法的成功，刻画人物的逼真，一些读者总觉得这些人物、故事不可能是虚构的，他们应该有生活原型。于是不少人去寻找原型，寻找的结果是令人失望的，我们对曹雪芹本人及其创作过程了解得实在太少了，寻找人物原型几乎是一个不可能完成的任务。

如果从艺术的角度来思考，这里就有一个问题：为什么《红楼梦》的人物形象如此逼真，曹雪芹究竟使用了什么高超的艺术手法？

To answer the question, we need to compare Cao's book with other works in the ancient Chinese literary history. Lu Xun sang the praises of the artistic achievements of *Honglou Meng*. In an article, "Changes in the History of Chinese Novels," Lu Xun commented, "The emergence of *Honglou Meng* broke all traditional thoughts and writing conventions." Then, what are the traditional methods of writing in terms of creating characters?

With its origin in story-telling, folk novel started in the Tang dynasty and became popular in the Song and Yuan dynasties. Story-telling is an art of audio and visual presentation. It differs from books because it needs to attract audiences. It has a set of developed skills in portraying characters. The major skills are: to use simple and plain language to sketch appearances, to use action and speech to manifest characteristics, and to focus on limited major characteristics to constantly strengthen the effect. There are also fewer descriptions of the scenery and thoughts. Early Chinese folk novels carried on the traditional art form of story-telling. The characters in Chinese ancient novels, such as *Romance of the Three Kingdoms* and *Water Margin*, are portrayed in such a traditional way.

One thing that needs to be pointed out is that there are two sides to everything. Story-telling depicts figures in its traditional special way and at the same time has its defects. It does not go into details and it lacks depth and innovation. It contains stories that are too dramatic and do not resemble real life stories. We can see novels that came later, such as *Jinping Mei,* demonstrate development in character building. In *Jinping Mei* the details of life and the people are close to those in daily lives; the characters also have richer and more complicated personalities that develop with the plots. In this way, another tradition of character-building is formed in the Chinese folk novels. The book *All Aspects of Novels* describes the characters created in the traditional form of story-telling as "flat characters," while the figures created in novels such as *Jinping Mei* are "round characters."

The characters in *Honglou Meng* are "round characters," like the characters in *Jinping Mei*. At the same time, it has "flat characters" like those who often appear in story-telling. In this way, *Honglou Meng* combines the two features and has achieved a higher literary level. In general, we can see several

　　要回答这个问题，必须将《红楼梦》放在中国古代小说的大背景中，和其他作品进行比较。鲁迅对《红楼梦》的艺术成就有着很高的评价，他在《中国小说的历史的变迁》一文曾这样说："自有《红楼梦》出来之后，传统的思想和写法都打破了。"那么，就人物塑造而言，传统的写法又是什么呢？

　　中国通俗小说萌芽于唐代，形成于宋元时期，是从民间说书发展而来的。说书是一种视听艺术，对它的欣赏和案头阅读不同，为了吸引观众及表演的需要，它在塑造人物上有一套很成熟的技法，主要特点是：用白描的方式勾勒人物外表，以动作和语言来塑造人物，突出人物性格中的一个或几个特点，并不断强化。较少人物外貌及周边环境的详尽描写，人物内心的描写同样不多。早期的通俗小说基本继承了民间说书的这一艺术传统，比如《三国演义》、《水浒传》等作品中的人物就鲜明地体现出这些特点。这是中国古代小说人物塑造的民族传统。

　　需要说明的是，任何事情都具有两面性，民间说书形成的人物塑造传统固然有其优点，但也存在着缺憾，那就是精细不够，缺少深度和变化，戏剧性强，不够真实，生活化。稍后的《金瓶梅》等小说描写世态人情，在人物塑造方面有新的发展，所塑造的人物贴近生活的原生态，人物性格不仅丰满复杂，而且随着情节的发展而不断变化。这样，就形成了中国通俗小说塑造人物形象的又一个艺术传统。这里借用《小说面面观》一书对人物形象的分类，将按照民间说书艺术传统塑造的人物形象叫"扁型人物"，将按照《金瓶梅》等小说艺术传统塑造的人物形象叫"圆型人物"。

　　《红楼梦》人物形象的塑造主要继承了《金瓶梅》等小说开创的圆型人物传统，同时又继承了民间说书的扁型人物传统，取两者之长，达到了一个新的艺术高度。总的来看，《红楼梦》

characteristics of character-building in *Honglou Meng*.

Firstly, the characters are not simply good or bad. They have rich personalities and they have complexity. In books before the time of *Honglou Meng*, only one major characteristic is emphasised for each figure. A distinctive feature is attributed to every character, just like the painted faces in Chinese operas. The audiences can tell by the faces who is the "good guy" and who is the "bad guy." The benefit of this kind of writing is that it leaves figures with distinctive characteristics that can be easily remembered by the audience. However, this kind of writing has a major setback: Each character could have only one single identity, and this does not represent the reality of life.

The painted-face strategy is not used in *Honglou Meng*. While depicting the major characters, it fully demonstrated their full and complex characteristics. All major characters in it had distinctive characteristics. Lin Daiyu, for example, is melancholy and sad; and Xue Baochai is very understanding. These features deeply impress the readers. However, these are not their only features. While being melancholy and sad, Lin Daiyu is at times humorous. Her words are often sarcastic but she is nice to those she likes. Xue Baochai, even though good at handling people, is honest after all. She may behave in a mature manner, but she is also an innocent and lovely girl, chasing after butterflies. She is considerate but that does not mean she would say yes to everyone on everything, of which the conflict between her and her brother Xue Pan is a manifestation.

Jia Baoyu's characteristics are even richer and more complex. He is normally nice and soft to girls, but sometimes he is rough and ill-tempered. He once sacked Qianxue and kicked Xiren. He followed his impulses and allowed Qingwen to tear up fans as she liked. He is at times weak and helpless. For example, he couldn't do anything when faced with Qingwen's expulsion, and even death. He does not like the self-indulgence of the male family members and he feels ashamed. On the other hand, he does not want to leave his family. He wants to enjoy the abundant resources. It is hard to judge if Jia Baoyu is a good person or a bad person, because his characteristics, speech and behaviours do not fall into just one category. Such is a real life person. *Honglou Meng* is able to deliver that. It discards the traditional way of writing, depicts persons

在人物塑造方面，有如下几个特点：

一是抛弃了那种好人全好，恶人皆恶的写法，充分展示了人物性格的丰富性、复杂性。此前的不少小说在塑造人物时，只突出人物性格中的一个方面，人物善恶分明，如同中国戏曲中的脸谱，将人物的好坏都写在脸上，是忠臣义士还是奸臣丑类，一望即知。这种写法的好处是人物性格鲜明，容易被人记住，但缺点也很明显，那就是人物较为单一，不符合生活的本来面目。

《红楼梦》没有采取这种脸谱化的写法，而是在突出人物主要性格的同时，充分展示人物性格的丰富性和复杂性。主要人物皆有着很鲜明的性格，比如说林黛玉的多愁善感，薛宝钗的善解人意，都使人印象至深，这是她们性格的主要特征。但是这并不是她们性格的全部，就林黛玉而言，她虽然比较多愁善感，可也有诙谐幽默的时候；尽管她说话有些尖刻，但对自己喜欢的人还是比较体贴的。再如薛宝钗，她虽然善于交际，但对人不失真诚；她虽然显得比较老成，但也未失少女的天真烂漫，偶有扑蝶之举；她善解人意，并不等于事事顺从别人，只要看一看她在家中和哥哥薛蟠发生的冲突就可以知道这一点。

至于贾宝玉的性格则更是丰富而复杂。他对女孩子十分温柔体贴，但也有粗暴蛮横的时候，比如他撵走茜雪，脚踹袭人；他喜欢任性而为，听凭晴雯撕去一把折扇，但有时候却相当软弱，面对晴雯的离去乃至死亡却束手无策。他不喜欢家族中男性们的胡作非为，为他们感到羞愧，但同时又离不开这个家族，享受着家族的优越资源。很难说这个人物是好是坏，因为人物的性格和言行并不都是那么截然分明，这才是生活的真实状态。《红楼梦》写出了这一点，它抛弃了人物传奇式的写

like those in real life and makes the readers feel they are real and genuine.

Secondly, Cao depicted the development and changes in a person's characteristics. The painted-face characters in the past, from the moment they appeared, exhibited no change. Event that happened later was simply adding a few more strokes to the painted face. Zhang Fei, in *Romance of the Three Kingdoms*, and Li Kui, in *Water Margin*, are such characters. However, such people do not exist in real life, where people do change with different environments.

People in *Honglou Meng* have different characteristics at different times. Jia Baoyu and Lin Daiyu are good examples. Even though they have a lot in common in terms of their life goals, the contrast between them is huge. Their difference leads to conflicts, as described in the first half of the book. Jia is an outward person and likes befriending different kinds of people yet he does not know how to handle relationships with females. Lin, on the contrary, is an inward person who deals with others seriously. She is jealous when Jia interacts with other girls. The conflicts between them are inevitable.

With tests and communications, the two have finally realised what they mean to each other and they have built up a strong sense of trust. In this way, their conflicts turn into mutual care. With the development of the plot, the conflicts become less and less while the tolerance grows greater and greater. These intricate changes are fully described in the book.

Another example is the relationship between Lin Daiyu and Xue Baochai. In the beginning, their relationship is very tense. Lin watches vigilantly as Jia makes friends with Xue, and would comment on Xue sarcastically. It is quite natural that girls in love want to exclude other girls. After all, love is not to be shared, not even with one's best friend. With the increased understanding between Lin and Xue, Lin gradually realises that the love between Jia and herself is unbreakable and that Xue has no intention of getting involved in their love affair. Moreover, Lin is later greatly touched by Xue's sincerity and passion. She knows she misunderstood Xue and they become very good friends.

The third feature in the book is that the author writes about the common characteristics of different people. Zhiyanzhai, the commentator, also noted

法，写出了生活化的人物形象，让读者感觉到十分真实、生动。

二是写出了人物性格的发展和变化。脸谱式的人物性格从出场时起，就不再有变化，此后发生的事件不过是在强化这一性格特征，比如《三国演义》中的张飞、《水浒传》中的李逵就属于这类人物。但这种人物这并不符合生活的真实面貌，因为随着个人处境和生活环境的变化，人的性格还是有所变化的。

《红楼梦》在塑造人物时，就很注意人物性格的发展和变化。比如贾宝玉和林黛玉，两人虽然志同道合，但彼此性格存在着明显的反差，这种反差使两人冲突不断，作品的前半部分有不少这样的描写。贾宝玉性格外向，喜欢结交朋友，与异性往来时往往把握不好分寸。而林黛玉恰恰相反，她性格较为内向，接人待物较为认真。因此，她对贾宝玉和其他女孩子的往来是十分在意的，冲突自然也就在所难免。

经过不断的试探和交流，两个人终于明白自己在对方心目中的地位，建立了一种十分默契的信任感。这样，彼此的冲突就变成相互间的关爱，随着情节的发展，两人较为尖锐的冲突明显减少，彼此多了一层包容。作品十分真实、细致地写出了这一变化过程。

再比如林黛玉和薛宝钗的关系，一开始也是比较紧张的。起初，林黛玉以警惕的目光关注着薛宝钗和贾宝玉的往来，不时对薛宝钗冷嘲热讽，这也符合恋爱中的女性的心理，毕竟爱情是排他的，不能与别人哪怕是最好的朋友来共享。随着彼此交往的增加，林黛玉渐渐意识到，她和贾宝玉之间的爱情是他人无法介入的，薛宝钗事实上也不愿意去介入。不仅如此，林黛玉还被薛宝钗的热情和真诚深深打动，觉得误解了人家。此后，两人关系变得较为融洽。

三是在相似中写出人物的个性，脂砚斋也注意到了这一点，

this and summarised it as "purposeful breach of writing rules," which means "intentional writings of similarities to make the difference more distinct."

Some characters in *Honglou Meng* have similar characteristics, for example, Lin Daiyu and Qingwen, also Xue Baochai and Xiren. Lin and Qingwen are both arrogant and sensitive, and they even have similar appearances. Xue and Xiren are both kind and understanding. However, there are still differences between these similar people. Lin is arrogant and sensitive but she is very careful. She does not want to say anything wrong and keeps a lot of words to herself. She even does not want to confide to Zijuan, her personal maid. Secondly, she is highly educated and has artistic charisma, and her sensitivity is manifested more in her deep contemplation of life. Qingwen is different. She is frank and outspoken and does not hold herself back, which leads to her tragic life. Compared with Lin, Qingwen is more straightforward and wilful.

Xue and Xiren are different in personality, too. Xue is educated and can see the essence of things easily. However she does not want to reveal the fact and would use a roundabout way, sometimes in an ostensibly stupid way, in her expressions. Xiren has more realistic considerations. She does not have Xue's foresight and can not hide her feelings as skillfully as Xue. Her persistence is her true personality and thought.

In *Honglou Meng*, Cao not only puts two people of similar personality together, he sometimes puts together a group of them. For example, Lin Daiyu, Qingwen, Miaoyu and Fangguan all have something in common while the differences among them are obvious.

This method of "purposeful breach" in writings is different to traditional writing methods of using opposite or similar figures for contrast. The use of different foils from different perspectives is to show the prominence of the main character, sometimes at the cost of sacrificing a less important character. For example, in *Romance of the Three Kingdoms*, in order to make Zhuge Liang a person of higer intelligence, the writer sacrifices Zhou Yu and makes him extremely narrow-minded and jealous. The use of "purposeful breach" could avoid such sacrifice by putting a group of people together. The

将其概括为"特犯不犯"，意思是说：故意写出人物的相似性，但人物的性格写得并不雷同。

《红楼梦》中有不少性格较为相似的人物，比如林黛玉和晴雯，薛宝钗和袭人。前者性格都有孤傲、敏感的成分，就连两人的长相也有几分相似。后者都较为温柔贤惠，善解人意。但是在两人性格相似的背后，则是个性的明显差异。林黛玉虽然孤傲、敏感，但还是很注意分寸的，许多话都埋在心里，不愿意和别人说，甚至就连身边的紫鹃都不愿意告诉。再者，她文化修养较高，具有诗人的气质，她的敏感更多地表现为对人生的深入思考。晴雯则不然，她性格较为刚烈，心直口快，没有城府，这也导致了她十分悲惨的人生结局。与林黛玉相比，她更加直率、任性。

再如薛宝钗和袭人，两人性格上也颇有不同之处。薛宝钗毕竟文化修养较高，一下就能看清事情的本质，但不愿意说出，以大智若愚的方式表现出来。而袭人则更多现实利益的考虑，看得没有薛宝钗远，也不如其会掩饰，她的痴是真实心态的流露。

在《红楼梦》中，作者不仅把两个性格相似的人物放在一起，有时甚至则把一组存在相似点的人物放在一起，比如林黛玉、晴雯、妙玉、芳官等人，在性格上确实存在一定的相似处，但彼此间秉性的差异也是十分明显的。

这种"特犯不犯"的笔法和一般的反衬、正衬有所不同。反衬和正衬尽管角度不同，但都有一个主次在，往往以次要人物来衬托主要人物，这种衬托有时候是以牺牲次要人物为代价的。比如《三国演义》这部小说，为了衬托诸葛亮的高明，不惜将周瑜丑化，极力渲染其嫉妒、狭隘的一面。"特犯不犯"的写法则可以克服这一弊端，因为在一组相似的人物中，大家

personalities of these people would be a foil to one another and would give each figure more features, thus achieving a win-win situation.

Cao apparently puts a lot of effort in character-building. His success is no coincidence.

II

In order to create genuine and vivid artistic effect, Cao not only puts a lot of effort into the descriptions of figures, he also uses a series of clever ways in the description of daily lives and also in the tempo of events. These make the readers feel like they were in the book, as if everything were happening in front of their eyes. They would feel like they are in the Grand View Garden and are drinking and laughing with the people there. It seems so true that they would not feel like they are merely reading a fabricated novel.

Even though the book is voluminous, the plots in it are relatively simple with few big events, such as the home-visit of Jia Yuanchun, the funeral of Qin Keqing and also Jia Baoyu's punishment by his father. Compared to *Romance of the Three Kingdoms* and *Romance of Sui and Tang* in which wars are fought, *Honglou Meng* is a simple book of few events. Compared with *Romance of the Three Kingdoms* and *Water Margin* in which big and unexpected events take place one after another, stories in *Honglou Meng* are simpler, and are about daily lives, for example, birthday parties, guest visits, festive celebrations, small chats, drinking and poem-writings and small arguments that we experience each day. It does not have too many dramatic coincidences as do other novels.

The writing of events in daily lives would determine the tempo of the book. In early folk stories, such as *Romance of the Three Kingdoms* and *Water Margin*, the time span is huge and stories are accounted in the unit of year. Only important wars and major events are described. The tempo of such books is fast. *Honglou Meng*, on the other hand, describes daily lives with shorter

相互衬托，通过相似使每个人的个性显露得更加鲜明，达到一种双赢的效果。

在人物塑造方面，曹雪芹还是很下了一番心思的，其成功绝非偶然。

（二）

为了达到逼真、形象的艺术效果，除在人物塑造上下功夫外，曹雪芹还在生活场景描写、叙事节奏等方面运用了一系列巧妙的艺术手法，使读者获得一种身临其境的现场感，仿佛一切都发生在眼前，自己置身大观园中，和众人一起宴饮、欢笑，并不觉得是在阅读一部想象虚构的文学作品。

《红楼梦》篇幅虽然很长，但就其故事情节而言，则较为简单，几乎没有写什么大事情，像元春省亲、秦可卿葬礼、贾宝玉挨打已经算是惊天动地的大事情了。这些事情在《三国演义》、《隋唐演义》这类以描写改朝换代、沙场征战的小说中，根本就不值得一提。与《三国演义》、《水浒传》那种大开大合、跌宕起伏、悬念丛生的写法相比，《红楼梦》的故事情节则大为淡化，更为生活化，作品所写更多的是每个人在生活中都会遇到的事情和场景：生日聚会、迎来送往、节庆欢聚、独坐闲聊、饮酒赋诗、斗嘴吵架，等等，很少有其他小说中常常发生的那些偶然和巧合。

事件、场景的生活化和写实化必然会带来小说叙事节奏的变化。在早期的通俗小说如《三国演义》、《水浒传》中，故事时间跨度较大，通常以年为单位，作品只写那些重要的战争和大事，因此情节的发展是快节奏的。《红楼梦》则不然，它更多的是日常生活场景的描写，故事时间跨度较小，其节奏比起《三国演义》、《水浒传》等小说要舒缓许多，和人们平日对时

time spans, and has a much slower tempo, close to that in real life.

Genunie characters, daily life occasions and the easy tempo are good demonstrations of Cao's success, giving readers a sense of authenticity, drawing them to the book with a strong sense of participation.

Another question arises here. The easy tempo of storytelling may satisfy the readers' tastes and create a sense of genuineness and being-there, but it may also have a negative impact. The readers may feel dull and bored. How to keep the readers interested and increase the readability becomes a huge task for Cao. Cao tries very hard and is very creative. In detail, he uses the following three literary methods.

Firstly, Cao strengthens the changes of venues in storytelling. He uses different venues in the stories as a major means of delivering changes, transposition, and tempo-adjustment. The scene is a basic unit of expression which helps to reduce the dragging of time and avoid tediousness.

Unlike *Pilgrimage to the West*, in which five centuries pass in a blink of eye, in *Honglou Meng*, many detailed descriptions of scenes and events make the tempo of the story go even slower than in real life. However, the readers of *Honglou Meng* would not be aware of the slow pace because the element of space is emphasised and used as a very important means of storytelling. The shifting of spaces is needed for the author's literary creation and it also satisfies the readers.

Secondly, there are changes in the storytelling which make the readers feel constantly refreshed. There are so many people in the Jia family. The description of the daily lives of the people there would involve a lot of repetitive events, such as conversations and banquets, which is quite natural. Repetition is the nature of daily lives. Colourful as the life in Jia family may be, it could not have twists and turns all the time. No one can help the repetition of daily routines such as dressing, meals, daily events, and festivals.

间的真实感觉十分接近。

真实的人物、日常的情景、舒缓的节奏，这些写实手法的运用十分成功，给读者一种十分逼真的感觉。这种真实感使读者与作品的距离大大拉近，产生了强烈的参与意识。

接下来又会有一个新的问题出现：极为舒缓的叙事节奏固然符合读者的日常生活体验，可以营造出一种真实感和现场感，但它也有负面效应，那就是容易造成较为沉闷、乏味的阅读效果，而如何保持叙述的趣味与张力，增加作品的可读性，就成为一个必须面对的新的艺术难题。作者在此方面还是下了不少工夫的，进行了许多创新。具体说来，他主要采取了如下三种艺术手法：

首先，强化空间叙事的功能，即以空间场景的转移作为叙事变化、转接及调整叙事节奏的重要艺术手段，将空间作为叙事的基本单元，以此来淡化时间流程过于缓慢所造成的沉闷和单调感。

在《红楼梦》中，大量场景的精细描绘使得叙事节奏等同甚至要慢于常态的生活时间，而不是像《西游记》等作品中所描写的那样，转眼就是五百年过去。此时，读者对时间已经不再那么敏感，空间的因素被大大强化，成为一种重要的叙事手段。因此，从这个方面来说，作者强化空间叙事的功能既是艺术创新的需要，也符合读者的接受心理。

其次，叙事稳中有变，保持叙述的新鲜感。《红楼梦》一书所写多为贾府众人的日常生活，显而易见，其中不少人物的言行举止、宴饮聚会等会不断重复，这也是正符合生活的原生态。日常生活原本就是如此，具有高度的重复性。贾府里的生活尽管丰富多彩，但也不可能每天变出一个花样，比如衣食住行、节庆民俗之类，重复是不可避免的。但问题在于，如果完

The problem is, if the author described life as it is, it would be a dull record without much attraction. It would be hard to avoid repetition because life is repetitive in itself. In order to solve this problem, Cao takes a bold initiative and uses "purposeful breach of writing rules."

The "purposeful breach of writing rules" is one of the concepts often brought up by Zhiyanzhai and others in their commentaries. In the past, researchers often try to understand that concept from the character-building perspective. Let's try another angle and analyse the breach from the perspective of narrative analysis.

In the first 80 chapters of the book, there have been a lot of purposeful breaches. Examples are, the descriptions of the first arrivals at Jia family of Lin Daiyu, Xue Baoqin and Xing Youyan (Chapters 3 and 49), flower-viewing events in the Mansion of Ning and Grandma Jia enjoying the Sweet Olive flowers (Chapters 5 and 38), Grandma Liu's two visits to the Mansion of Rong (Chapter 6 and Chapters 39 to 42), Xue Baochai's butterfly-chasing and Lin Daiyu's flower-burying (Chapter 27), the death of Jinchuan and Qingwen (Chapters 30 and 32), Jia Baoyu's commemoration on Jinchuan and Qingwen (Chapters 43, 70 and 78), the forming of poets' societies by Jia Baoyu and the girls (Chapters 37, 38, 49 and 50) and the funerals of Qin Keqing and Jia Jing (Chapters 13 to 15, 63 and 64).

It needs to be pointed out that the purposeful breach is not only for the contrast of two events, but also for the contrast among three or more events. For example, Jia's first encounter with Qin Zhong, Shui Rong of Prince Bei Jing and Jiang Yuhan (Chapters 7, 14, 15 and 28); Jia Jing and Jia Zheng's birthday celebrations and also the birthdays of Xue Baochai, Wang Xifeng and Jia Baoyu (Chapters 11, 16, 22, 43, 44 and 63).

Those people and events appeared in the same chapters and sometimes chapters apart, for example, Xue's butterfly-chasing and Lin's flower-burying. This kind of purposeful breach of repetition achieves a structural stability in the book, maintaining a balanced outlook. At the same time, Cao applies some minor adjustments to the stability and balance, making the writing unique.

全按照生活的原生态来叙述，作品会显得单调乏味，缺少吸引力。如果完全不重复，则又不符合生活的原貌，也很难做到。为了解决这一艺术难题，作者大胆创新，采取了"特犯不犯"的叙事方法。

"特犯不犯"是脂砚斋等人在批点《红楼梦》时多次提出的一个见解。以往的研究者通常从人物形象的塑造这一角度来理解，不过，我们还可以换个角度，对"特犯不犯"一语进行叙事学层面的观照。

在《红楼梦》前80回中存在着大量特犯不犯的描写，如林黛玉、薛宝琴、邢岫烟等人的初进贾府（第三、四十九回），宁国府赏花、贾母赏桂（第五、三十八回），刘姥姥的两进荣国府（第六、三十九—四十二回），宝钗扑蝶、黛玉葬花（第二十七回），金钏、晴雯之死（第三十、三十二回），贾宝玉的祭奠金钏、晴雯（第四十三、七十、七十八回），贾宝玉等人的两结诗社（第三十七、三十八、四十九、五十回），秦可卿、贾敬的丧葬（第十三—十五、六十三、六十四回），等等。

需要指出的是，这种特犯不犯并不仅仅表现为两件事之间的对应比照，有时还表现为三件事乃至更多事件之间的对应比照，比如贾宝玉初识秦钟、北静王水溶、蒋玉菡（第七、十四、十五、二十八回），贾敬、贾政寿辰，宝钗、凤姐、宝玉等人生日宴庆的描写（第十一、十六、二十二、四十三、四十四、六十三回）等。

这些人物、事件有些相隔数回乃至数十回，有些则出现在同一回中，如宝钗扑蝶、黛玉葬花的描写。这种"特犯"人物、事件的重复和分布使全书在叙事结构上保持了一种稳定性，呈现出一种较为对称均衡的结构布局。与此同时，作者在这种稳定、匀称的基础上又进行了一些新的调整，即"不犯"。虽然作品所写

There are a lot of similarities among the people and events described in the book, such as festivals and banquets. Due to the differences of seasons, time, venues, participants, and the feelings of participants, there are a lot of differences as Cao writes from various perspectives and uses different writing skills. Take the descriptions of birthdays of different people for an example. For Jia Jing and Jia Zheng, Cao only keeps routine records of them without many details while he puts a lot of effort into Jia Baoyu's birthday, making it colourful and interesting. There are also differences in Xue's butterfly-chasing and Lin's flower-burying. Even though both events take place in spring, and both characters are young girls, the two different characters with different personalities and views of lives take different actions. Cao designs similar environments for the two girls to perform their acts yet achieves quite different results that manifest their personalities quite vividly. The stability and evenness of the events and descriptions give the readers a sense of genuineness, a taste of renewal in the plain narratives. The readability of the book increases. Compared with other novels, *Honglou Meng* has achieved a new height in the art of narration.

Furthermore, the writing method strengthens the atmosphere of the narratives, maintaining the momentum of the stories. In *Honglou Meng*, most stories are petty daily issues. But Cao does not simply record the routines of life each day. On the contrary, he, apart from keeping the original flavour of the stories, digs deeply into the petty issues and explores deeper meanings. In other words, the lives are of highly literary features. The truthfulness of lives is the truthfulness of art.

The story of Xue Baochai's butterfly-chasing is nothing unique. Any young girl would do that in spring. But when Cao tells it, the story becomes quite unique. Xue is a reserved person and she hides her feelings quite well, which makes her somewhat mysterious to some readers. The butterfly-chasing event shows her other side—a more genuine, innocent side of Xue as a young girl. In the absence of other people when she is not on her guard, she lets out her true feelings, in sharp contrast to her normal disposition. A small event it may be, yet it is unexpected for the readers who can savour it for a moment. This story, echoing with Lin's flower-burying event, is another example of the

的人物、事件有颇多相似性，如节庆、宴饮等场面的描写，但由于节令、时间、地点、参与人数、人物心态等主客观条件的不同而显现出不同的特点，作者在叙述这些事件时，着眼点不同，所用的笔墨也是不一样的。比如同是生日场面的描写，写贾敬、贾政就基本上是例行公事，泛泛而写，没有用太多的笔墨，而对贾宝玉的生日则浓笔重写，突出其新鲜别致。再如宝钗扑蝶和黛玉葬花，虽然两者所写都是少女在春天的故事，但两人性格气质、人生态度迥然不同，行为方式自然也就很不一样，作者着意为两人设置了一个基本相同的活动环境，特犯不犯的手法将两人的形象刻画得栩栩如生。稳定和匀称使作品获得逼真的写实艺术效果，稳中有变则使叙事保持着新鲜感，避免叙事的呆滞沉闷，增强了作品的可读性。较之其他小说作品，《红楼梦》的叙事艺术确实达到了一个新的高度。

再次，增加叙事的情调和意境，以保持叙事的张力。《红楼梦》一书所写，大多为日常生活琐事，但作者并非照相式地复制、摹写生活，而是在保持高度真实感的前提下，注意挖掘琐事细节中的情调和趣味。也就是说，作者笔下的生活是一种高度艺术化的生活，其真实是一种艺术化的真实。

比如宝钗扑蝶，就故事本身而言，并没有多少特别之处，这是许多少女在春天都会做的事情。但在作者笔下，却显得十分别致。由于薛宝钗平日以端庄、稳重的面目出现，内心世界藏而不露，城府较深，对一般人来说，颇有些神秘感。扑蝶之举则生动形象地展示了这位青春少女的另一面，也是更为真实的一面，那就是她的天真烂漫。在没有外人在场、心理不设防的情况下，她终于流露出自己的真性情，与平日的稳重、端庄形成鲜明对比。看似寻常小事，但对读者来说则是一种意外收获，感到意趣盎然，余味无穷。宝钗扑蝶与同一回中的黛玉葬

magic brush of Cao.

Cao is a poet. He observes the outside world so carefully that he finds beauty in small things all the time. In his narratives, he adopts poems by other poets in the past. Baochai's butterfly-chasing, Daiyu's flower-burying, Lingguan's rose-painting and also Shi Xiangyun's nap after getting drunk are all petty events in daily lives but are described poetically and are highlights of the book, which have greatly increased its readability. This pratice is a great innovation in writing. It highly enhances the effectiveness of expressions and literary status of plain language literature. It also has a great and long-lasting impact on future works.

It is the successful employment of such narrative skills that makes *Honglou Meng*'s stories slow yet not boring, real yet not just routine, petty yet not messy, normal yet not mediocre. It has achieved a very high literary level, impressing readers deeply for generations.

Ⅲ

Readers who are familiar with the book would have noticed that the endings of stories and characters are often revealed beforehand. Cao would often use different forms of literature, for example, poems and riddles, to hint at the fate of characters. This technique has made the whole book peppered with mystery and sadness, thus more soul-touching.

Ancient Chinese novels, especially folk novels, use pre-narration extensively within the narrative. However, the narrative functions in the ancient novels are straightforward, and often do not play a major role. The frequent and repetitive use of tales, references to exploits in stories to and also the dexterous employment of stories by Cao himself is second to none. Cao uses a system of forewarning throughout the book and weaves a complete and thorough system of narration, enriching the content and implications of the book while arousing the readers' interests to read and participate.

花相映成趣，都是作品中的神来之笔。

作者具有诗人气质，对外界观察细致入微，时时能发现生活中的诗情画意，他大胆借鉴古代诗词，将其意境化用到小说的叙事描写中。如宝钗扑蝶、黛玉葬花、龄官画蔷、湘云醉卧等，尽管都是日常生活中很平常的琐事，但都写得极富诗意，别具情趣，成为作品中的精彩段落，读后一点都不感到沉闷、乏味。这是十分了不起的艺术创新，它大大提高了白话文学语言的表现力与艺术品位，对后世小说的创作有着十分深远的影响。

正是成功地综合运用上述这些叙事艺术技巧，使《红楼梦》的叙事节奏舒缓而不沉闷，真实而不呆滞，琐细而不凌乱，平常而不低俗，达到很高的艺术水准，打动了一代又一代的读者。

（三）

熟悉《红楼梦》的读者可能都会注意到这样一个现象：作品采取预先叙事的手法，提前将故事、人物的结局透露出来，并不时借助其他形式比如诗歌、谜语等，来暗示人物未来的命运，使整部作品带有一层神秘、感伤的色彩，增加了作品的感人魅力。

中国古代小说特别是通俗小说虽然较多地使用预叙这种叙事方式，但形式、功能均较为单纯，且在全书中的分量并不重。像《红楼梦》这样大量、频繁、集中地使用，充分挖掘其艺术功能，运用得如此之丰富、如此之巧妙者，再找不到第二个，真可以说是前无古人，后无来者。曹雪芹创造性地使用预叙这一形式，并将其贯穿全书，构建了一个完整、严密的预叙系统，大大丰富了作品的内涵和意蕴，同时也增强了读者阅读、参与的兴趣。

The method of revelation in advance is applied throughout the book. As early as in Chapter 1, a Buddhist monk and a Taoist priest predict that Yinglian is "ill-fated" and would "bring trouble to her parents." In Chapter 5, a story is told about "a Dream of the Land of Illusion where the destiny of the twelve beauties is explained" and that "after celestial wines, the dream of the red mansions is illustrated." In Chapter 22, we see Jia Zheng's sad lantern riddles with ill omens. In Chapter 79, there are writings of "I am not destined to live under silk-panelled windows. And why would you have to die young and be buried in the yellow earth?" We can say without exaggeration that such kinds of predictions and hints are everywhere in the previous 80 chapters of the book.

In *Honglou Meng* we can see various ways of revelation in advance. It can be purely descriptive, as shown in Chapter 3 when Jia Yucun escorts Lin Daiyu to the capital. "Hence, [Jia Zheng] treated Yucun uncommonly well and did all he could to help him. The day Jia presented a petition to the throne and Yucun was rehabilitated without much difficulty. He was ordered to await an appointment. Within two months, a post became available in the prefecture of Yingtian in Jinling and Yucun took it. He bid farewell to Jia Zheng, chose a day and set off for the post. But no more of this." These events, happening after Lin's arrival at the Mansion of Ning, yet are accounted for before the descriptions of Lin's arrival. This is how Cao reveals in advance. The descriptions often end with "But no more of this" or "Details will be told later." Cao also gives predictions of future events through words spoken by the characters. In Chapter 13, Qin Keqing, after her death, appears in Wang Xifeng's dream and makes reference to the "decline in the future." "When convicted of crime, everything would be confiscated by the court" and "on decline" are all revelations in advance on the future of the Jia family.

However, in general, such kinds of obvious revelation are not overwhelming. Cao uses more hints in various forms to do the job. The forms include paintings, such as the "Main Volume of the Twelve Beauties", "the Supplementary Volume, and the Supplementary Volume II" in Chapter 5. Also found in Chapter 5 are "Songs of the Dreams of the Red Mansions." Riddles are used in Chapter 22 where riddles texts are composed, as well as drinking games, like those at Jia Baoyu's birthday banquet in Chapter 63.

Cao links up all the characters and events in the book by using a complete and well-structured system and forms a revelation in advance. Those revelations mostly take the forms of poems, riddles that are sometimes

《红楼梦》全书都贯穿着预叙，从作品第一回一僧一道对英莲命运"有命无运、累及爹娘"的预测，到第五回的"游幻境指迷十二钗 饮仙醪曲演红楼梦"；从第二十二回的"制灯谜贾政悲谶语"，再到第七十九回的"茜纱窗下，我本无缘；黄土垄中，卿何薄命"。毫不夸张地说，在前80回中，随处都可以找到一些具有预言性、带有暗示色彩的语句。

《红楼梦》进行预叙的方式也是丰富多样的，它可以是一般的讲述，比如第三回贾雨村送林黛玉入京后的一段描写："因此优待雨村，更又不同，便竭力内中协助，题奏之日，轻轻谋了一个复职候缺，不上两个月，金陵应天府缺出，便谋补了此缺，拜辞了贾政，择日上任去了。不在话下。"这些事情都发生在林黛玉进贾府之后，但却在此之前讲述出来，显然是属于预叙。这种预叙往往用"不在话下"或"这是后话"等词语作标志。它也可以通过故事中的人物之口道出，如第十三回秦可卿给凤姐托梦，其所述"将来败落"、"有了罪，凡物可入官"、"败落下来"等语来看，明显是在暗示贾府将来的命运，同样属于预叙。

不过总的来看，《红楼梦》中像这样较为明显的预叙还不是太多，作品更多的是采取种种暗示手法来进行预叙，具体的形式也是灵活多样、不拘一格的：或通过图画，如第五回所写的"金陵十二钗正册"、"副册"、"又副册"；或通过诗词曲，如第五回所写的《红楼梦》套曲；或通过谜语，如第二十二回诸人所制谜语；或通过酒令，如第六十三回贾宝玉生日聚会上所行的酒令等。

作者将这些预叙与对全书人物、事件的描述紧密地结合在一起，构成了一个较为完整、严密的预叙系统。这些预叙大多是以暗示的形式进行，之所以如此，也与诗词、谜语等文学样

ambiguous and with double meanings. The double meanings of the text have double functions, too. On the one hand, they serve as a device for the narration of the stories. On the other hand, they are predictions and have symbolic meanings. From the point of view of artistic expression, the book becomes richer because of the hidden text, as readers can be engrossed in the artistic enjoyment of riddle-solving.

To find out the form and charateristic of revelation in advance is not difficult. However, it is difficult to evaluate that narrative method objectively and fairly, and to find the profound meanings behind this literary method for a better understanding of this great book.

Judging from the fact that this method is repeatedly employed in the book, we know that the author does not do so by chance. He must have purposefully used this method and the reason behind it is worth contemplating.

From a narrative perspective, the employment of revelation in advance corresponds with the very important flashback narration at the beginning of the book. It is mentioned previously that a stone which "was not good enough to be used to repair the sky and changed its form and went into the earthly world." The stone "experienced the joy of union, the sorrow of departure, the cold and warmth of the world." It tells us "its own stories that happened in the society it reincarnated into" (Chapter 1). For the stone, it tells what it has already experienced. Because of this, it knows the endings of all people and events, and it gives away hints throughout the book. The revelation of the future is quite natural in this sense. That is why we say revelation in advance is the preconditon of flashback narration and it is quite natural and logical.

However, the stone is not a real person but a fabricated character. In the book, the stone is an embodiment of the author and it says things for him. Here comes one question. Since the fate of all people could be found out by readers in the later part of the book, why must the author use pre-narration and suggest their fates in advance? What are the reasons for him to do so?

式本身所具有的模糊性、双关特点有关，它使作品中的不少语句获得双重蕴涵：一方面以字句表面的含义参与、完成作品的叙事，另一方面则隐藏着具有预言、象征性的意义。从艺术表达的角度看，它使作品的蕴涵更为丰富，读者在阅读时，有一种近乎猜谜的艺术享受。

归纳出《红楼梦》预叙这一叙事手法的存在形式及特点并不算困难，问题在于如何对这一叙事手法进行客观、公正的评价，并探讨这一文学现象背后所蕴涵的意义，以便更为深入地理解这部优秀作品。

从预叙在作品中大量、频繁运用这一现象来看，这并非作者的无心插柳，而是他有意识地加以运用的结果。其背后的动因，确实是耐人寻味的。

从叙事的角度看，预叙的运用与卷首那段统摄全书的倒叙有着密切的关系。前面已经讲到，全书故事的主要讲述者是那位"无材补天，幻形入世"、"历尽离合悲欢炎凉世态"的石头，它讲述的是自己"坠落之乡，投胎之处，亲自经历的一段陈迹故事"（第一回）。对石头来说，他实际上是在回顾那些已经发生过的往事。也正是因为这个缘故，他对故事中人物未来的命运和归宿了如指掌，不时地提前进行交代和暗示，这种超时空预叙也是合情合理的。可以说，《红楼梦》里的预叙是以倒叙为前提的，合乎艺术自身的逻辑。

自然，这位石头叙事者并非真有其人，他不过是作者虚构的一位艺术形象。在作品中，他是作者的化身，发挥着代作者立言的功能。不过这里有一个问题：故事中人物的命运、归宿到作品后面肯定都会——写到，读者到时一看便知。既然如此，作者为什么一定要运用预叙手法，提前对人物的命运、归宿进行交代呢？他这样做，究竟是出于什么考虑呢？

Many researchers say that *Honglou Meng* is a book filled with fatalistic thoughts. The reason for this theory is the repetitive use of revelation in advance. The fates of the main characters in the book are pre-determined even before their reincarnation, and are recorded in the volumes, such as the Main Volume of *the Twelve Beauties* , the Supplementary Volume, and the Supplementary Volume Ⅱ. The characters are like puppets, with different appearances and personalities, and would perform their duties accordingly. They would be happy, sad, talkative, or silent and their behaviours are controlled by a pair of invisible hands. Fatalism does exist in this kind of pre-arrangement. Furthermore, most of the characters in the book end up in tragedy, which shrouds the whole book in depression and sadness. A pall of sadness is cast all over the characters due to the application of revelation in advance.

However, the author's intention goes beyond that. There must have been other reasons for him to spare no efforts in compiling the book, apart from the venting of feelings and the expression of fatalistic thoughts. From all those detailed descriptions we know that the author knows what he is doing. He is recalling the events and thinking about those characters with a strong sense of repentance and reflection, even though he has added some fabricated and imagined events.

At the beginning of the book, Cao says there are two reasons for him to write the book. One is to "write the stories of the girls into history" and that "even though I am corrupt, there have been some females of strong and good personalities. I can't, for the protection of my own shortcomings, let them perish without a trace." The second reason is that "I have let down my father and brothers who had educated me, and have ignored my teachers and friends who had persuaded me to follow the virtuous path. Hence, I have acquired few skills, and have already wasted half of my life. Now I want to compile my stories into a book and use it to warn the others" (Chapter 1). Many researchers have paid due attention to the first reason and there have been many works on it. The second reason, because it does not comply with the common reception that the book is anti-feudalism and pro-democracy, is intentionally or unintentionally ignored by researchers.

Obviously, while writing *Honglou Meng* and trying to "write the stories of

不少研究者指出《红楼梦》一书具有宿命色彩，他们之所以会产生这种印象，应该说与作品中预叙的反复运用有一定的关系。作品的主要人物从出生开始甚至早在投胎转世的时候，其命运就已经被决定，记在《金陵十二钗》正册、副册、又副册之类的册簿中。他们仿佛演剧的木偶，虽然从表面上看，个性各异、面目不同，在人生舞台上各自进行着或欢喜、或悲惨、或热闹、或静默的表演，但实际上他们的所作所为，无不被一双看不见的大手牢牢控制着。不可否认，这种安排设计确实有宿命的成分在。加上作品中这些主要人物的命运和归宿基本上都可以不幸和悲惨来形容，很少有善终的。因此，这些预言无疑强化了全书的悲剧色彩，并营造出一种忧伤、压抑的悲剧氛围，使作品中的人物、事件始终笼罩在一层不祥的阴影中。

不过，作者的目的并不仅止于此。他之所以要花费如此大的心血来创作这部小说，在感情的宣泄、宿命观念的表达之外还有别的原因。从作品的具体描写来看，作者的头脑是十分清醒的，他知道自己在做什么。他是以忏悔和反思的态度来重温那些曾经发生的人物和事件，尽管其中有不少属虚构和想象。

按照作品开篇所述，作者主要有两个创作目的：一是"使闺阁昭传"，"我之罪固不免，然闺阁中本自历历有人，万不可因我之不肖，自护己短，一并使其泯灭也"；二是"将已往所赖天恩祖德，锦衣纨绔之时，饫甘餍肥之日，背父母教育之恩，负师友规训之德，以至今日一技无成、半生潦倒之罪，编述一集，以告天下人"（第一回）。对前一个创作目的，研究者给予了充分重视，相关著述甚多，这里不再赘述；后一个创作目的因不符合对《红楼梦》主旨反封建、民主主义之类的流行认知，因而被研究者有意或无意地忽略。

显然，曹雪芹在创作《红楼梦》时，除"使闺阁昭传"外，

the girls into history," Cao also wants to educate the readers. The predictions and revelations in advance are for that purpose. From the detailed descriptions, the repentance and reflections are profound and complicated. They are not totally fatalistic and the sense of regret is something we need to pay special attention to.

We can see the sense of regret from the descriptions of Jia Baoyu and Wang Xifeng.

In Chapter 5 when Jia Baoyu is dream-travelling in the Land of Illusion, revelation in advance is used. The Fairy Disenchantment is sent to provide guidance for Baoyu by his ancestors, Duke Ning and Duke Rong. The two seniors know that the family is "at the end of their times and not salvageable." That being said, the two ancestors still want to try their best to save their off-spring. They have great expectations for Baoyu. They hope the Fairy Disenchantment could use erotic events to warn him of his stubbornness, and hope that could enable him to escape disillusion and hence take the proper path in life. Even though the Fairy Disenchantment does do as the two Dukes say, warning everyone of their destiny and persuading Baoyu to "think about this thoroughly in the future and repent and correct his wrongdoings, to study the thoughts of Confucius and Mencius and also to devote himself to the betterment of society," Baoyu does not come to the realisation of all that. When he wakes up from his dream, he is the same as before, without any change. Later, Qin Zhong, before dying, also persuades him, his father Jia Zheng severely punishes him, Xiren and Shi Xiangyun all try to guide him, but their efforts are in vain.

In Chapter 13, Qin Keqing, on her deathbed, appears in Wang Xifeng's dream and tells her that she should "in glorious times prepare for the times of decline." Qin also warns Wang of "two unfinished tasks." This is also rendered by using revelation in advance. Even though Wang Xifeng says, "What you've said is quite right," she does not take Qin Keqing's advice. After Qin's death, Wang becomes even more manipulative. She uses all her powers to gain personal benefits, and leads the Jia family onto a declining road of no return. Wang is chiefly responsible for the family's decline.

Cao is very serious when writing such stories. There is no trace of ridicule

还有总结人生教训的重要目的，作品中大量预叙的运用正是为了贯彻这一创作意图。通过作品的具体描写来看，忏悔和反思的内容是十分深刻而复杂的，并非完全指向和等同于宿命，其中作者通过预叙所流露出的惋惜之情是应该给予特别关注的。

作者通过预叙所表达的惋惜之情可以从贾宝玉、王熙凤这两个主要人物身上看出来：

作品第五回，贾宝玉梦游太虚幻境，这一回集中使用了预叙这一叙事方式。按照作品的描写，警幻仙姑是受宁、荣二公之灵的委托特意来点化贾宝玉的，因为他们已经预先知道自己的家族"运终数尽，不可挽回"。尽管家族的命运注定如此，但宁、荣二公还是想作一番努力来挽回，对贾宝玉寄予了很大希望，希望警幻仙姑"以情欲声色等事警其痴顽，或能使彼跳出迷人圈子，然后入于正路"。警幻仙姑虽然按照宁荣二公的嘱托，提前告知家族未来的命运，规劝贾宝玉"今后万万解释，改悟前情，留意于孔孟之间，委身于经济之道"。但贾宝玉并未因此醒悟，当他从梦中醒来之后，依然故我，思想行为并没有因此而发生丝毫改变。其后，又有好友秦钟临死前的劝告，父亲贾政的训斥，袭人、史湘云等人的开导等，但都没有产生什么实际效果。

作品第十三回，秦可卿临死前托梦给王熙凤，劝她"于荣时筹画下将来衰时的世业"，并明确告诉她还有"两件未妥"的重要事情要办。这里也同样运用了预叙手法。王熙凤虽然表示认同："这话虑的极是。"但她显然并未听从秦可卿的这番劝告。秦可卿死后，她反而变本加厉，玩弄计谋，损公肥私，最终将家族一步步带向不归之路。家族的破败，她是要负主要责任的。

作品在写到这些地方时，态度是十分严肃、认真的，看不

or sarcasm in his tone. These revelations, unlike the vague and ambiguous poems and riddles, are down-to-earth. Jia Baoyu and Wang Xifeng are important people in the Jia family and they undertake major responsibilities. As long as they were willing, they could have changed the fate of the family. The fall of the family has been revealed to them in advance, which serves as an expression of regret. Cao is trying to tell the readers, if these two important people would listen to the advice from others, and if they would change their behaviours, they could have changed the destiny of their family. At least there is such possibility. Cao's attitude is quite clear. He wishes that the two people could change the destiny which has been prearranged by heaven. But, to everyone's disappointment, they do not grasp the chance and still behave as they did in the past. They eventually fall with the decline of the family. The regret is the author's reflection. He uses the revelation to express his thoughts that, in the process of the family decline, there have been many opportunities and there have been many methods by which the family could have been salvaged. But the chances slip through the fingers of those in charge. Those who lead the family to the abyss are the key figures in the family, like Jia Baoyu and Wang Xifeng. They are all responsible. They are victims and culprits at the same time.

Cao has two perspectives over the issue of destiny. One is that he recognises there is a destiny but he does not want to be controlled by it. He knows the divine will is not to be disobeyed. However, he does not want to let go the last hope and opportunity to change destiny. Cao uses ample revelations in the book that not only serve as expressions of his sorrow and create an atmosphere of sadness and suppression, but also suggest to the readers that, while the destiny of man is prearranged by heaven, it could be changed through hard work, or at least there exists hope and opportunities. If man could be well-prepared, he would have minimised the loss and the ending may have been less miserable.

出其中有反讽或调侃的意味在。这些预言的内容都明白无误地告诉当事人，不像诗词那样含糊不清，产生歧义。贾宝玉、王熙凤二人都是贾府里的重要人物、家族责任的主要承担者，只要他们愿意，是可以改变家族命运的。将家族未来衰败的结局提前告诉他们，显然是在表达一种惋惜之情。使用预叙手法，作者实际上是在进行一种假设：假如这两人听从他人的劝告，改变自己的行为方式，是有机会挽救家族的衰败命运的，最起码是存在这种可能性的。作者的态度也较为明确，他希望这两位重要人物能够改变上天已经规定好的命运，但令人遗憾的是，他们都没有把握着机会，依然我行我素，直至随着整个家族走向没落。这种惋惜正是作者反思的结果，他运用预叙这种形式表达了自己思考的结果：在家族走向破败的过程中，是有很多次机会、多种方法可以挽回的，但这些机会都被家族的主要成员们白白地浪费掉了。因此将家族带向深渊者，正是那些家族的主要人物，如贾宝玉、王熙凤等人，他们每个人都有责任，既是受害者，又是加害者。

在承认命运存在的同时又不甘心接受命运的随意摆布，知道天命不可违，但又不放弃改变命运的最后希望和机会，从作品的具体描写来看，这正是作者命运观的两个方面。他在作品中大量使用预叙，一方面借此流露忧伤、惆怅的悲剧心绪，营造不祥、压抑的不和谐气氛；另一方面也在进行提示读者：人的命运尽管早已被造化规定好，但它是可以靠个人努力改变的，最起码是存在希望和机会的。如果提前做好准备，最起码等悲剧到来时，可以最大限度地减少损失，也许结局就不会太悲惨。

贾宝玉画像

Portrait of Jia Baoyu

六　艳情人自说红楼 ——《红楼梦》的续书

Chapter Ⅵ　Beauty Lovers' Account: The Continuation
of *Honglou Meng*

This is definitely a miracle in Chinese literary history and in world literary history, too: An incomplete script of 80 chapters has become the pinnacle of achievement of the ancient literature, representing the highest achievement of folk novel by Chinese people. At the same time, the remaining 40 chapters, written by someone else for the sake of completeness, are accepted by readers of all levels as the genuine continuation of the original book. Because of their acceptance, the latter 40 chapters are considered to be an organic part of the book. The original part and the continuation by others coexisted harmoniously. The continuation of someone else's book is a tough job and often receives little appreciation due to the poor quality ending. However, the latter 40 chapters of *Honglou Meng* are an exception. They have achieved a breakthrough, a unique literary miracle like restoring the missing arms of Venus.

When talking about Cao Xueqin and his *Honglou Meng*, we cannot avoid talking about Gao E and the latter 40 chapters written by him, as well as other different versions of continued works resulting from *Honglou Meng*.

I

Before discussing Gao E and the latter 40 chapters, we need to discuss another issue. How does Cao design the fate of the characters and the endings of the book? A very important criterion of judging whether a continued work is good or not, is to see if the continuation is consistent with the characters and plots in the former part of the book.

According to the verses and divertimento in Chapter 5 and contents in other chapters and in the commentaries by Zhiyanzhai, Cao has an overall design of the characters and plots and he did write chapters beyond Chapter 80. We could say that he had almost completed the majority of the book except that he did not have the chance to go over the final editing of it. It is a pity that the manuscript is lost and we could not see it now. However, according to the descriptions and hints in the book, and the commentaries by Zhiyanzhai, we still could have a general understanding of Cao's design of the ending of the book.

From the overall layout of *Honglou Meng*, we can see that the main story line is the tragic decline from glory of the Jia family. This is quite obvious from the descriptions and hints throughout the first 80 chapters. We can

这注定是中国文学史乃至世界文学史上一个空前绝后的奇迹：一部小说以其残存的80回竟然成为一个古老民族文学艺术的巅峰之作，代表着该民族小说发展的最高成就；与此同时，为完成全璧而续补的后40回竟然能达到乱真的程度，与原著一起被读者广泛接受，家喻户晓，妇孺皆知。读者的认同和喜爱已使后40回续作成为《红楼梦》的有机组成部分，原作和续书构成了一种良性共生的关系。续书的写作本来是一件吃力不讨好的事情，通常会有狗尾续貂之讥，但《红楼梦》的后40回则不然，它取得了突破，这种给维纳斯续残臂式的成功创造了一个前无古人后无来者的文学奇迹。

说到曹雪芹和他的《红楼梦》，不能不提起高鹗和后40回续书，自然也不能不说说围绕这部名著所产生的一批续书。

（一）

在谈论高鹗和后40回之前，我们首先要探讨一个问题：曹雪芹本人对《红楼梦》一书的结局是如何考虑和安排的，因为是否与原书的人物、情节保持一致，这是评价续书的一个重要标准。

从作品第五回的判词、套曲、其他章回的内容以及脂砚斋批语所透露的信息来看，曹雪芹对全书人物、事件的安排是有着通盘考虑的，而且他确实写到了80回之后，可以说是大体写完，只是没有来得及完成全书最后的修改。可惜这部分稿子已经迷失，现在无法看到。不过根据作品中的相关交代、暗示及脂砚斋的批语，我们还是可以大体了解作者对全书结局的安排情况的。

从《红楼梦》的整体布局来看，贾氏家族从鼎盛到衰落的悲剧描写是全书的主线，从前80回的相关描写和暗示中可以很

envisage a great tragedy after Chapter 80. The happy times of the young men and women in the Grand View Garden are to be ended by heartbreaking deaths and departures. The whole family, broken after the impact of several major incidents, would be destroyed, just like the descriptions in the book that it is "like the fall of a high building and the diminishing of an oil lamp." The actual decline of the family and its displaced people are only hinted in the first chapters. The descriptions should come after Chapter 80.

The trigger for the tragedy is the "revelation of the incidents." The reason for the raid of the Jia family is not hard to guess. There is enough evidence in the first 80 chapters. Jia She robs others and kills someone for a few antique fans. Wang Xifeng, for the sake of 3 000 taels of silver, manipulates the litigation papers and causes an innocent couple to die. Jia Lian, who indulges himself in wine and women, takes someone else's wife by force. Other disgraceful conducts, such as inducing officials, loan-sharking, recruiting bandits, arranging illegal gambling and visiting brothels, are only a few examples of the flaws in Jia family. If one is to seriously investigate even one of the events, the Jia family could be on the brink of being ruined. The descendents of the Jia family have long forgotten the hardship their ancestors went through when creating the glory of the family, and they have become corrupt and indulged themselves in sensual enjoyments. Even if the Jia family had not been raided, it would only be a matter of time for the family to decline in the hands of those trouble-making parasites. The raid only speeds up the decline. Leng Zixing says in Chapter 2, "though the external structure may still look fine, the inside is nearly empty."

The above introduction is only a general outline of the situation. The stirring and seething tragedy is to be described with vivid characters and events in the book, especially those major characters, like Jia Baoyu and the twelve beauties in Jinling. Those people are the major characters in the family and they will be the sufferers of the great tragedy. Their destinies have all been revealed vaguely in the verses and divertimento in Chapter 5 and will be the focus of the latter part of the book. However, because of the vagueness of the

清楚地看到这一点。可以想见，80回之后必将是一场大悲剧的上演，大观园里青年男女的欢乐时光注定要用极为悲惨的生死离别来画上句号，整个家族也将在一连串的打击之后分崩离析，家破人亡，彻底走向没落，正如作品中所描写的："忽喇喇似大厦倾，昏惨惨似灯将尽。"意思是说家族的破灭像大厦倾倒一样迅速，像油灯燃尽一样凄惨。至于贾府究竟是如何败落、流散的，前80回只留下伏笔，并没有具体的描写，这些内容应该都在80回之后。

走向悲剧的导火线是"事败"，"事败"就是事情败露的意思。导致抄家的原因也是可以想见的，前80回对此已有了较为充分的描写和铺垫，要么是贾赦的强取豪夺，为几把古扇逼死人命；要么是王熙凤的包揽词讼，为三千两银子坏人姻缘，平添一对冤魂；要么是贾琏纵情酒色，夺人之妻。其他如交通外官、放高利贷、招纳匪类、聚赌嫖娼等恶行，在贾府可以说是屡见不鲜，见怪不怪了。认真追究起来，哪一件都足以使这个家族破败衰亡。贾家的那些不肖子弟们早已抛弃祖先艰难创业的遗风，彻底堕落，沦为一群酒肉利欲之徒。即使没有后来的抄家，仅是这些膏粱子弟们坐吃山空、荒淫无耻、惹是生非的行为，这个家族迟早会走向败落，抄家只不过是加速了这一过程而已，正如作品第二回冷子兴所形容的："如今外面的架子虽未甚倒，内囊却也尽上来了。"

上面所勾勒的不过是一个大体的轮廓，这场轰轰烈烈的大悲剧还需要通过具体可感的人物、事件的精细描写体现出来，特别是那些作者着力塑造的主要人物，如贾宝玉和金陵十二钗。他们既是家族的主要成员，同时也是这场大悲剧的承受者，他们的结局和归宿无疑是后半部的重心所在。作品通过第五回的判词、红楼梦套曲及其他部分的暗示已经有所交代，但由于诗

poems and hints, disagreement arose as to their implications. Luckily, Zhiyanzhai has revealed many important messages that could satisfy the readers who are concerned with the main characters' fate to a certain degree.

Let's firstly look at Jia Baoyu. After Chapter 80, with the decline of the family, the worry-free rich nobleman's joyful time comes to an end. His life falls into extreme difficulty. From Zhiyanzhai's comments, Jia is even sent to prison after the raid. What is worth mentioning is that in the latter part of the book, people of little significance, like Qianxue and Xiaohong, become major players making great contribution to the family. Qianxue and Xiaohong are not mentioned in detail in the first 80 chapters but, apparently, Cao must have put them in the first 80 chapters for later use. Without Zhiyanzhai's commentaries, it would be hard to notice the link. This is another example of Cao's well-conceived designs.

What the writer focuses on and readers would like to know most eagerly is the result of Jia Baoyu and Lin Daiyu's love. A lot of effort is put into the descriptions. This is, for sure, the important plot in the latter chapters. Jia and Lin's love story has to come to an abrupt end and Xue Baochai eventually becomes Jia's wife. Even if Cao's plan on the ending of the love story between Jia and Lin was similar to what we read from the current latter 40 chapters the development of the story may have been different. Cao may not create the dramatic bride-swap, because even if there was no such bride-swap, Jia and Xue could simply lead a quiet and boring life. Wouldn't a marriage as such also be a tragedy?

The ending of Jia Baoyu is also hinted in the first 80 chapters that Jia would renounce his worldly life and become a Buddhist monk. Zhiyanzhai mentions several times that Jia would "let go of the cliff," meaning he would let go the worldly life in desperation. This is fairly consistent with Jia'sthoughts all along.

Being the core figure in *Honglou Meng*, Lin Daiyu's ending would no doubt be the trump card in the continued works. This beautiful, sensitive and over-anxious, learned and talented young lady, suffering from physical illness and emotional stress, is not able to taste the sweet fruition of her love before

词及暗示的含糊性和多义性，难以有特别确切的了解，由此产生争议也就在所难免。好在脂砚斋批语中透露出不少重要的信息，可以在一定程度上满足读者对这些主要人物命运的牵挂和关注。

先说贾宝玉。80回之后，随着家族的破败，这位富贵闲人无拘无束、自由自在的快乐时光也宣告终结，生活很快陷入极端困顿的状态。从脂砚斋批语所透露的信息来看，贾宝玉在抄家的过程中还曾遭受过牢狱之灾。值得注意的是，在这部分内容中，一些小人物如茜雪、小红等大显身手，成为关键人物。茜雪、小红在前80回中着墨不多，作者写到她们，显然有千里伏线的用意在。如果没有脂砚斋批语的交代，后人是很难想象到这些情节的。由此可见作者对整部作品考虑、安排得十分周密。

作品着力描写、读者也最为关心的宝玉婚恋问题在后文中当有精彩之笔，这是可以想见的。宝、黛二人刻骨铭心的恋情因黛玉的早逝戛然而止，宝钗最终将成为宝二奶奶。尽管结果与现在所看到的后40回基本一致，但过程很可能完全不同，特别是那个极富戏剧性的调包计，曹雪芹未必会这样写。结婚之后，宝玉、宝钗的生活相当平淡乏味，这样平淡乏味的婚姻不也是一场悲剧吗？

关于宝玉最后的归宿，作品前80回也屡有暗示，贾宝玉最后是弃家为僧的。脂砚斋批语还多次提到后文有宝玉悬崖撒手的描写，"悬崖撒手"意味着对尘世的彻底绝望，这一安排应该说是符合贾宝玉的一贯思想的。

作为作品的核心人物，林黛玉结局的描写无疑会成为后半部中的重头文章。这位天生丽质、敏感多虑、极富诗人才情的贵族少女在病痛与情感的双重折磨下，未能尝到爱情的蜜果就

dying in tears. Her death, from the hints in the previous 80 chapters, should not be so dramatic as the bride-swap. Some researchers say she died of her illness while some say she died of suppression. Some even say she threw herself into a river. However, these are merely presumptions and may not reflect the intentions of Cao. Perhaps Cao would have some unexpected ideas.

Faced with Lin's death, how would Jia react? This must be very hard for the author to tackle and could be a test of Cao's skills. Unfortunately, the manuscript is nowhere to be found.

The description of another heroine in the book, Xue Baochai, is another sign of Cao's delicate design. After Lin's death, Xue becomes the lady of the Jia family. However, at this time, there remain only a handful of servants in the family, such as Sheyue. Jia and Xue could have lived as a respectful couple in harmony with the old time friendship. However, this hanging-on relationship with no excitement would never match up to the harmony developed within the arguments and quarrels between Jia and Lin. The final act by Jia, "letting go of the cliff," is a manifestation of his choice and also his attitude to marriage. He has had a breakthrough. He is relieved, leaving all suffering and pain to Xue. Xue seems to have a better ending than Lin Daiyu, Wang Xifeng, Jia Yingchun and Miaoyu, but what does she get in the whole process, from a chaste girl praised by all to a discarded wife without hope in life? Isn't she a main victim, too?

The results of other people, such as Jia Yuanchun, Jia Tanchun, Shi Xiangyun, Wang Xifeng, Miaoyu, Xiren, Xiangling and Granny Liu, along with the "List of Lovers" to be released at the end of the book, would also be in the mind of Cao. Hints can be found in the first 80 chapters and from Zhiyanzhai's comments.

Now we know Cao had a comprehensive plan for the book and that he completed the majority of the book. The question now is how many chapters he has written in the original book. Does it have the 120 chapters as the current version? Some researchers have made a study on this. Zhiyanzhai and others, having read the manuscripts, provided very important information for the solution of that problem. According to the information and clues, Cao would

泪尽而逝。至于具体的细节和情景，从前80回的描写来看，应该不像调包计那样戏剧化。有的研究者认为她是死于疾病，有的认为她死于迫害，也有研究者认为她是投水自尽，但这些也只是推测而已，未必符合作者的原意，曹雪芹说不定会有出人意料的写法。

林黛玉死后，贾宝玉的反应如何，这实在是很难写的一笔，于此可见作者的笔力、功夫，可惜这些文字现在已无法看到。

作品中另一位主人公薛宝钗归宿的描写同样可见作者的匠心与才情。她在黛玉去世后成为贾府的女主人，此时，守在他们身边的，也只有麝月等少数仆从了。贾、薛二人固然可以做到"齐眉举案"，有旧情可谈，但这种不即不离、缺少激情的夫妻关系与贾、林在不断争吵、试探中达到的心灵默契是无法相比的。由贾宝玉的最后悬崖撒手不难看出他的感情取向，不难看出他对这桩婚姻的态度。他超脱了，留给宝钗的却是无尽的苦痛和失落。对薛宝钗而言，似乎她的结局比林黛玉、王熙凤、迎春、妙玉等人要好些，但是，从众口皆碑的贤德淑女到前途无望的弃妇怨女，她在这一过程中得到的是什么？她不也是一位悲剧的主角吗？

其他如元春、探春、惜春、史湘云、王熙凤、妙玉、袭人、香菱、巧姐、刘姥姥等人的归宿，如小说结尾的情榜等，作者在后面也都会写到，这可以从前80回的暗示及脂批中得到一些线索。

既然曹雪芹对全书有着通盘的考虑，而且还大体上写完了全书，那么原书究竟有多少回呢？是不是也像现在所看到的续书那样有120回呢？研究者对这一问题也进行了探讨。脂砚斋等人曾看到过后面的原稿，他们在批语中流露的信息为解决这一问题提供了十分重要的线索。根据这些线索推算，原作的回

have had 110 chapters in his original book, 10 chapters shorter than the current version. Some have suggested that there should be 108 chapters in the original book.

If there were 110 chapters in the original book, it would have a very hasty ending. All events, such as the raid, the fall of the Jia family and the displacement of the people, would have to happen in 30 chapters. If Cao had a plan like this, he could have had his reasons. From the contents in the first 80 chapters, the last 30 chapters should be very colourful. The loss of the manuscript is most unfortunate indeed.

Ⅱ

Researchers in the academic field normally think that the last 40 chapters of the current 120-chapter version are not written by Cao but are the earliest version of continuation by someone else. They have three reasons. Firstly, according to records, as in Zhang Wentao's foreword in a poem, "To Gao Lanshu (Gao E) in the Same Year," "it is said that the part after Chapter 80 was written by Lanshu." Secondly, all existing hand-written copies from the earliest times contain 80 chapters only. Zhiyanzhai also commented that the chapters after Chapter 80 were borrowed by others and went missing. The third reason is that some events in the last 40 chapters do not match the comments by Zhiyanzhai.

In 1921, Hu Shi published an essay, "Textual Researches on *Honglou Meng*," and discussed that issue thoroughly. In the book, Hu says that the latter 40 chapters in the current version that contains 120 chapters were not written by Cao Xueqin. It is Gao E who wrote it. Researchers in the field all accepted Hu's view. Thus, Gao became the author of the latter part of the book and has been severely criticised by many. Many researchers blamed on Gao the inavailability of the complete version of the original book. Some claimed Gao was guilty of manipulating *Honglou Meng* and some even painted Gao as a "special cultural agent" who had his own agenda. Gao became a resented figure in the literary world and his image was paraded as a negative example. It was not until recently that, with further researches, people have started to view that issue more objectively and tolerantly. People start to recognise and to pay respect to Gao E for his effort to safeguard *Honglou Meng*. The much-

数当为110回，比续书少10回。不过也有不同的意见，如有的研究者认为原作应有108回。

仅仅30回的篇幅，就将抄家、破败、子孙流散等许多头绪一一了结，似乎显得仓促、紧张了些。不过曹雪芹如果这样安排的话，自然有他的道理，从前80回的内容来看，后30回一定相当精彩。可惜原稿已失，形成了一个永远无法弥补的缺憾。

（二）

学界通常认为120回本《红楼梦》的后40回并非出自曹雪芹之手，它是最早的一部《红楼梦》续书，这主要基于如下三条理由：一是相关的记载，如张问陶《赠高兰墅（鹗）同年》诗序云："传奇红楼梦八十回以后，俱兰墅所补。"意思是说，小说《红楼梦》80回以后，都是高鹗所补的；二是现存《红楼梦》早期的抄本都是80回，而且脂砚斋在批语中曾明确说，80回以后的部分被借阅者迷失；三是后40回的故事情节与脂砚斋在批语中所透露的不够一致。

1921年，胡适在其《红楼梦考证》一文中详细论证了这一问题，提出通行120回本《红楼梦》的后40回为续书，不是出于曹雪芹之手，其作者是高鹗。此后学界普遍接受了胡适的这些观点，高鹗被当作续书的作者，受到了许多严厉的批评和指责，甚至谩骂。不少红学家将无法看到《红楼梦》全璧的不满和怨气全撒到高鹗身上，将其视为篡改《红楼梦》的罪人，还有的红学家将他描绘成用心险恶、受人指使的"文化特务"。其结果是，高鹗以丑角形象在一部部文学史教材中被当作反面人物游街示众。直到近几年，随着学术研究的深入进行，人们才开始用比较公允和宽容的目光来重新审视这段文学史上的公案，为保全《红楼梦》而付出辛勤劳动的高鹗终于得到应有的

criticised last 40 chapters start to have some new meaning and colour in the eyes of the Hong experts.

In fact, whether Gao E is the author of the latter part of the book is still arguable, as some strong evidence of the reversed views exists. Furthermore, Gao E never admitted that he was the author. No matter what the situation was, Gao did put in a lot of effort editing the book before the formal printing. He made his own contributions to the printing and promotion of the book. His efforts were all in the current version which contains 120 chapters. His editing was in it and he could be regarded as the author of the latter 40 Chapters from this perspective. However, he was perhaps not the main author or the original creator of the book. This is something we need to keep in mind. It would be hard to determine which parts he edited. It is necessary to write something about the man who contributed a lot in the printing and circulation of the last 40 chapters, and who received a lot of criticism because of those chapters.

Gao E, pen-named Lanshu and nicknamed Honglou Waishi (Historian of the External Honglou). His ancestors came from Tieling in northern Liaoning province and was in the Yellow Flag Internal Affairs Bureau in the Han army. He could be best described as "extremely talented" and was "frustrated due to dejection." His experiences were like those of Cao. He was talented enough to undertake the task of continuating Cao's work, and his work was one of the best of continued books. If Gao were to write a book of his own, he might have achieved a higher level of renown.

Due to the lack of information, we could only see a very sketchy outline of him, from his own descriptions and other scattered records. He was a successful candidate in the imperial examinations at the provincial and municipal levels. When he finally obtained qualifications to use his talents, he was already over 50, a time to be expecting retirement. He was later appointed to various but powerless official positions, such as the inner court scholar, Shuntian Village Examiner, imperial inspector to southern Yangtse River, and assistant to the office of prosecution. Those appointments extremely disappointed and saddened him. In many of his poems, he wrote about being "dejected, pitying himself while walking on a muddy path." Because of those experiences, he was able to understand Cao completely. However, his talent and eloquence, "a surprise to his audience," were a compensation for his

尊重和肯定，饱受贬斥的后40回在红学家眼里也有了新的色彩和内涵。

其实，高鹗到底是不是后40回的作者还是存在争议的，因为存在着相当有力的反证，何况当事者高鹗本人就不承认自己是作者。不管怎样，高鹗在《红楼梦》刊刻前曾做过一番整理修订工作，对该书的刊印和传播是有贡献的。120回本的《红楼梦》倾注着他的心血，其中有他增补的文字，因此从这个角度说他是后40回的作者也有一定的道理，不过他未必是主要作者或原创者，这一点是要区别开的。至于究竟哪些地方出自他的手笔，现在已无法确考了。对于这位为后40回的刊印流传做出很大贡献，又为后40回受到许多指责、谩骂的高鹗，是应该为他写点什么的。

高鹗，字兰墅，号红楼外史。祖籍辽东铁岭，汉军镶黄旗内务府人。用"困厄失意"、"才华过人"八个字足可概括他的一生。落魄不遇，使他与曹雪芹有着类似的人生体验；才华独具，使他修订的后40回在众多续红之作中脱颖而出。以高鹗的见识与功力，如果他另外去写一部小说，也许在后世可以得到更高的声誉。

十分遗憾的是，因资料的缺乏，高鹗在我们的视野中也是一个面目模糊的身影，从其夫子自道及其零星的记载中可窥见其人生的一鳞半爪。他虽中过举人、进士，可等他得到这些施展才学的资格时，早已年过半百，油然而生夕阳之叹了。随后而来的内阁中书、顺天乡试同考官、江南道御史、刑科给事中等有职无权的谏官、学官官衔，让颇有胸襟的高鹗感到失落和惆怅。在不少诗文中，他流露出一种"泥途悲潦倒"的感叹。早年的科场淹滞、晚年的平淡仕途使他始终处于悲苦困厄的心绪体验中，这使他能够在情感上理解和贴近曹雪芹。其过人的学识、出众的才华、生花的口才据说是"凡在有目，谅皆欣赏"，

misfortune in office.

We also know that Gao was an honest and gentle man. He often encouraged young people to be filial, to contribute to the betterment of society and to take a scholarly career path. He was good at writing *bayu*, the formulated writing style, with forceful words and keen insights. In his writings and poems, we can see some thoughts relating to Buddhism and Taoism. Traces of those can be found in the latter 40 chapters of *Honglou Meng*.

Gao was unfortunate, yet he was also fortunate in another way, both because of *Honglou Meng*. Were it not for *Honglou Meng*, who would have paid attention to a dejected scholar, given that there would be thousands like him then?

Ⅲ

To continue someone else's book is a difficult work with little reward, especially when the book is *Honglou Meng*. The second writer's work would inevitably be compared with and judged against the work of Cao Xueqin, the original writer and first runner of the relay. The continuation would be dwarfed by the previous part and would receive disadvantaged treatments. Perhaps it was out of an impulse that the second writer undertook the task. Had he known the criticisms on the book after his death, would he still have done it? Naturally, he knew that if he hadn't taken on the task, he would not have been in the spotlight of discussions, and he would only be among the second or third class writers, ending up with only some books placed on the dust-laden bookshelves among many others.

It seems there should be another perspective for evaluating and judging continued works. The one daring enough to take over a relay baton from Cao Xueqin should be expected to have outstanding performances. The problem is, what kind of performances would be considered satisfactory? There have been no yardsticks in the history. Gao's continued version is far better than many other attempts, such as *Xu Honglou Meng* (*Red Chamber Dream Continued*), *Honglou Meng Bu* (*Red Chamber Dream Addition*), *Honglou Huanmeng* (*Illusionary Red Chamber Dream*), *Honglou Fumeng* (*Return to the Dreams in Red Chamber*), *Honglou Zhenmeng* (*True Dreams of Red Chamber*), and *Honglou Zaimeng* (*More Dreams of Red Chamber*). In these books, Lin Daiyu is dug out of the grave, Jia Baoyu is pulled back from an ancient Buddhist

这也许是失意人生的一种补偿吧。

此外，我们还知道高鹗为人忠厚，常常勖勉、规劝弟子们恪尽忠孝，走举业之路。他的八股文写得很好，思力精到，笔力雄健。在诗文中，他还常将人生如梦的感伤情怀抹上一层佛老色彩。所有这些，我们在《红楼梦》的后40回中都可依稀感觉到。

高鹗是不幸的，但他又是幸运的，这一切都是因为他和《红楼梦》的特殊缘分。没有《红楼梦》，今天还会有谁去关心这位失意落魄的文人呢？要知道在那个时代，有着同样命运的文人可是成千上万。

（三）

写续书是一件吃力不讨好的工作，何况是为《红楼梦》写续书，与曹雪芹的接力赛跑注定使人们用前者的标准来衡量后40回的作者，使他在前者的辉煌中暗淡失色，从而受到不公正的对待。也许这位续书作者当年续写《红楼梦》只是一时的冲动，假如他预知百年后自己的举动会招来那么多是是非非，他还敢动笔吗？自然，他也该知道，如果他不续写《红楼梦》，后人也就不会那么动情地注视他。在文学史上，他也只能与成群结队的二三流作家一样尘封于图书馆古籍书库的一排排书橱中。

对续书的评价和定位，似乎应该有另一种眼光。既然从曹雪芹手中接过了接力棒，人们自然渴望他有超水平的发挥。问题在于，他写到什么程度才会让人们点头认可呢？此前此后都没有现行的范例可循。与那些将林黛玉从坟墓中挖出，将贾宝玉从古寺中拉回，强配鸳鸯的《续红楼梦》、《红楼梦补》、《红楼幻梦》、《红楼复梦》、《红楼真梦》、《红楼再梦》们相比，后40回续作不

monastery, and they are united in marriage. However, the readers expect much more. Here comes another question: If we were able to find the original book of Cao, how fascinating would it be?

The extraordinary folk novels in the Chinese literary history, for example, *Romance of the Three Kingdoms*, *Water Margin*, *Pilgrimage to the West* and *The Scholars* often have a stirring first half but the second half are mediocre and disappointing. Is it true that there is always a Burmuda Triangle in the creation of long novels? Cao, no matter how great and outstanding he might be, could only demonstrate the talents bestowed on him to such a limit and he could go no further. He is only human, not god, just like Newton who could not have invented the Theory of Relativity. If Cao did complete the whole book, would he have broken through the limits? Would he be able to maintain a high standard like that in the first 80 chapters and be many times better than the continued work? No one has the answer. We could only guess.

My personal view is that the continued 40 chapters of the book have brought more values than damage. The achievements could be manifested in the following two aspects.

Firstly, it has maintained the completeness of *Honglou Meng* and promoted circulation. We can imagine that, traditionally, Chinese readers would not easily accept an incomplete novel. The continued work, the 40 chapters, has made *Honglou Meng* a complete literary work. Over more than two centuries, readers have regarded it as an integrate part of the book, a fact that could not be altered by some objections of Hong experts. This is full recognition of the continued work. Had its style been inconsistent, or been too different from the orginal work, the continued work would not have been accepted. Another question can be raised: If readers had not been told about the fact that the latter 40 chapters had been writen by someone else, would they have noticed it? Seeing the circulation and acceptance of the whole book, most readers couldn't have noticed that, nor could some critics who have done in-depth studies on novels. Would those meticulous researchers who overcritised the latter 40 chapters have more acute observations? Not necessarily.

Secondly, the continued work has achieved a rather high artistic standard.

知道要高明多少倍，但人们还是有着更高的期待。进而我们又想到一个问题，如果我们今天果真有幸看到曹雪芹原作的话，它会精彩绝伦到什么程度呢？

中国古代那几部我们引以为自豪的小说如《三国演义》、《水浒传》、《西游记》、《儒林外史》等，前半部无不写得轰轰烈烈，惊心动魄，但一到后面，顿然黯淡失色，令人大失所望。是不是真的存在一个长篇小说创作中的"百慕大三角区"呢？曹雪芹再伟大、再杰出，也只能将上天所赋予的才华与机遇发挥到所允许的极限，而不可能走得再远，就像牛顿提不出相对论一样，毕竟他是人，不是神。曹雪芹如果写完全书的话，他一定会走出文学创作中的这种雷区吗？其内容一定能保持前80回的水准，比后40回续作高明千万倍吗？谁也说不准，这终究只是无奈的猜想。

在笔者看来，后40回续书是功大于过。这个功主要表现在如下两个方面：

一是它保持了作品的完整性，有利于《红楼梦》的广泛流传。可以想象，依照中国人的欣赏习惯，一部残缺的作品是很难被接受的。后40回续书使《红楼梦》成为一部完整的文学作品，200多年来，人们一直将它和前80回当作一个艺术整体来阅读欣赏的，少数红学家的反对并不能改变这个事实。这也是对后40回续书的充分肯定，如果它的风格与原作明显不一致，相差太大，人们是不会认可它的。这里还可以再提出一个问题：如果不知道后40回为续书这个前提，人们能看得出来它是续书吗？从200多年来《红楼梦》流传和接受的情况来看，多数人是看不出来的，就连那些对小说下过很大功夫的批评家也看不出来。那些苛求后40回的研究者的眼力是不是比前人更敏锐、更深邃呢？未必。

二是具有较高的艺术水准。在众多的红楼续书中，以后40

Among the many continued attempts, Gao's continued work is of the highest standard. His work, in general, has followed Cao's architectural designs and ended the book with a tragedy. The writing style is close and it has many excellent proses at times. Hu Shi commented in his revised "Textual Researches on *Honglou Meng*," saying that, "Objectively, I think the latter 40 chapters by Gao E, even though not as good as the previous 80 chapters, do have some amazing parts. He had some excellent descriptions in Siqi's death, Yuanyang's death, Miaoyu's tragic encounter, Wang Xifeng's death, and Xiren's marriage. The most notable is the fact that all these people ended in tragedy. The most important of all is the Wood-Stone Predestination. Gao E was bold enough to even make Lin Daiyu die of illness, and make Jia Baoyu leave his family for a monastery, which broke the normal expectation of a happy ending like many Chinese novels. Simply from this tragic ending we should say that Gao is to be admired... he must also be thanked."

Gao E manages to follow the hints in the previous 80 chapters where a tragic environment, figures and events are established and he responds to them in the latter 40 chapters. He also creates some touching stories which enabled the unity between the two parts. He is as skilful as Qingwen, who dexterously mends a winter dress with sparrow fur as inner layers.

Up to today, some people are still criticising that the latter 40 chapters has done too much, and that the taste is not too high. They complain of the unnecessary light of hope added at the end of the book, where there is a prosperous scene that "both orchid and sweet olive are fragant" and the family is picking up again. The criticism is that the continued work falls into the usual ending of grand reunion. I must say that the mentioning of good ending is a minor issue, given that so many excellent descriptions of life and death, sad departures and the decline of a great family. Even though we can say that such description does reduce the impact of the tragic ending, the motive of Gao may not be of worldly pursuit of fame, as suggested by some. Why couldn't we view Gao's motive from another perspective? Maybe Gao is soft-hearted; he loved the young men and women in the book for their youth so much that he did not want to see them end up too miserable and depressive, and therefore let some light into the dark and sad environment. He wanted to give some comfort to readers and to himself. After all, some survived these tragedies and need to

回续书的艺术水准最高，它大体上遵照曹雪芹原作的安排，为全书设计了一个悲剧性的结尾，与原书风格较为接近，且时有精彩之笔。胡适在《红楼梦考证》（改定稿）一文中曾有这样的评价："平心而论，高鹗补的40回，虽然比不上前80回，也确然有不可埋没的好处。他写司棋之死，写鸳鸯之死，写妙玉的遭劫，写凤姐的死，写袭人的嫁，都是很有精彩的小品文字，最可注意的是这些人都写作悲剧的下场。还有那最重要的'木石前盟'一件公案，高鹗居然忍心害理的教黛玉病死，教宝玉出家，作一个大悲剧的结束，打破中国小说的团圆迷信。这一点悲剧的眼光，不能不令人佩服。……我们不但佩服，还应该感谢他。"

在总的悲剧气氛中，后40回续书的作者将前80回中已露端倪的人物、事件一一做了合情合理的安排和交代，还别出心裁地设计了不少动人的情节，使前80回和后40回成为一个和谐的艺术整体。他仿佛小说中补缝雀毛裘的晴雯，显示出高超的艺术功力。

但直到今天，仍有人埋怨后40回画蛇添足，境界太低，给《红楼梦》弄了个"兰桂齐芳"、"家道复初"的光明尾巴，落入大团圆结局的窠臼。平心而论，在后40回中，与众多人物的生生死死、离离散散，整个家族的日暮途穷、摧枯拉朽相比，这种光明尾巴是轻描淡写，微不足道的。即使我们承认此举对全书的悲剧色彩有所冲淡，但其动机也未必如有些研究者所说的是庸俗的名利思想使然。为什么我们不能从另一个角度来体察这位作者的动机和用心呢？他太善良了，太喜爱那些洋溢着青春气息的少男少女了，实在不忍心让结局过于悲惨，令人过于抑郁，所以在浓重的悲剧阴云中透出几丝亮色，给还要生活的读者、给自己留下一点安慰。毕竟在饱受风霜、历经苦难后

live on. I'd rather think positively about Gao's intentions, which could well be his genuine intentions. If he were a short-sighted shabby scholar who would only pursue some small benefit, he could have abandoned the sad ending and made Jia and Lin wed happily, and made other girls Jia's concubines. He could have further made Jia achieve highly in academic examinations which would make him government officials so that he could lead his family to its former glory. Xia Jingqu wrote in his book, *Yesou Puyan* (*Straight Words of a Wild Man*), about someone of that experience. However, Gao didn't do that. He did not indulge himself in rejected scholar's daydreaming. On the contrary, he sings a sad verse for that once grand and noble family. The ending of the family in the latter part of the book is that Jia family tumbles down with the rich men and elegant women either dead, displaced or living on in monkhood. How could there still be fragrant orchid and sweet olive? How could there be restoration of the former glory? Would the sight of a small recovery after the tumult truly spoil Cao's vision of the ending? Jia Baoyu left; Lin Daiyu, Grandma Jia and Wang Xifeng died; Jia Tanchun and Shi Xiangyun married afar, and Miaoyu was taken away by robbers. With the insignificant ones remaining, would the Jia Mansion be the same? Would the heartbreaking trauma be over simply because Jia Lan, a minor in the family, achieved some scholarly success? Gao has bulldozed the whole building and left a small thatched shed using the material remaining from the demolition of the Jia family. Although he has not truly responded to Cao's prediction by "leaving a piece of empty bleak land," Gao has done good enough. We shouldn't blame him for the minor issues but should remember him as the chief director of the last part of *Honglou Meng*.

Let's have a closer look at the final part of the book. The Jia family collapses, and "once the big tree falls, the monkeys have to scatter away." With the Combination of Gold and Stone in the foreground, the Wood-Stone Predestination became an eternal sorrow on Lin Daiyu's death. Jia Baoyu becomes a monk, leaving Xue Baochai to endure a boring ordinary life. For the three, the ending of the love story is filled with blood and tears. Grandma Jia, in her deathbed, comes back to her senses at the critical moment of the family's fall and dies shortly afterwards. Wang Xifeng, the calculating woman, also dies in disgrace and disappointment. The tragedies of others, such as Jia Tanchun, Jia Yingchun, Jia Xichun, Yuanyang, Siqi, Miaoyu, Xiren, and Xiangyun, just

还有存活者，他们还要活着。我们宁愿将续书作者的动机朝好处想，这也许是他的本心，如果他真是那种目光短浅、没有眼界、为蝇头小利而取悦读者的庸俗文人，他完全可以抛弃那个大悲剧，让宝玉和黛玉欢天喜地地结合，并将众多的女孩子纳为姨娘、小妾，然后再让宝玉科场得意，使贾府中兴，就像此前的小说家夏敬渠在《野叟曝言》中所描写的那样，高官厚禄，位极人臣，子孙繁衍，大富大贵。但这位作者没有沉湎于这种潦倒文人的白日梦中，他不无沉痛地用自己的笔为高贵显赫的世家唱着凄绝的挽歌，在他的笔下，盛极一时的贾府颓然坍塌，家破人亡，到书的最后，贵戚富哥，闺秀娇女，死的死，亡的亡，出家的出家。"兰桂齐芳"，又能怎么芳呢？"家道复初"，真的会复初吗？看到那种浩劫过后的所谓小康，我们会有欢天喜地的欣慰之感吗？宝玉走了，黛玉、贾母、王熙凤仙逝，探春、湘云嫁人，妙玉被劫，只留下一些可怜兮兮的偷生者，这还叫贾府吗？那种刻骨铭心的伤痛和失落靠一个小道学贾兰的中举就能抚平吗？这位作者推倒了一座大厦，仅在一片废墟上用残砖碎瓦搭设了一座小窝棚，这也许还未真的达到那种"落了片白茫茫大地真干净"的地步，但我们能忍心再去责备续书作者吗？他做的已经很不错了。我们不要忘记，笔在他手上，他是《红楼梦》后半场的总导演。

在悲悲切切的哀乐声中，贾府轰然倒塌，大树既倒，猢狲烟消云散。伴着金石姻缘的锣鼓喧闹，木石前盟随林黛玉的魂归离恨天而成为一种永恒的缺憾。宝玉的撒手而去，使宝钗于无望的平淡岁月中饱受煎熬，一场交织着血泪恩怨的爱情就这样终场。贾母在大起大落的转折关头，回光返照，随即溘然长逝；工于心计的王熙凤终于在心力交瘁的无奈中含辱而去。其他如探春、迎春、惜春、鸳鸯、司棋、妙玉、袭人、湘云等，

to name a few, lie in either death or the departure from the Jia family. The tragedies run one after the other and tears of those people could have formed a river. This is what the continued work presents to us.

Obviously the continued work cannot be the same as the original. There are no two writers whose thoughts and literary skills are the same, after all. It would be even more impossible to expect others to be as good as the talented Cao with his extraordinary life experience. The last 40 chapters, when being compared with the previous 80 chapters, are often criticised for the following reasons.

Firstly, the fates of the characters do not fully correspond with Cao's original designs. Many have pointed that out. For example, Shi Xiangyun is left out, and Xiaohong is not mentioned in the end; Xiangling and Wang Xifeng's endings are different from the predictions and hints in the previous 80 chapters. The difference is clear when we read the commentaries of Zhiyanzhai. Some researchers say Gao has distorted Cao's original intentions. Such a view may sound reasonable but it has ignored a very important issue. Could Cao's original intentions and the designs of the endings, which seem obvious for ordinary readers, not be detected by Gao? From what Gao wrote in the final 40 chapters, we know that he is a more talented writer than his critics; he is also in a better position to read the early hand-written copies of the original book as well as Zhiyanzhai's commentaries. Obviously, it is not that he was not able to comprehend Cao's designs and arrangements; he might have his own reasons.

If we accept some researchers' argument that the last 40 chapters is the work of Cao, or Cao's work is contained in them, the answer to the problem would become very easy to get. It is natural for Cao to have changed his mind and for the last part to become inconsistent with the previous parts. This would be understandable, but we will need more evidence. Another argument is that the author of the continued work is a strong-minded writer who follows his own ideas, not Cao's designs, and ends the last part of the book so differently from the way Cao has planned. We know that before the Cheng version came out, *Honglou Meng* had been copied by hand. It is impossible for Gao to have missed it or Zhiyanzhai's commentaries. If he intended to fully comply with

亡的亡，散的散，一个悲剧接一个悲剧，汇成血泪之河，这就是续作所展示给我们的景象。

自然，既然是续书，就不可能与原作完全一样，毕竟这个世界上没有哪两个作家在思想观念、艺术修养上是一模一样的，特别是像曹雪芹这样具有奇特身世的天才作家是不可复制的。较之前80回原作，后40回续书大体在如下几个方面受到人们的批评：

一是全书人物结局的安排与曹雪芹原先的设计不尽吻合。已有不少研究者指出这一点，如将史湘云丢开，小红完全没有结果，香菱、凤姐的结局与前80回的暗示不符等，将其与脂批所透露原作后半部内容进行对比，可以看得更为清楚。有些研究者据此指责它歪曲了曹雪芹的原意。这种指责看似有理，但失之肤浅，因为它忽略了一个重要问题，那就是原作的创作意图与结局安排连一般的普通读者都可以推知，难道续书作者就看不出来吗？从后40回的内容来看，这位续书作者的文学修养并不比那些批评、指责他的红学家低，而且他阅读早期红楼梦抄本及脂批的条件比我们更好。显然，并不是这位续书作者感知力差，看不懂曹雪芹原作对全书结局的安排，也许是另有原因。

如果照有的研究者所说，后40回本来就是曹雪芹所作，或其中含有作者的原稿，那问题就迎刃而解了，因为曹雪芹在创作过程中想法有所改变，未能与前80回一致，这是可以理解的。但这一说法还需要更多过硬材料的支持和更为充分的论证。另一种可能的理由就是，续书作者是一位颇有个性的作家，他有自己的想法，不愿意完全按照原作的意图来写，因此才出现如此明显的不一致。可以想象，在程本刊印之前，《红楼梦》一直是以抄本的形式流传的，他不可能没见过这些抄本，不可能没

the design in the previous 80 chapters and Zhi's commentaries, Gao, having such literary talents, could have written the latter part so well that no one could tell it from Cao's work. Why did he want to leave some defects? He must have his own reasons that we have no way of finding out now.

Secondly, there is inconsistency in ideology. In the last part, Gao adds a prosperous ending that "orchid and sweet olive are fragant" and the Jia family is restored. As well as this, the slight favour towards the imperial scholarly examination system was criticised. Because of these, many researchers blamed the writer of the last 40 chapters for being conservative and behind times.

This criticism seems to be reasonable. However, it is not without its problems. Firstly, many criticisms are based on the presumption that Gao E is the writer of the continued work, and on Gao E's personal life experiences. When such presumptions are undergoing increased challenges, the critics should re-evaluate their presumptions and their validity. Secondly, we see that some ideologies in the last 40 chapters do not seem proper to us but we know we are seeing them through modern eyes. We don't know the thoughts of people 200 years ago, in the middle of the Qing dynasty. We do not know how Cao would think about Gao's ideology. Cao criticises the ugly defects of the Jia family in the first 80 chapters, but this does not mean he has no feelings for his family. Judging from his respect for the founders of the family, we know that Cao is not able to see through the nature of the feudal families and the determination to separate from them. It seems to some researchers that the harsher the descriptions of the family decline, the higher moral ground the author would be on. Even though no critic has presented that kind of views so clearly, many researchers are judging Gao's work against current ideological standards. However, Cao's dilemma is that he wants to relentlessly expose the dark side of the family, and at the same time, from the bottom of his heart, he wants to cling to his family. Gao's last 40 chapters are proof of those kinds of feelings. A great tragedy is planned yet a little hope is kept. We may well say

见过脂批。如果他愿意按照前80回及脂批的提示来写的话，以他的文学功力，是完全可以做到以假乱真，滴水不漏的。他何以要流露出这些破绽，肯定有自己的理由，只不过我们不知道而已。

二是后40回的思想与原作不一致。其中最受人诟病的是其安排了一个兰桂齐芳、家道复兴的结局。此外，对科举态度的细微变化也屡受人们的批评。于是，研究者纷纷指责后40回的作者思想庸俗，保守落后等。

这一指责看似有理，但也不是没有问题。首先，很多对后40回的批评是建立在高鹗为续书作者的基础上，并结合高鹗的身世经历进行批评。当越来越多的材料动摇这一前提时，那些批评者就有必要重新审视自己的立论前提和有效性了。其次，从现代人的立场来看，后40回所流露的思想确实有些不合时宜，但问题在于，在二百多年前的清代中叶，人们是怎样来认识这一问题的，尤其是曹雪芹本人，他是如何来认识这一问题的。在前80回中，曹雪芹对家族的种种弊端确实流露出深恶痛绝的批评态度，但这是不是就意味着他对家族已毫无感情，没有一点留恋。老实说，从对家族创业者的崇敬态度看，他恐怕还没有达到那种看清封建家族制度本质、与封建家庭彻底决裂的思想高度。将贾府的破败写得越悲惨，好像作者的思想就越深刻，以家族、人物的悲惨程度来衡量作品的优劣，虽然没有批评者这样明确提出过，但他们实际上是按照这种标准来评价后40回的，这实际上是以今人的观念来苛求古人。对家族种种黑幕无情揭露的同时，在内心深处又保留一份对家族辉煌的眷恋，爱之愈深，责之愈切，从曹雪芹的身世经历及其在前80回的相关描写来看，这才是他对家族的全部态度。后40回的描写恰恰符合这一思想，在大悲剧的前提下，留下一点希望，应该说这位

that Gao has a reasonable command of Cao's intentions. It is unreasonable for those researchers to criticise the minor details of the family restoration and to ignore the tragic endings. While the last 40 chapters may not have achieved as high a literary level as the previous 80 chapters have, nor are they without any merit at all.

Thirdly, there is inconsistency in the descriptions of the characteristics of people and in the plots, as many researchers have pointed out. For example, Lin Daiyu becomes too sensitive and Grandma Jia becomes too indifferent to Lin Daiyu. The bride-swap plot comes so breathtakingly and is the highlight in the last 40 chapters. However, it may not correspond to Cao's original intentions, and it is not in harmony with the atmosphere and tempo in the previous 80 chapters. The reason for this may be related more to Gao's understanding of the previous 80 chapters. It could also be the weakness of Gao's writing skills.

To judge a piece of continued work, we need to look at its consistency in characters, plots and styles with the original work. At the same time, we should take into consideration the artistic quality of the continued work. We must see the problems and also the outstanding achievements, especially the latter. The work on the last 40 chapters, overall, is not so good as the original book, as we naturally expect more from it. However, even so, despite some defects, it does have some exceptional highlights and it has maintained overall consistency with the original work. Among hundreds of continued works, it can be considered the best. It can also be considered one of the bests of all ancient Chinese novels. The proof lies in the recognition and acceptance it has received over the past two centuries.

It is totally inappropriate to judge the social morals of the literature of the past against modern attitudes and norms. Critics should put themselves in others' shoes. Would they have done better if they were living in ancient times? No one can be sure. Those who expected too much from predecessors in turn would receive the same demands from descendents. My view concurs with that of Chen Yinke, a famous scholar, that we should be more tolerant with the scholars in ancient times.

续书作者对曹雪芹创作意图的把握还是比较准确的。只看到兰桂齐芳、家道复兴的局部细节而忽略整个后半部大悲剧的描写，这显然是以偏概全，不够公允的。后40回也许没有达到曹雪芹在80回中所表现的思想和艺术境界，但也不能简单地以庸俗视之，将前80回与后40回人为地对立起来。

三是人物性格的描写、情节的安排与原书不尽一致。这种情况确实是存在的，研究者也多有提及，比如将林黛玉写得过于神经质，将贾母对林黛玉的态度写得过于冷漠等。调包计也确实写得惊心动魄，不同凡响，为后40回续书中最为动人之笔，但它未必符合曹雪芹的原意，与前80回的气氛和节奏也未必和谐。之所以出现这一情况，可能与续书作者对原书理解的偏差有关，也可能与续书作者的功力不够有关。

评价一部续书，既要看它在人物、情节及风格的描写、安排等方面与原作保持一致，同时也要看其自身的艺术水准；既要看到其不足，也要看到其佳处，特别是后者。总的来看，后40回续书确实没有原著写得那么好，与我们对它的期待还有一定的距离，但同时也必须看到，它基本上保持了与原作的一致，尽管存在着不少败笔，但也时有精彩文字。在中国古代数百部续书作品中，它应该算是最好的一部。即使放在全部中国古代小说作品中，它也是较为突出、优秀的。二百多年来，人们对它的认可和接受足以说明问题。

站在今人的立场上来批评、指责古人，除了证明自己拥有时间的优势外，只能说明自己的无知和尖刻。不妨设身处地想一想，自己如果生活在古人所处的那个时代，是不是就一定比他们高明呢？未必。自己如此苛求前人，后人将来又会如何看待自己呢？笔者觉得还是应该像著名学者陈寅恪所说的，对古人要抱以理解之同情。

IV

Honglou Meng, after it came out, has been loved by people from all walks of life and enjoyed great circulation. It has made far-reaching influence on Chinese folk novels. More continued works and related books keep appearing, which has become a unique cultural phenomenon.

The first book to come, after Cao's attempt, was Xiaoyaozi's *Hou Honglou Meng* (*Later Dream of Red Mansions*), written between the latter part of Emperor Qianlong's reign and the reign of Emperor Jiaqing. From then to the reign of Emperor Daoguang, a number of books emerged and formed an upsurge in the creation of *Honglou Meng*. It was after Daoguang's times that the trend started to diminish because readers' tastes had changed. Due to the great influence of *Honglou Meng*, the creation of continued works on the book is still going on. Every now and then we can find news about *Honglou Meng* on TV or newspapers. According to statistics, there are as many as 98 continued books. This is unique in the literary history in the world that a novel can lead to so many continued works, which also shows the attraction of *Honglou Meng*.

The major characteristics of the continued works are as follows:

Firstly, the continued works mainly appeared in a period between the reign of Emperor Jiaqing and that of Emperor Daoguang. In that period, *Honglou Meng* was very popular and had attracted interest from all levels of society. The continued books became popular because of the fact that *Honglou Meng* was a great book and enjoyed a wide readership, and also the fact that the circulating original book was incomplete. The continued books were welcomed as a great compensation for the readers' sense of loss and disappointment at the lack of an ending.

Secondly, the ideologies and contents are similar. Most continued works were written for the sake of complementing the incomplete original work. From there we can see the attitude of the Chinese towards tragedies. Even though there are differences in the arrangements in characters and plots in the continued works, for example, the Jia family being restored to its former glory, Jia Baoyu marrying Lin Daiyu, Jia Baoyu becoming a great scholar and also achieving great military success, becoming a high rank official, having a bevy of concubines and enjoying the luxuries of life. The writers of the continued works all extended their dreams on paper. Some even went further by using supernatural methods. They either brought Lin Daiyu and Qingwen back to

（四）

《红楼梦》面世之后，受到社会各阶层读者的喜爱，广泛流传，对中国通俗小说的创作产生了深远的影响，其后，受《红楼梦》影响而创作的续书和仿书也不断出现，成为一个独特的文化现象。

继后40回之后出现的第一部续书是逍遥子的《后红楼梦》，成书时间约在乾隆末年至嘉庆间。其后续书、仿书不断出现，并在嘉庆至道光年间形成一股创作的热潮。道光之后，随着人们欣赏趣味的变化，这股热潮才逐渐消歇。由于《红楼梦》的广泛、深远影响，围绕该书进行的续书创作直到今天都没有停止过，我们时常可以从电视、报刊上看到此类消息。据统计，从《红楼梦》面世以来，各类续书多达98种。一部小说竟然引来如此多的续书，这在中外文学史都是绝无仅有的，由此可见《红楼梦》的巨大艺术魅力。

总的来看，这些续书有如下一些特点：

一是创作、刊印的时间较为集中，主要集中在清嘉庆、道光年间。这一时期，《红楼梦》广泛传播，受到社会各个阶层的关注。这些续书利用《红楼梦》的名著效应和群众基础，满足了读者阅读原作产生的缺失、遗憾心理，因而受到欢迎。

二是思想、内容较为接近。这些续书大多为弥补原书的缺憾而作，由此也可看出中国人对悲剧的态度。尽管这些续书具体的人物、情节安排不尽相同，但内容不外乎贾府复兴，宝、黛结合，宝玉中进士，点翰林，立战功，做高官，妻妾成群，尽享人间富贵之类。这些续书的作者们利用文学创作，做了一场纸上的白日梦。由于原作中有不少主要人物如林黛玉、晴雯等已去世，续书作者只好采取超自然手法，或让死者复生，或

life, who had already died in the previous 80 chapters, or used spiritual connections between the alive and the dead. To those writers, whether their works make sense or not was irrelevant.

Thirdly, the writers tried to follow Cao's writing style. Let us take Qin Zichen's *Xu Honglou Meng* as an example. The ideology in his work put aside, he successfully maintained the essence of Cao's vivid description of scenery and style of language. Continued works are normally short. Apart from *Honglou Fumeng*, which has 100 chapters, the normal length of continued work is between 20 and 40 chapters, because of their intention to make the original complete and to create a grand reunion. They did not want to create something extra, or, something like a new *Honglou Meng*. For a grand reunion, 20 to 40 chapters are enough to do the job.

The continued works all based their writings on the 120-chapter version but with differences. Most started after Chapter 120 but some started from Chapter 97, like Qin Zichen's three books called *Xu Honglu Meng*, *Honglou Meng Bu* and *Honglou Huanmeng*. The reason for him to start from Chapter 97 is that he did not want Lin Daiyu to die and he had to do some ground work for the next chapter titled "The spirit of bitter flower returning to the sky of no hatred." Another book, *Zengbu Honglou Meng* (*Honglou Meng Appendix and More*), is even more unusual. It is a book to continue the stories in *Bu Honglou Meng* (*Addition to Red Chamber Dream*). This is a sequel to a sequel, a very rare case in China's novel history.

Apart from this, the main characters in the original book appeared differently in the continued books. Mostly the writers continued the plots in the original books and some wrote about the stories of the next generation. *Honglou Xumeng* (*Continuing Red Chamber Dream*) is a series of stories of the relationship among four people. They are, firslty, Xiaoyu, son of Jia Baoyu and Xue Baochai; secondly, Shunhua, daughter of Shi Xiangyun, a reincarnation of Lin Daiyu; thirdly, Tongxia, daughter of Xing Youyan, and finally Bixiao, daughter of Baoqin. In *Honglou Fumeng*, Zhu Mengyu, Jia Baoyu's reincarnation, was reborn in Dantu County, Jiangsu Province. He and Xue Baochai had dear relationship, and the two rebuilt the Jia family together. Other books adopted the same writing style, such as *Xu Honglou Meng* and *Zengbu Honglou Meng*.

Overall, those continued books not only distorted Cao's original intentions

阴阳相通，往往写得人鬼混杂，至于是不是合乎情理，也就顾不上了。

　　三是在写法和风格上，这些续书尽量从各个方面模仿原作。比如秦子忱的《续红楼梦》一书，且不管其思想内容如何，在景物描写、语言风格等方面是颇得原作神韵的。这些续作的篇幅通常都比较短，除《红楼复梦》长达100回外，其他多在20至40回左右。这也与续作者的创作意图有关，因为他们的主要目的很明确，那就是弥补原作的缺憾，达到大团圆的目的，并不想节外生枝，像不少仿作那样另起炉灶，也照葫芦画瓢写出一部《红楼梦》来。仅仅完成一个大团圆的结局，有20至40回的篇幅也就够了。

　　至于续法，各书虽然基本上是以120回为基础，但具体情况则略有不同。这些续作大多从120回续起，不过也有从第97回续起的，如秦子忱的《续红楼梦》、《红楼梦补》、《红楼幻梦》这三部续书。之所以从第97回续起，是因为原作的下一回为"苦绛珠魂归离恨天，病神瑛泪洒相思地"，续书作者因不愿意看到黛玉的死亡，故从这一回续起。《增补红楼梦》则更为特殊，它接续《补红楼梦》而写，可谓续书之续书，这在中国小说史上还是颇为少见的。

　　此外，续书对主要人物的设计安排也不尽相同，多数作品直接利用原书的人物来展开故事，也有一些是写下一代人的故事。如《红楼续梦》中，宝玉转生为宝钗之子小钰，黛玉转生为湘云之女舜华，故事在他们及邢岫烟之女彤霞、宝琴之女碧箫之间展开。再如《红楼复梦》中，宝玉转生江苏丹徒，名祝梦玉，与宝钗情同姐弟，共同振兴家族。其他如《续红楼梦》、《增补红楼梦》等也采取了这一写法。

　　总的来看，这些红楼续书不仅违背了曹雪芹创作《红楼梦》

but lacked his high-level taste. They failed to mactch up with the uncomparable literary quality of the original work. Therefore, the continued works have always been ranked low by researchers. However, being low quality does not deny the continued books of their merit in research. In the long history of Chinese novels, these continued books were not regarded as good books. Nevertheless, we can find some issues from the creation of these books.

For instance, continued works tell us Chinese people's preference of literature and their aspiration in life. The majority of the continued works share the same plots, which means the ideology expressed in these works represent the similarity of the public. The writing and printing of novels in ancient times were highly commercialised, and the readers' tastes and aspirations strongly restricted the writers. It explains some phenomena in the development of ancient China's novels, for example, the continued books kept appearing and most of ancient novels end with grand reunions.

From the continued works emanating from *Honglou Meng*, we can see the exemplary function and influence of a great classic work. Most authors of the continued works had tried to follow the original styles, even though they might not have done a very good job, and in so doing they helped promote the literary skills of the original writer, and lifted the overall level of novel writing. This is like the existence of a great calligrapher who inspired a lot of people to follow his style and in the end the overall quality of calligraphy in society has been raised. By comparing the continued works with romance books prior to *Honglou Meng*, we can see their influence on ancient China's novel. From this perspective, we should acknowledge the value of continued works.

Through the continued works, we can also have a glimpse of the acceptance of *Honglou Meng* at that time. The creation of continued books is something special. It is a creation based on the original work. The writers expressed their ideas creatively, rather than in the form of commentaries. Their attitudes towards the original book were expressed in a covert way through the descriptions of the characters and the arrangement of plots in their work.

的原意，而且思想平庸、格调不高。至于艺术水准，那更是无法与原书相比，故研究者对这些作品的评价历来较低。不过，艺术水准低并不等于这些书没有研究价值。确实，放在整个中国小说史上，这些续作的艺术水准并不高，但从这一创作现象中还是可以看出一些问题的。

比如由此可见中国人的欣赏趣味和人生理想。大量续书情节内容的一致，说明它们所体现的思想意识具有共同性和代表性。古代小说的创作、刊印具有很强的商业性，读者的审美趣味和人生理想对其构成了很强的制约，由此可以解释古代小说发展演进中的不少现象，如续书的不断出现、古代小说颇多大团圆结局的描写等。

由红楼续书的大量创作也可以看出经典小说在古代小说创作中的示范和推动作用。这些续作大多刻意模仿原作的写法和风格，尽管模仿得不一定像，但它客观上使原作高超的艺术手法得到普及，从整体上提高了古代小说的创作水平。就像出现一位大书法家，众人临摹模仿，提高了整个社会的书法水平一样。只要将这些红楼续书与先前的才子佳人小说进行比较，可以很明显地看到《红楼梦》面世后带给中国古代小说的新变化。对此应该从正面来看，给予适当的肯定。

通过这些续书可见当时人们对《红楼梦》的接受情况。续书是一种特殊的创作，一种面对原作的创作。它以创作而不是点评的形式表达对原作的看法，从其人物形象的塑造、对情节的安排等方面可见其对原作的态度，只不过表达得较为隐蔽、含蓄而已。

薛宝钗画像

Portrait of Xue Baochai

七　传神文笔足千秋——《红楼梦》的流传

Chapter Ⅶ　The Everlasting Expressive Writing: The
Circulation of *Honglou Meng*

This book has gone from a folk novel looked upon with contempt, to a literary classic that is now known to people throughout the world; from a small circulation of handwritten copies to a worldwide publication; from a banned book by the Qing government, to a classic recommended by the Education Ministry in China. The ups and downs of *Honglou Meng* are dramatic, and are the source of much discussion. Nowadays, the study of *Honglou Meng* has become a discipline—Redology. It attracts broad interest from readers and experts. Throughout the 20th century, books dedicated to research on *Honglou Meng* have exceeded 1 000. *Honglou Meng* is a miracle in its own right, as is its influence on China and the world. There are so many questions and puzzles to be solved, and there are so many words to be said about it. The popularity of the book is obvious and we can also learn the socio-cultural attitude of the readers who like the book so much.

I

There are many different versions of *Honglou Meng*, due to constant revision, copying and printing during its writing and spreading process. Differences do exist in those versions, and some differences are huge. The differences exist in story plots, in characters and in speeches. When reading or researching on *Honglou Meng*, we need to be aware of the version we are reading, so as to make sure that the reading and research is based on a correct and authoritative version. The same applies to other traditional novels in the Chinese literary history, such as *Romance of the Three Kingdoms, Water Margin* and *Pilgrimage to the West*.

The numerous versions of *Honglou Meng* are an important and difficult problem for researchers. Ordinary readers may not need to know the details of how versions differ but because many researchers often emphasise these differences, it wouldn't be a bad idea for readers to be aware of some

从残缺不全、受人歧视的通俗小说到享誉中外、妇孺皆知的文学名著，从小范围的传抄到全世界的风行，从早年清政府的查禁到当下教育部门的推荐，《红楼梦》的流传过程充满戏剧色彩，其间有许多值得一说的现象和话题。如今，《红楼梦》研究已经成为一门显赫而热闹的学问——红学，吸引着全世界成千上万的读者和专家。整个20世纪，全世界有关《红楼梦》的研究专著至少在一千种以上。《红楼梦》本身就是一个奇迹，它面世二百多年来在中国及世界的流传和影响，这同样也是一个奇迹。围绕着《红楼梦》这部奇书，有太多的谜团需要揭开，有太多的话要说。从中不仅可见人们对这部小说的喜爱程度，更可由此透视人们通过阅读这部小说所流露出的社会文化心态。

（一）

《红楼梦》在创作、流传过程中，经过不断的修改、抄写和刊印，出现了多个版本。这些版本之间存在着不少差异，有些甚至是较大的差异，其中既有故事情节方面的，也有人物形象方面的，更有语句文字方面的。因此，无论是阅读《红楼梦》，还是研究《红楼梦》，都必须了解自己所看的是哪一种版本，以保证阅读和研究建立在正确、权威的文本基础上。实际上这也是中国古代小说在流传过程中出现的一个普遍现象，阅读《三国演义》、《水浒传》、《西游记》等小说，同样要注意版本问题。

版本问题是《红楼梦》研究中一个重要而繁难的问题，对一般读者来说，不需要了解得特别详细，但由于不少研究者很喜欢强调《红楼梦》版本之间的差异，因此相关的基本知识还是需要知道一些的，否则遇到内容有差异的不同版本，便会感

differences to avoid any confusion.

Broadly speaking, there are two major categories of versions of *Honglou Meng*. The first category is the Zhi (yanzhai) version and the second one is the Cheng version. The Zhi version refers to those versions circulated before the formal printing of *Honglou Meng*, including other published versions originating from them. There are twelve books of Zhi version. The features of the Zhi versions are that they are all hand-written copies, mostly with early commentaries by Zhiyanzhai, and have only 80 chapters. The other category refers to those publications based on Cheng Weiyuan and Gao E's compilations, including other versions originating from them. Features of the second category are that they have been printed without Zhiyanzhai's comments and they have 40 more chapters.

There is clear evidence that the Cheng versions originated from the Zhi versions. However, it is not possible to identify from which Zhi versions the Cheng version evolved. Due to the many different features of the two categories, e.g., the differences in the content and the form of publication, we normally do treat them as two different categories. The Zhi versions were copied early, closer to the author's time. They were usually considered to have reflected the genuine features of the original novel. However, the incompleteness is a big problem. Of the twelve existing versions, none is complete; the Zheng Zhenduo version has only two chapters. The circulation of the Zhi versions is not extensive. The Cheng versions, despite their differences from the original versions, are complete, and they are significant in the circulation of *Honglou Meng*. We can even say that for the 200 years of time in which *Honglou Meng* has been in existence, readers have been able to appreciate *Honglou Meng* mainly because of the Cheng versions.

There are differences between the two major categories, in story plots, expressions and even in the titles of the chapters. Examples are, the conversation between the Buddhist Monk and the Taoist Priest in Chapter 1, Jia Baoyu's behaviours and speeches in a farm house in Chapter 15, the descriptions of Qin Zhong's death in Chapter 16, You Sanjie's actions and speeches in Chapter 65, the death of Qingwen in Chapter 77 and also Jia Zheng's punishment of his son in Chapter 78. These are the examples of major differences, but the biggest difference is that the Cheng versions have an extra

到困惑和迷茫。

大体说来，《红楼梦》的版本可以分为两个系统：一个是脂本系统，一个是程本系统。前者主要指《红楼梦》刊印之前、以传抄形式流传的版本，同时还包括依据这些抄本为底本传抄、刊印、评点的后出版本。目前所知见脂本系统的早期抄本有12种，其特点是：这些版本都是以抄本的形式存在，多数带有脂砚斋等人的早期批语，内容只有前80回。后者主要指程伟元、高鹗整理并刊印的《红楼梦》版本及依据程本翻印的各类版本。这一系统的版本很多，其特点是：以刊印本的形式存在，没有脂批，且皆有后40回的内容。

程本系统是由脂本系统演变而来的，两者有着明显的渊源关系，至于程本依据的底本究竟是哪一个版本，目前已难以确考。由于两者内容文字及刊印形式等方面的显著差异，通常被研究者区分开来，作为两种不同的版本系统来对待。脂本传抄时间较早，距作者时间较近，通常认为它更接近作品原貌，其不足是缺失较为严重，目前所知见的12种脂本抄本中，没有一种是完整的，有的甚至只有两回，比如郑振铎藏本，而且脂本的传播范围较小。程本虽然对作品改动较多，但它十分完整，对《红楼梦》广泛传播的贡献甚大。可以说，自《红楼梦》面世以来的200多年间，人们主要是通过程本来了解这部优秀小说作品的。

从文本内容来看，两个版本系统从情节到人物、从文句到回目都存在着较为明显的差别。比如第一回一僧一道与石头之间的对话、第十五回宝玉在农家的言行描写、第十六回秦钟去世前的相关描写、第六十五回尤三姐的言行描写、第七十七回晴雯之死、第七十八回贾政教子等处，人物、情节皆有较大的

of 40 chapters.

The languages used in the two categories are different, too. The Zhi versions use elegant language in ancient styles while the Cheng versions are more colloquial. The conversation between Wang Xifeng and You Erjie is a typical example where traditional style language is used in the Zhi versions while colloquial language is used in the Cheng versions. The two langauge styles are different and as a result the two characters are also shaped differently.

One more point must be made here that not only are there differences between the two major categories, but differences exist within the same category, too. This makes the problems of the versions more complicated. Of the Zhi versions, the Jiaxu version contains a table of contents and also a 400-odd word conversation among the Buddhist Monk, the Taoist Priest and the stone, which does not appear in any other copies of the Zhi versions. The two Cheng versions, Version One and Version Two, published one year apart, differed a lot. Version Two, in comparison with Version One, has 19 568 words revised or deleted, of which 14 376 were in the first 80 chapters. These include changing the language style from classical to colloquial, the insertion of folk languges, the modification and insertion of words and even the change of story plots. It is clear that the analysis of different versions is a very important work for conducting research on *Honglou Meng*.

None of the copies of the different versions should be simply categorised as good or bad. Each has its own values and should be treated objectively. The Zhi versions should not be overvalued and the Cheng versions should not be undervalued. We must take an objective approach in identifying the differences in order to sort out their relationship to each other before making any judgement.

Of the current versions, the two published by the People's Literature Publishing House could be considered superior and their influence is considerable. One of them is based on Cheng Version Two which makes references to other versions. Brief commentaries are included as footnotes. Since its initial printing in October 1957, that version has been reprinted more than ten times, with several million copies now in circulation. No other version can compare to it. The other version, based on a relatively early version, the Gengchen Version, was prepared by *Honglou Meng* Research Institute within

差异，且不说程本还多出了后40回。

此外，两个版本系统的语言风格也颇为不同，脂本较为典雅，多用文言语句，程本则较为口语化。比如第68回凤姐初见尤二姐的那段说辞就很有代表性，脂本用的是文言，程本用的是白话，语言风格明显不同，由此塑造出的人物形象也存在着差异。

这里还要说明的是，不仅两个版本系统之间存在着较大差异，实际上，即使是同属一个版本系统的版本在文字内容上也会存在差异，《红楼梦》版本问题之繁难主要体现在这里。比如同为脂本，甲戌本卷首的几条凡例、第一回僧、道与石头之间400余字的对话等内容，为该书所独有，而不见于其他脂本。再比如程甲本和程乙本的刊印虽然只相差短短不到一年的时间，但也存在着很大的差别。据统计，程乙本对程甲本的删改多达19568字，其中仅前80回就删改了14376字。这种改动包括变文言词语为白话、俗话词语、润色文字、增删词语、改动情节等多个方面。可见版本问题确实是红学研究中的一个重要问题，值得深入探讨。

平心而论，无论是哪个版本系统的版本，各有其优劣之处，自有其独特的价值，因此，不可一概而论，要客观谨慎对待，而不能偏执一端，好则好极，坏则坏透，将脂本夸到天上，将程本贬得一钱不值。避免情绪化的宣泄，冷静、认真地比勘各版本间的差异，理清源流，明其优劣，探求真相，以定取舍。

在《红楼梦》的众多整理本中，以人民文学出版社出版的两种较为精良，影响也较大。其中一种以程乙本为底本，参校了其他版本。注释在每页下，简明扼要。从1957年10月初版至今，已印刷十数次，印数高达数百万册，远非其他校注本可比；另一种由中国艺术研究院红楼梦研究所校注，选用抄本中

China National Research Institute of Arts. With careful selecting and editing, it reflects the original features of Cao Xueqin's book. At the same time, it provides a clear explanation of the social systems, codes, relics and difficult languages used in the book. It is aimed at readers at a medium level of education. There have been over two million copies circulated since its initial publication.

II

According to the commentaries by Zhiyanzhai, *Honglou Meng* was in circulation as it was being written. Zhiyanzhai and fellow scholars started their commentaries at the same time when the book was being written. They even participated in the creation of the book. No other book in the world has ever been completed in such a unique way. At the beginning, the chapters were only hand-written copies circulated among Cao's friends and relatives. Later, it was printed for publication and circulation. The book soon became popular and went abroad. It was appreciated by readers worldwide and became a well-known classic Chinese novel.

Over 200 years have elapsed since the creation of *Honglou Meng*. The circulation of *Honglou Meng* has occurred through the following periods: the hand-copy period, the printing period, the quality printing period, and the multi-facet period.

The first period, the hand-copy period, started with the writing of *Honglou Meng* in the middle of Emperor Qianlong's reign, when Zhiyanzhai and others provided commentaries. It ended in the year 1791, the 56th year of Emperor Qianlong's reign, when the book was printed using block printing by Cheng Weiyuan and Gao E.

At the beginning, hand-written copies of *Honglou Meng* were circulated among Cao's friends and relatives. Some copies were made and kept in Prince Yi's Residence and Prince Mongolia's Residence. According to records, only a few people, including Zhiyanzhai, Fucha Mingyi and Yongzhong, were able to read those copies. Later on, *Honglou Meng* was distributed to a more general public; some copies were even sold after further copying. Due to the huge length, it was hard to do mass production, so the costs of copies were high and

年代较早、较为完整的庚辰本为底本，取舍较为审慎，力求反映曹氏原著的面貌。同时还对小说作品所涉及的典章制度、名物典故及难解用语进行了比较详尽、准确的注释。该书将读者对象定位为中等文化水平，便于初学者阅读。自出版以来，已发行二百多万部。

（二）

从脂砚斋批语所透露的信息来看，《红楼梦》还在创作、修改的过程中就已经开始了流传，脂砚斋等人一边阅读，一边批点，并亲自参与了小说的创作，这在中外小说史上也是绝无仅有的。起初作品只是以抄本的形式在曹雪芹亲友这个小范围内流传，其后，得到刊印，在社会上一纸风行，被迅速广泛传阅，并跨越国界，受到全世界读者的喜爱，成为享有盛誉的小说经典。

从《红楼梦》创作、流传至今，已有二百多年的历史，根据它在不同时期传抄、刊印及阅读、接受的情况和特点，可以将其流传过程分成四个不同的历史阶段，即传抄阶段、刊印阶段、精印阶段和多元阶段。

从清代乾隆中期《红楼梦》创作、脂砚斋等人进行评点到乾隆五十六年即1791年程伟元、高鹗首次以活字版刊印，这是《红楼梦》流传的第一个阶段，即传抄阶段。

起初，《红楼梦》主要以抄本的形式在曹雪芹亲友的小范围内流传，其中一些是在怡亲王府、蒙古王府抄成、收藏的。从相关文献的记载来看，只有脂砚斋、富察明义、永忠等少数人能读到这部作品。稍后，《红楼梦》开始流传到社会上，阅读的范围稍有扩大，还有人抄录之后拿到外面出售。由于作品篇幅较大，抄写不易，购买一部得花不少钱，故价格昂贵，流

the circulation was limited. During this period, not many people got to read this book, let alone discuss and comment on it. Even if famous scholars like Yuan Mei had only heard of, rather than having read, the book.

In the 56th year of Emperor Qianlong's reign, after being edited and compiled by Cheng Weiyuan and Gao E, and eventually published using moveable type, *Honglou Meng* began its second period of circulation. The period extends to 1921 before the Yadong Library of Shanghai published a new edited version of *Honglou Meng*. This period was called the formal printing period.

The advantage of formal printing is obvious when compared with hand-copy in terms of the cost (time and money). The number of copies increased rapidly. The cost was lowered, which enabled a wider circulation of *Honglou Meng*. Many printing houses printed their own copies of *Honglou Meng*. Notwithstanding the quality of Cheng Weiyuan and Gao E's job, the printing houses had contributed greatly to the accelerating and the wide circulation of a final version of *Honglou Meng*. Readers relied mainly on the Cheng versions of *Honglou Meng* in the 100-odd years after its publication, which is an undisputable fact.

Cheng Weiyuan printed the book twice, commonly known as Version One and Version Two. Version Two, perhaps because of the small number of copies, was not as widely used or as influential as Version One. Version One was published without Zhiyanzhai's commentaries. So was Version Two. It was only in 1811, the 16th year of Emperor Jiaqing's reign that a version of *Honglou Meng* was printed by Dongguan' ge Printing House with commentaries. After that, a trend was formed to comment on *Honglou Meng*. A number of commentators emerged, such as Wang Xilian, Zhang Xinzhi, Yao Xie. Commentary became one of the ways of discussing *Honglou Meng*, and was widely accepted. Apart from that, comments appeared in the form of poetry, essays and paintings. Many people continued the stories of *Honglou Meng*, and many dramas and musicals were written based on *Honglou Meng*. The influence of *Honglou Meng* was obviously extensive. There was a common

传的范围仍然较为有限。因此，这一时期阅读、了解这部书的人并不多，谈论、评赏的人则更少，甚至连袁枚这位才子也只是听说而已，并没有真正见到过原书。

乾隆五十六年，程伟元、高鹗将经过整理订补的《红楼梦》以活字版刊印，开辟了《红楼梦》版本及流传的新阶段。从这一年到1921年上海亚东图书馆校勘整理《红楼梦》，这是《红楼梦》流传的第二个阶段，即刊印阶段。

与抄写的费时费力、价格昂贵相比，刊印的优势无疑是十分明显的，不仅印刷速度快、印量大，而且还大大降低了成本，它使《红楼梦》真正得到广泛的传播。此后，各家书坊争相刊印，形成了《红楼梦》出版的热潮。不管程伟元、高鹗对作品的改动和处理是好是坏，他们为大众提供了一个《红楼梦》的定本，并使其快速、广泛地流传，其对《红楼梦》传播的贡献是不可否认的。人们在此以后的一百多年间主要是靠程本来了解《红楼梦》的，这是一个不争的事实。

程伟元总共刊印了两次，第一次刊印的俗称程甲本，第二次刊印的俗称程乙本。可能是程乙本印量不大、流传不广的缘故，在一百多年的时间里，影响最大的还是程甲本。程甲本删去了脂砚斋批语，属于白文本，后出的程乙本也是白文本。直到嘉庆十六年（1811年），东观阁书坊重刊时才开始带有评点，其后不断有新的评点本刊出，在道光至光绪年间形成了一个《红楼梦》评点的高潮，并涌现出王希廉、张新之、姚燮等清代著名评点家，评点成为人们评论《红楼梦》的主要形式之一，受到读者的欢迎。此外，人们还以诗词、笔记、绘画等形式来评论这部作品。围绕《红楼梦》所写的续书、仿书也有不少，据此改编的戏曲、曲艺等多种艺术形式的作品，数量也相当多。由此可见《红楼梦》对其后小说乃至通俗文学创作的重大影响。

saying during that time claiming that "conversations without discussion of *Honglou Meng* were conversations in vain."

During this period, *Honglou Meng* was translated into Manchurian and Mongolian and was loved by readers of those minorities. A Mongolian noble man, Hasibao, translated and contracted it to a 40-chapter Mongolian *Honglou Meng*, titled *Newly Translated Honglou Meng*. He also wrote the forewords on how to appreciate *Honglou Meng*, and added general commentaries and connotations, all of which demonstrated his original perspectives on the book. This was a unique commentary among so many in the Qing dynasty.

Contrary to the public circulation of *Honglou Meng*, some so-called moralists launched their criticism on *Honglou Meng*, branding it an erotic book. In the Qing dyansty, *Honglou Meng* appeared many times on the list of banned books. What was more interesting was that the emperors and queens in those times liked to read the book and they would discuss it in the imperial court, while they forbade the general public to read it. The overall situation was that the voice of banning the book was as loud as the thunder but the action was like a drizzle. Considering that nearly every household had a copy of it, the ban was merely a formality. Even if it had been executed, it would not have achieved any major effects; as a matter of fact, many people were against the ban at the time. Some printing houses, in order to avoid censorship, changed the name of *Honglou Meng* to *Jinyu Yuan* (*The Stories of Gold and Jade*), *Daguan Suolu* (*Memories of the Grand View Garden*) and *Jinghuanxian Ji* (*Stories of the Illusory Fairy*).

The year 1921 was a year of unique importance to *Honglou Meng* and the research on it. In this year, Hu Shi published "Researches on *Honglou Meng*," initiating the founding of the discipline. After that, the study of *Honglou Meng* became a study to which great importance was attached. At that time, with the assistance of Hu Shi, Chen Duxiu and others, the Yadong Library of Shanghai published a version of *Honglou Meng* edited by Wang Yuanfang with punctuation. This was a milestone in the research of *Honglou Meng*. The period starting from the year 1921 up till the 1980s was considered the third period of *Honglou Meng* circulation, which was the quality printing period. Quality printing means that, other than commercial printing, researchers started to treat *Honglou Meng* in a more scholarly manner. Researchers even adopted

当时《红楼梦》盛行的景况可以用时人"开谈不说红楼梦，纵读诗书也枉然"这一诗句来概括，意思是说：如果谈话的时候不说《红楼梦》，即使读了不少诗书，也是枉然的。

值得一提的是，这一时期《红楼梦》还被翻译成满文、蒙古文等少数民族文字，受到其他民族的喜爱。尤其是蒙古族的哈斯宝，他不仅将《红楼梦》节译、改写成40回的蒙古文《新译红楼梦》，而且还为之撰写了序文、读法、总评及评注等，对作品有自己独到的看法，在清代众多《红楼梦》评点家中独具特色。

与大多数人传阅、喜爱形成鲜明对比的是，这一时期也有不少人从教化卫道的角度将这部小说视作淫书，大加指责。在清代，《红楼梦》还被官府定为禁书，多次遭到查禁，在各类禁书目录上，皆有《红楼梦》的名字。有意思的是，当时的皇帝、皇后们却很喜欢《红楼梦》，他们自己在宫廷里阅读、谈论，却不允许一般的百姓去看。总的来看，这种查禁雷声大，雨点小，在《红楼梦》已家置一编、妇孺皆知的情况下，并没有人去认真执行，也不会取得多大的效果，何况当时就有人明确反对。有些书坊主为了对付官府的查禁，将《红楼梦》改名为《金玉缘》、《大观琐录》、《警幻仙记》等，继续刊印发售。

1921年对《红楼梦》的流传和研究来说，无疑是一个特别值得纪念的年份。这一年，胡适的《红楼梦考证》一文发表，标志着新红学的建立。从此，红学成为一门具有现代学科性质的专学，受到学界的重视，对其后《红楼梦》的研究影响深远。当时的亚东图书馆在胡适、陈独秀等人的帮助下，推出了汪原放校勘整理的新式标点本《红楼梦》，开始了《红楼梦》流传的新阶段。从这一年到20世纪80年代，是《红楼梦》流传的第三个阶段，也就是精印阶段。之所以叫精印，是因为从这一时期开始，《红楼梦》的刊印在商业目的之外，已开始有了较为明确的学术意识，人们

the methods used in exploring historical works to check over *Honglou Meng*, which greatly improved the quality of the book. This kind of scholarly research had never existed in the past.

Initially, the Yadong Library used a copy called Shuangqing Xianguan version, a version based on Version One of the Cheng versions. Later, Hu Shi loaned his precious Version Two of Cheng versions, based on which the Yadong Library published a version in 1927. Wang Yuanfang was again in charge of editing and putting in punctuations. This book was well received and, by 1948, it had been reprinted 16 times. For half a century that followed, Version Two became the most read and most influential copy of *Honglou Meng*. Even though some Zhi versions were published during this period, they were either published by photocopying or mainly used for research purposes, not for general readers, such as the 80-chapter version edited by Yu Pingbo published in 1963 by the People's Publishing House.

The Yadong Library publication inspired other publishing houses to publish their own versions. By 1949, more than 10 edited versions had flooded the market and most of them were decent publications. It was because of this that the editing of *Honglou Meng* became an important part of Redology.

The 1980s saw *Honglou Meng* entering a new period. *Honglou Meng* Research Institute of China National Academy of Arts published a new version of *Honglou Meng*, based on the Gengchen Version. This was the first carefully edited version of the Zhi version, and it marked the fourth period of *Honglou Meng*'s circulation, the multi-facet period. In this very prosperous period, the methods of publication (edited or photocopied), the motives of publishers, and the targeting of readers made it a much more multi-faceted period than any of the previous periods of *Honglou Meng* publication. There is an enormous contrast between this and ealier periods where one version dominated.

In this period, nearly all important versions of *Honglou Meng* were reprinted by photocopying. Based on different approaches, different versions were chosen to work on. The methods of editing also varied, satisfying the needs of different readers. At the same time, *Honglou Meng* was being

开始用过去治经史的方法来校勘整理《红楼梦》，作品的质量有了明显的提高，这种科学、认真的态度在以前是不曾有的。

亚东图书馆最初是以程甲本的翻刻本双清仙馆本为底本进行校勘整理的。后来，胡适将自己珍藏的程乙本出借，亚东图书馆又于1927年推出以这个版本为底本的整理本。该书仍由汪原放句读，出版之后，受到读者欢迎。到1948年，该书再版达16次之多。在此后的半个多世纪里，程乙本成为读者最多、影响最大的一个《红楼梦》读本。其间虽然也有脂本的出版，但它们要么以影印的方式出版，要么如俞平伯整理校点的《红楼梦八十回校本》（人民文学出版社1963年版），主要供学术研究之用，并不适合一般的读者阅读、欣赏。

受亚东图书馆的影响，其他出版机构也纷纷推出了自己的整理本。截止到1949年之前，共出版了10多种整理本。态度大多还比较认真。也正是为此，从这一时期开始，《红楼梦》的校勘整理成为红学研究的一个重要组成部分，受到研究者的重视。

进入20世纪80年代，《红楼梦》的流传进入一个新的阶段。1982年，由中国艺术研究院红楼梦研究所校注的《红楼梦》出版。该书以庚辰本为底本，是第一个经过认真校勘整理的《红楼梦》脂本普及读本。以此为标志，《红楼梦》的流传进入了第四个阶段，即多元阶段。之所以称多元，是因为这一时期无论是脂本还是程本，无论是校勘整理还是影印出版，整理出版的动机、目的、形式以及读者面都是多元的，读者可以有不同的选择，这与此前一本独盛的景象形成了鲜明对比。

这一时期，几乎所有现存的《红楼梦》的重要版本都得到了影印出版，校勘整理出于不同的考虑而选择底本，整理的形式也有多种，基本上满足了各层次读者的需要。同时，

translated into the scripts of five minor ethnic languages, namely, Mongolian, Korean, Tibetan, Kasakh and Uygurian. Readers today enjoy better resources than readers of any previous period.

Ⅲ

Apart from its local popularity, *Honglou Meng*'s foreign reception was excellent, too. It was distributed overseas and was loved by the peoples around the world. *Honglou Meng* was introduced abroad long ago and was translated into many languages. The overseas researchers have formed an important force in the research on *Honglou Meng*. Cao has won worldwide renown for Chinese literature.

Honglou Meng was first introduced to China's neighbouring countries, such as Japan, Korea and Vietnam. According to records, not long after the printing of *Honglou Meng*, a total of 18 sets of 9 volumns of the book were brought to Japan from Zhapu in Zhejiang Province in 1793. Various versions of *Honglou Meng* were later introduced to Japan, where *Honglou Meng* was also printed. In 1905, *Zengping Butu Shitou Ji* (*Illustrated Stories of the Stone with Additions*) was reprinted by the Tokyo Imperial Printing Company. This was an indication of how much Japanese people loved the book.

At the same time, *Honglou Meng* was brought to Europe and America by merchants and priests. For example, in 1832, the 12th year of Emperor Daoguang's reign, a Russian religious delegation brought from Beijing to Russia a hand-written copy of *Honglou Meng*, known as the Leningrad version. It is a Zhi version that has important value for research. Currenlty, in public and private libraries in Japan, Russia, the United States and Korea, there are a number of valuable copies of *Honglou Meng* in their collections. According to Li Fuqing, a well-known Russian sinologist, libraries in Russia have a collection of over 60 versions of *Honglou Meng* and related works. Libraries in South Korea have also collected over 20 versions of *Honglou Meng*. These

《红楼梦》还被翻译成多种少数民族文字出版，共有蒙古文、朝鲜文、藏文、哈萨克文、维吾尔文等5种文字的版本。现代读者阅读《红楼梦》的条件比以往任何一个历史时期都要好。

（三）

在中国本土的流传之外，《红楼梦》还跨越国界，在世界范围内得到较为广泛的传播，受到各国、各民族人们的喜爱，成为世界级的文学名著。总的来看，《红楼梦》在海外的流传不仅时间早，而且影响大，被翻译成多个语种的译本。在红学研究的大军中，还有一支不可忽视的海外力量。曹雪芹为中国文学赢得了世界性的声誉。

《红楼梦》最早传入的是日本、朝鲜、越南等亚洲近邻国家。据记载，《红楼梦》被刊印不久，1793年，即由商船从浙江的乍浦传到日本，而且传去的作品数量还不小，共9部18套。其后各种《红楼梦》的刊本不断传入日本。同时，在日本本土也有《红楼梦》的刊印，如1905年，日本东京帝国印刷株式会社就翻印了《增评补图石头记》。由此可见日本读者对《红楼梦》的喜爱程度。

与此同时，《红楼梦》还随着传教士、商人的足迹流传到欧美各个国家，比如道光十二年即1832年，一个俄国宗教使团将一部珍贵的《红楼梦》抄本从北京带到俄国，这就是通常所说的列藏本，它是一个具有重要研究价值的脂批抄本。现在日本、俄罗斯、美国、韩国等国家的公私藏书机构里都藏有不少《红楼梦》的珍贵版本。据俄罗斯著名汉学家李福清介绍，在该国的图书馆中收藏有60多种《红楼梦》及其续作和改编作品。韩国的各类藏书机构也藏有20多种《红楼梦》的各种版本。从

figures are an indication of how people in those countries loved *Honglou Meng*.

Apart from treating *Honglou Meng* as a literary work, many foreigners use *Honglou Meng* as a language textbook because it is written in pure and elegant Mandarin. The lively descriptions in the book are also a resource for contextual studies of Chinese culture and traditions. Many countries started to translate part of the book for that purpose. In the 19th century, translations of *Honglou Meng* could be seen in languages like Russian, English, Korean, Japanese and Mongolian.

In the 20th century, with the development in cultural exchanges between China and other countries, *Honglou Meng* was further introduced to the world. Fully translated versions appeared in several languages, such as English, Japanese and others.

According to statistics, by the 1990s, there have been more than 70 versions of *Honglou Meng* translated into 17 languages. Among those, high quality influential versions include English versions, by Qiao Li (1892, China Post Publishing House, Hong Kong), Wang Jizhen (1929, Duran Publishing House), D. Hawkes (1973, Penguines) and also by Yang Xianyi and Gladis Yang (1978, Foreign Languages Press); the German version by Kuhn (1932, Leipzig Press); the French version by Li Zhihua (1981, Gallimard Press); and the Russian version by Panasiuk (1958, Literature and Art Publishing House of former Soviet Union). The existence of so many translated versions made it very easy for readers around the world to read *Honglou Meng*.

Honglou Meng, a book with a plethora of stories and plots, covers many aspects of life. It would be hard for the Chinese to fully understand all of the complex meanings, let alone translate them. The translation of *Honglou Meng*

这一数字可以看出，这些国家的人民对《红楼梦》还是十分喜爱的。

除了文学上的欣赏之外，还有不少外国人将《红楼梦》当作学习汉语的语言教科书。因为《红楼梦》使用纯正、典雅的北京口语，小说中有许多生活化的描写，对外国人来说，这确实可以作为学习汉语和了解中国社会文化的教科书使用。这样，《红楼梦》不断被译成外文，起初大多数都是摘译、节译，后来开始出现全译本。在20世纪之前，已有俄文、英文、朝鲜文、日文、蒙古文等多个语种的译本。

进入20世纪之后，随着中国与世界各国之间学术文化交流的增加，《红楼梦》开始有了更为广泛的传播，并出现了多个语种的全译本，有不少语种如英文、日文等还出现了多种版本的全译本。

据相关资料的综合统计，截止到20世纪90年代，《红楼梦》至少共有17个语种的译本70多种。在上述这些译本中，质量较高、比较有影响的主要有乔利的英译本（1892年香港中国邮报社刊印），王际真的英译本（1929年由杜兰公司出版），霍克思的英译本（1973年由英国企鹅公司出版），杨宪益、戴乃迭的英译本（1978年外文出版社出版），库恩的德译本（1932年德国某比锡岛社出版），李治华等人的法译本（1981年法国的利玛出版社出版），巴纳秀克的俄译本（1958年国家文艺出版社出版）等。有如此多而且优秀的译本，世界各地的人们阅读欣赏《红楼梦》已经非常方便。

《红楼梦》内容丰富，头绪繁多，涉及到各个方面的生活，别说翻译，就是中国人正确地阅读理解《红楼梦》都不是一件容易的事情，由此可以想象，翻译这部小说是一项相当困难的工作。在众多翻译家的不懈努力下，《红楼梦》陆续被翻译成

has always been hard work. Thanks to the arduous work of some translators, *Honglou Meng* has been translated into many languages and, in entering the world stage, has shared the Chinese culture with people all over the world.

Furthermore, many famous encyclopedias and dictionaries have included entries of *Honglou Meng* and Cao Xueqin and highly acknowledge this piece of art, i.e., *Encyclopedia Britanica* of Britain, *Laros Encyclopaedia* of France, Germany's *Encyclopedia of World Literature*, *Encyclopedia of World Literature in the 20th Century*, *American Encyclopedia* and *International Encyclopedia*, and *The Great Soviet Encyclopedia*. Outside China, sinologists have also written many excellent books introducing *Honglou Meng* to the world and they have contributed significantly to modern research on *Honglou Meng*.

Honglou Meng belongs not only to China but also to the world. It is a spiritual treasure that should be shared by the whole world. When Cao wrote it, he was afraid that no one would understand him, hence putting down these lines of sad words, "Everyone says the author is insane, yet who really understands the message in the book?" He would never have known that, 200 years later, what he did is not in vain. His work has won him worldwide glory. We can imagine that in the future, his work will still be loved by future generations. *Honglou Meng* is eternal.

多种译本，为此我们要感谢那些辛勤的文明使者——翻译家们，是他们的辛勤劳动使《红楼梦》真正走向世界，使世界各国的人民也得以分享中国传统文学的巨大艺术魅力。

此外，国外许多著名的大百科全书、辞书，如英国出版的《英国百科全书》、《大条目百科全书》，法国出版的《大拉罗斯百科全书》、《通用百科全书》，德国出版的《世界文学百科辞典》、《二十世纪世界文学百科辞典》，美国出版的《美国百科全书》、《国际百科全书》，苏联出版的《苏联大百科全书》等，都曾专门设置"《红楼梦》"、"曹雪芹"等条目，向读者介绍《红楼梦》的基本情况，并对该书的思想及艺术给予极高评价。海外的汉学家们也出版了许多优秀的论著，为《红楼梦》研究做出了很大的贡献。

在今天，《红楼梦》不仅仅是属于中国的，它同时也是全世界人民共同拥有的宝贵精神财富。当初曹雪芹创作《红楼梦》时，似乎还有些担心没有人能真正理解、喜爱自己的作品，发出了"都云作者痴，谁解其中味"这样有些悲观的感叹。自然，他绝对想不到，二百多年之后，全世界都有他的知音，他的心血并没有白费，这部作品为他赢得了世界性的声誉。在可以想象的将来，《红楼梦》仍然会像过去、现在这样，受到一代代人们的喜爱，它的生命力是永恒的。

《红楼梦》法译本封面

Cover of the French Version

尾声　一部小说和它创造的奇迹

Epilogue　A Novel and Its Miracle

A novel, once regarded erotic and unorthodox and thus banned, has now become a well-known literature throughout the world and has resulted in Redology, the study of *Honglou Meng*, and kept attracting more and more experts' efforts. This novel, an incomplete literature in a few hundred years, has made the society crazy about it and has led to national political movements, bringing ups and downs for many people. There is no other book in the world that could have done the same. Not to mention the great artistic charm of the novel, the various social and cultural phenomena described in it, either solemn or funny, have provided materials good enough for researchers on the study of public attitude and morality.

It is worthwhile for those researchers and lovers of the book to have spent time reading it and writing hundreds of articles on it. After all, this is a book of genius that shows all the talents of a writer. It also represents the highest achievements of Chinese literature. Even though for the fact that the book is, after many revisions, incomplete and that some distortion occured in circulation and many errors were found in it, the defects could not overshadow the glory. Those defects were minor ones and were minicure, compared to the achivements it has made. The book coud endure the test of time and repeated deliberation; even the fuzziest readers would surrender to the exellence in it, be it the deep thoughts, the delicate plans, the well structured sentences or beautiful proses. The artistic charm of it cannot be replaced by any other novel. There have been a few novels of splendour in the Chinese history, for example, *Stories of the Three Kingdoms, Water Margin, Pigrimage to the West and The Golden Lotus* and *The Scholars*. These novels have not reached the high level *Honglou Meng* has achieved. Reading the book should be regarded as having a conversation with a great writer. The abstract theories one learns in class should be turned into spiritual experiences and artistic enjoyment. In this way, one can fully enjoy the beauty of literature and of language. The incompleteness of the book and the lack of historical materials become the magnetic force that drives readers more and more to solve the puzzles. They would try very hard to

　　一部曾被视作淫词邪说、遭到查禁的通俗小说日后竟然成为享誉世界的文学名著，并由此形成一门人称红学的学问，让众多专家学者为之呕心沥血；一部残缺不全的文学作品竟然在几百年间让整个社会为之痴迷不已，并由之引发轰动全国的政治运动，带来不少命运际遇的沉浮兴衰。这部小说和它所创造的种种奇迹在古今中外的文学史上恐怕再也找不出第二例来。且不说原书本身所蕴涵的巨大艺术魅力，仅由该书所引发的或庄重、或滑稽的种种社会文化现象，已足以成为透视世态人心的绝佳材料，为研究者们所注目。

　　毫无疑问，众多专家学者及业余爱好者在这部书上花费大量时间和精力并为之写出成百上千部研究著作是值得的，毕竟这是一部凝结着天才作家毕生心血的杰作，代表着中国古典小说艺术的最高成就。尽管这部作品几经修改仍未最后完成，在流传过程中出现不同程度的失真现象，于情节、字句间留下了不少破绽，但瑕不掩瑜，这不过是细枝末节，无损于其辉煌的艺术成就。这是一部耐得住反复推敲的佳作，即使是最挑剔的读者也不能不为该书处处闪耀的艺术光彩所征服，无论是其深邃的思想、绝妙的构思，还是严整的结构、优美的字句。其独特的艺术魅力是其他小说作品所无法替代的，尽管在中国古代风华绝代的小说名著还有不少，比如《三国演义》、《水浒传》，比如《西游记》、《金瓶梅》，比如《儒林外史》，但都还未能达到《红楼梦》的这种艺术高度。阅尾声曹雪芹读该书实际上是在与一位伟大的作家进行跨越时空的心灵对话，在课堂上学到的抽象文学理论将化为刻骨铭心的情感体验和艺术享受，由此得以充分领略文学之美、语言艺术之美。该书因作品缺失、文献不足等原因形成的诸多谜团更是对各个阶层的读者形成强大的吸引力，让人欲罢不能，苦苦寻找着也许永远都无法得到的

find answers, yet they may not get any.

Judging from the background of and the process of its creation, *Honglou Meng* should be an isolated or incidental phenomenon. There must have been other writers who would have had similar experiences like that of Cao. Maybe there were quite a few. But only Cao wrote *Honglou Meng* that will last forever. Cao was unfortunate, yet he was fortunate in a way. The novel was written by him but does not belong to him alone. It belong to the times he lived, to all Chinese people and to a culture. It could not have appeared in the Wei and Jin periods in ancient China, nor could it appear in Tang and Song dynasties. Nor could it appear in Ming dynasty. It could only appear on the eve of the downfall of an empire. This was decided by the law of development of literature, by the socio-cultural elements at that time and also by Cao's unique personal experiences. It came to this world via the words of a genius writer, demonstrating the essence of the culture and the art of a people, and it has reached the pinnacle of the Chinese ancient novels. Without the development of the novels prior to it, it would not have succeeded. There is a saying that through one tiny drop of water one can observe the whole world. Through this great novel, one could see the characteristics of the Chinese people and taste the great traditional culture of China and its people.

We can say that there is validity for the research of *Honglou Meng*. We cannot negate the necessity of the researchs only because a few researchers had some indecent behaviours. Current bold prediction that the Redology would go bankcrupt would only win a few clicks on the internet and some commercial benefit; it would have no impact on the progress of academic research. The novel itself, and the various cultural phenomenon evolved with it are worth studying. In fact, this is the precondition and basis for the foundation of Redology as a study. It is *Honglou Meng* that gave birth to Redology, not that Redology made *Honglou Meng* popular. This simple truth is not easily understood by some in today's chaotic field where the norm in academic studies is lacking. There has already been a saying in the past which goes, "conversation without the discussion of *Honglou Meng* are conversations in vain," but the high status of *Honglou Meng* didn't come until the 20th century,

答案。

　　就创作背景与成书过程来说，《红楼梦》的出现应该说是一个个别或者说偶然的现象，在中国古代文学史上具有类似曹雪芹家世、生平与才华的作家不能说是一个没有，甚至可以说还有不少，但最终写成像《红楼梦》这样的传世名作者则只有他一人。曹雪芹是不幸的，却又是幸运的。这部小说固然是作家的个人创作，但它并不仅仅属于曹雪芹一人，它属于一个时代，属于一个民族，属于一种文化。它不可能出现在魏晋，不可能出现在唐宋，也不可能出现在明代，而只能出现在一个古老帝国破败的前夜，这是由文学自身的发展规律与那个时代的诸种社会文化因素、个人的独特机缘所决定的。它通过一个天才作家之手，展现了一个民族文化艺术的精髓，达到了中国古代小说的巅峰。没有前代小说的发展作为铺垫，就决不会有这部小说的成功。一滴水可以观整个世界，通过这部巨著可以透视中国小说的民族特色与艺术品格，领略中国传统文学艺术和民族文化的巨大魅力。

　　可以说，研究红学有着无可置疑的正当性和合理性，不能因为某些研究者的不规范之举就否定整个学科存在的必要性。当下主流红学破产之类的豪言壮语除了博得一些点击率和商业利益之外，在学术层面不会有任何实际进展。无论是这部小说自身还是围绕它所产生的种种社会文化现象，都是值得认真探讨的，而事实上，红学研究也正是以此为研究对象展开的，这正是红学得以成立的前提和基础。是《红楼梦》这部优秀小说催生了红学，而不是红学捧红了《红楼梦》，看似十分浅近的道理在红学研究喧闹异常、学术规范缺失的今天，反倒不容易看明白。尽管古人早有"开谈不说红楼梦，纵读诗书也枉然"之言，但《红楼梦》真正获得应有的声誉和地位却是在20世纪，

even though it's been 200 years too late for Cao Xueqin. It was in the 20th century that the biased folk novel entered the main shrine of literature, entered the classrooms in universities and was accepted into the modern academic system. With efforts from Wang Guowei, Hu Shi, Lu Xun and Yu Pingbo, *Honglou Meng* has achieved paramount status in the literary history, and Redology has become a special study in the limelight of the development of modern Chinese studies and has also become a leading studies of the time. The amount of attention and participation of researchers has made Redology a study as important as Tunhuangology and Oracle-bone Studies. Redology has experienced a lot of attention and many achievements have also been made. Many imporant records were found and many excellent articles were dedicated. Redology certainly is one of the highlights in modern Chinese studies.

Honglou Meng has undergone tremendous setbacks while enjoying the highest status. After many willful and rude cover-ups, it has lost its original appearance. It has been violently distorted and become strange to the readers. Looking back on the entire 20th century, the reading of and the research on this book went far beyond the literary and cultural sense and became a daily activity for people from all walks of life. The whole nation paid attention to it and it was attacked by the forces of politics and business alike. Because of that, the book was manipulated by some so-called Redologists, or used as either an encyclopedia that provides guidance to life or an encrypted code book that contains great secrets of historical importance, as well as a medical encyclopedia which contains cures for all diseases. New explanations on the book emerged with all sorts of crazy ideas. All of them sounded rather reasonable in their own claims. During such big mess, Redology was reduced from academic research to a performance art. In one word, *Honglou Meng* was considered everything but a novel. This may sound rediculous yet was so true. The contempt and trample on academic norms has made Redology a public bin. Whether the strange interpretations on the dreams, or Qin Xue, studies on

虽然对曹雪芹来说，这一切都来得太迟了。正是在这个悲喜交加的世纪里，昔日受人歧视的通俗小说赫然进入文学家族的核心，并走上大学课堂，被纳入现代学术体系。在此背景下，经王国维、胡适、鲁迅、俞平伯等先驱者的不断努力，《红楼梦》获得了文学史上至为崇高的经典地位，围绕它产生的红学也终于成为一门受人注目的专学，在中国现代学术建立的过程中大出风头，成为一种时代学术风向标。整个社会空前的重视与众多学者的参与使红学成为与敦煌学、甲骨学并称的显学，一直喧闹纷繁，热点不断，取得了十分丰厚的收获，这有大批不断发现的重要红学文献为证，有大批相继出现的优秀学术著作为证。在现代中国学术史上，红学研究是可以大大写上一笔的。

但同时也要看到，在获得至高经典地位的同时，《红楼梦》这部小说也付出了沉重的代价，在一次次刻意、粗暴的涂抹和装扮中，它逐渐失去其本来的面目，被严重扭曲和异化，变得模糊而陌生。回望整个20世纪，对这部小说的阅读和研究早已超出文学和文化的范围，变成全民参与的日常行为，举国关注，受到政治、商业等因素的轮番冲击。于是，这部小说被自以为是的专业或业余的红学家们随意装点，或被打扮成指点迷津的人生教科书，或被打扮成隐藏着重大历史内幕的密码本，或被打扮成包治百病的百科全书，等等。有关这部小说的解读可以说是众说纷纭，热闹非凡，什么千奇百怪、匪夷所思的说法都有，都不会让人感到意外和惊奇，而且个个都是理直气壮，气吞山河。在种种喧嚣和吵闹声中，没有门槛的红学逐渐从学术研究蜕变成一种行为艺术。反正《红楼梦》什么都是，它就不是小说。看似荒唐，却是眼前活生生的现实。对学术规范的漠视和践踏，使红学不可避免地成为一个人人得以利用的公共垃圾箱，不管是非驴非马的解梦派红学，还是沙滩起高楼的秦学，

Qin Keqing, the Redology by Tu Mo're or the claim that Redology is going to bankrupt, all use Redology to attract attention.

It was improper for people to push a good novel to a rediculously high level and to manipulate it at will. It was disrespectful for the author. The imbedded meanings and the delicate plans in the book were wrongly interpreted and manipulated by those people's wild guesses. If those people were right, that *Honglou Meng* was a text book on history, an encrypted code, an encyclopedia, what else could they turn it into other than a deformed object? What could they have achieved more? We need no more deformed creatures. We need more excellent novels like *Honglou Meng*. It is because of its outstanding literary achievement, not anything else, that *Honglou Meng* became a great book in the Chinese literary history.

Let's return to the text, to the novel, and to literature. Let's follow normal academic methods and base the studies on the book. Let's discuss issues based on truth, and do not over-elaborate. Let's talk about Cao Xueqin, about *Honglou Meng* and reveal the truth of it. Let's appreciate the beauty of literature, of language, and of merits. These should be our fundamental stand. In this chaotic world where new and abrupt interpretations emerge, it would not be a welcoming act of me to call on everyone to go back to the basics. Even though it may not sell well and may not attract the attention of the media, I believe this is the right direction that Redology should develop in. This is the right place where we should make our efforts.

An excellent novel written by a talented writer does not need awards and flowers to highlight its glory. The achievements and contributions it has made in literal art are enough for it to last forever.

不管是创建新体系的土默热红学，还是宣告主流红学的破产，都可以利用红学的招牌招摇过市，吸引人们的眼球。

将一部本为文学作品的优秀小说漫无边际地拔高，随心所欲地曲解，看似十分重视，实则是对作者的失礼，对作品的不尊重。因为在种种脱离文本的无端猜测中，作者凝结在字里行间的才华和匠心被忽视和扭曲了。退一步讲，即使这些人的观点能够成立，《红楼梦》确实是历史教科书，确实是密码本，确实是百科全书，这种做法除了将《红楼梦》变成一个畸形怪胎外，又能给这部小说带来什么呢？毫无疑问，它并不能为这部小说增辉，反而会损害其价值。因为这些东西我们并不缺少，我们缺少的是像《红楼梦》这样优秀的小说。《红楼梦》之所以在文学史上获得如此崇高的经典地位，就是因为其巨大的文学成就和艺术魅力，而不是别的。

回到文本，回到小说，回到文学，遵照基本的学术规范和方法，一切从作品出发，实事求是，拒绝过度阐释，拒绝牵强附会。回到曹雪芹，回到《红楼梦》，返璞归真，还作品以本来面目，从中领略文学之美、语言之美、才情之美，这就是我们的基本立场。在红学研究乱象不断、新说纷出的今天，提出这个简单至极的主张尽管不合时宜，而且缺少卖点，不会引起专门制造轰动效应的媒体的关注，但我们相信，这才是红学研究的正确方向，这才是应该努力的方向。

一部天才作家创作的优秀小说不需要什么不相干的奖杯和鲜花来为它贴金添彩，仅仅是其在文学艺术上的巨大成就和杰出贡献，便足以使它不朽。

Notes from Translators

Cao Xueqin is the author of *Honglou Meng* (often known as *The Dream of Red Mansions*), one of the richest and the most complex novels in China's literature history. The book *Cao Xueqin* provides readers with a brief history of Cao and the Cao family, the essence of and the debate around *Honglou Meng*.

As the writer states that "*Honglou Meng*, to a certain degree, is like a celestial novel that contains too many puzzles and is hard to comprehend," and to thoroughly understand *Honglou Meng* and Cao Xueqin is "like finding fragments of a delicate vase that was broken 200 years ago that can only give us a rough picture of what it looked like." The book *Cao Xueqin* serves as a guide for readers to further their own interest and explorations of the novel that presents China's colourful literature, rich culture and complex society in an elegant and sophisticated manner.

Over the past 40 years Chinese film producers have produced movies and TV series based on *Honglou Meng*, presenting the grandness and elegance of the Chinese novel.

The translation captures the main contents of the original book to serve western readers, in particular young readers, other than a word-by-word translation. For the title of the book, Chinese phonetic translation of *Honglou Meng* is adopted to preserve and present the nature and literary beauty of the Chinese language.

图书在版编目(CIP)数据

　曹雪芹:汉英对照/苗怀明著:(澳)陈杨国生,
(澳)海(Hay,T.), (澳)爱博译. —南京:南京大学
出版社，2010.3
　(中国思想家评传简明读本)
　ISBN 978-7-305-06610-8

　Ⅰ.曹… Ⅱ.①苗…②陈…③海…④爱…
Ⅲ.曹雪芹(？～1763)—评传—汉、英　Ⅳ.K825.6

中国版本图书馆CIP数据核字(2009)第239789号

出 版 者　南京大学出版社
社　　 址　南京汉口路22号　邮　编　210093
网　　 址　http://www.NjupCo.com
出 版 人　左　健

丛 书 名　《中国思想家评传》简明读本(中英文版)
书　　 名　曹雪芹
著　　 者　苗怀明
译　　 者　Guosheng Yang Chen, Trevor Hay & Bo Ai
审　　 读　李　寄
责任编辑　陈颖隽　　　　编辑热线　025-83595509

照　　 排　江苏凤凰制版印务中心
印　　 刷　江苏凤凰盐城印刷有限公司
开　　 本　787×1092　1/16　印张　14.75　字数　279千
版　　 次　2010年3月第1版　2010年3月第1次印刷
ISBN 978-7-305-06610-8
定　　 价　35.80元

发行热线　025-83594756
电子邮箱　Press@NjupCo.com
　　　　　Sales@NjupCo.com (市场部)